# DESIGN
# BOOK
# FOUR

P9-BJS-159

# Fine WoodWorking®

# DESIGN BOOK FOUR

320 photographs of the best
work in wood
by 332 craftspeople

Selected by the editors
of Fine Woodworking magazine

The Taunton Press

Front cover photograph:

*BRYAN SMALLMAN* (see page 41)
South Norwalk, CT
Table

Back cover photographs:

*MICHAEL CABANISS* (see page 3)
Davenport, CA
''Trastero'' adaptation of a Spanish colonial
cupboard

*RALPH ASHMEAD* (see page 146)
Inverness, CA
Viola d'amore

*MICHAEL FORTUNE* (see page 81)
Toronto, ON Canada
Dining chairs

Typesetting: The Taunton Press, Inc.

Newtown, Connecticut 06470

Printed in Italy

©1987 by The Taunton Press, Inc.
All rights reserved

First printing: August 1987

International Standard Book Number 0-918804-83-3

Library of Congress Catalog Card Number 77-79327

A Fine Woodworking Book

Fine Woodworking® is a trademark of The Taunton
Press, Inc., registered in the U.S. Patent and Trademark
Office.

The Taunton Press, Inc.
63 South Main Street
Newtown, Connecticut 06470

# Contents

# Introduction

The idea for this book was born ten years ago, when we decided to publish photographs of the very best work in wood sent to us by readers of *Fine Woodworking*. This, then, is *Design Book Four,* the fourth photographic survey of the state of the woodworker's art.

*Design Book Four* contains photographs of 320 objects made of wood, the pick of some 10,000 photos we received from nearly 1,600 makers during the fall of 1986. Over a period of two months, the editors of *Fine Woodworking* pored over this daunting collection, selecting photos that we hope have produced both an attractive book and a representative sampling of the creative range and vitality of contemporary woodworking. All kinds of wooden objects are displayed here—bowls, doors, musical instruments—but this is primarily a book about furniture. In keeping with our craft's emerging interest in vibrant paints and lacquers, the book is, for the first time, printed in full color.

When we decided in the winter of 1985 to go ahead with a fourth design book, we had serious doubts. Only two years and a few months had elapsed since publication of the previous volume, and we wondered if woodworking had changed enough to warrant another look. Would a fourth book in ten years turn up new work or would it simply rehash old ideas in full color? To my eye, the photographs in this book do reveal a craft in rapid evolution.

While it's true that the forebears of the modern apartment dweller never had need for a coffee table or a cabinet to hide the television set, there's really little that's fundamentally new in furniture design. A dining chair still needs a seat and a back, a table needs four legs to lift its flat surface above the floor. Indeed, many contemporary craftsmen find great satisfaction in reproducing popular period designs that haven't changed measurably in two centuries. For others, the overwhelming challenge is to apply fresh ideas, inventive techniques and untried materials in the execution of less familiar forms. At a decade's distance, it is possible to measure how far we've come.

If any convincing stylistic verdict emerged from the 600 photos published in our first design book, it was a single-minded infatuation with wood as a material. Artisans of the mid-1970s were much taken with the idea that furniture could also be sculpture, a notion frequently expressed in massive lumps and slabs of wood fashioned into interpretations of everyday furniture. The wood, selected for its rich figure and sanded smooth, was usually left unadorned, save for a thin coat of clear oil.

As the contemporary craft-furniture movement has matured, its view of wood—both as a material unto itself and as a convenient medium for advancing an idea—has become less hidebound. Even in 1975, when we published our first tentative coverage of craft woodworking, the promise of new materials seemed ever present, hovering just offstage but never playing an important role. The pages that follow offer delightful proof that woodworkers of the late 1980s have learned to comfortably combine wood with fabric, leather, metals, plastics, stone and especially colorful paints and lacquers.

Still, the most successful work in this book—whether furniture or not—speaks less about mastery of materials and technique than it does about a sophisticated understanding of design. Craftspeople in general and woodworkers in particular, seem to have always struggled to learn how their work fits into the larger scheme of art, craft and design. Many have satisfied this intense curiosity through serious study of design history, their investigations leading them to obscure books and to museums— here and abroad—to examine the best examples of what's gone before. This volume documents the success of those explorations. Seen against the brash but often unresolved work in our first book, much of the work displayed here is not only more refined in execution but also more mature in concept.

Among its 220,000 subscribers, *Fine Woodworking* counts three amateur woodworkers to every professional. Yet professionals account for the majority of the work in this book, primarily, I suspect, because they are accustomed to sending slides to juries and clients and are therefore more attuned to the promotional advantages publication sometimes affords. Entries came to us from all over the United States and Canada, Europe and Australia, from one-man professional shops and from busy cooperatives, as well as from the basement workshops of talented amateurs. Some of the professionals represented here are self-taught craft converts, having abandoned other careers to pursue what they thought might be a more spiritually rewarding life of designing and building beautiful things of wood. Others, sharing the same sense of purpose, are practicing graduates of one of about 20 schools that specialize in the training of furniture designer-makers. Still others have acquired their training through apprenticeships with master craftsmen, in the United States or abroad.

**How this book was judged**—As did its precursors, *Design Book Four* began with an invitation to *Fine Woodworking* readers to send in photos of the best work they had done since the last volume was published. Through the summer and fall of 1986, a slow trickle of mail grew into a furious torrent as the October entry deadline approached. Our job was to sift through this mountain of transparencies in search of the 320 photographs for a book.

We first performed a light table triage, culling obviously unpublishable photos as well as plainly flawed work. This proved more difficult than we had imagined for as craftsmen have become better designers and makers, they have also learned to promote their work through photos of equivalent quality. Our decision to make this book the most selective and graphically spacious of the series complicated our task. With room for only one picture in 30, we could accept only the very best photographs. We turned away much worthy work simply because the photos were badly cropped or too dark or too light, or the color skewed. We intended our final choices to reflect the striking harmonies and provocative contrasts we encountered in judging the photos. Thus, a page of colorful art furniture might be followed by a spread of well-made examples of enduring period woodwork, a rustic bowl beside a luxuriously inlaid jewelry box.

*Design Book Four* represents a great deal of work by many people. I am grateful to the *Fine Woodworking* staff for taking time from regular magazine duties to judge the photos and to Susan Gardner, who unfailingly matched every slide to its proper entry blank. Hundreds of readers entrusted us with photographs that had obviously taken a great deal of time and money to produce and to them I owe special thanks, for without them there could be no book. I hope our efforts in editing this book have rewarded that trust.

Paul Bertorelli
April 28, 1987

# DESIGN
# BOOK
# FOUR

# Cabinets

Chests of drawers are the most political of all furniture. Just because of sheer size and difficulty of building, they are very expensive. They are inherently ostentatious: while they may hide their contents, they reveal just how much stuff you possess.

It's not inappropriate to think of chests as small houses, their design and building as architecture. The function and the size determine the plan, how large the drawers will be, and so on. Engineering follows several proven paths. Structural choices for a piece of furniture this size were thoroughly explored centuries ago; even new materials like plywood and laminate haven't changed them. But chests are easily underbuilt, so care must go into the structure.

Visually, the designer is pretty much left with figuring out a facade. Since depth will be very shallow, low relief at most, this is basically a two-dimensional problem. In this, chests differ from most other furniture, which is best designed in the round, as a three-dimensional object. Chests almost always go up against something like a wall. So, they have a back. This means you look at the front. (The sides hold the two apart to provide room for the stuff inside.) The chest designer, working with plans and elevations, is using the same orthogonal process as an architect.

The guys who made the chests we now revere as antiques put most of their attention into the facade. Structure was usually a compromise between speed and quality. Speed often won; for instance, many drawer glides were glued and nailed cross-grain, inevitably causing cracks in dry weather and breaking glides loose during wet spells.

It may be impossible to do it "right." Chests have to be lightweight enough to be moved, but sturdy enough to resist stress. If they sit on an uneven floor, they have to resist racking, or else the drawers won't slide. The whole construction will have to expand and contract smoothly with changes in humidity, without drawers getting too tight or too loose.

Of course, the best antique work, like the best contemporary work, expresses thoughtful devotion to every detail on the part of the makers. Construction of such large objects on a commercial scale has always demanded specialization of labor, and these days specialization has been carried to the industrial extreme of the assembly line. The solitary woodworker is left to make exceptional one-of-a-kind pieces. One reason contemporary chests tend to be less fancy is that financial and time pressures prevent the single worker from mastering all the processes that went into a classic highboy. This required the skills of the designer, joiner, veneer specialist, turner, carver and finisher, not to mention office management.

Another reason for visual simplicity is a change in the politics of home furnishings. Furniture is an expression of its age. Those revered old cabinets were made for Europeans (and their American descendents) who, with the rapid spread of wealth and learning, fancied themselves glorious, new Romans. So they appropriated motives and styles of the classic civilizations for their furniture. Elements of imperial architecture appeared, especially on chests. These owners were proud of their empires, believing God gave them the world and its peoples to exploit. They used their furniture to express this pride.

Two world wars and a clearer anthropological view of humanity have taught us that "civilization" is not congruent with "technology," and that true savagery is not located among the nude peoples. It is no longer possible to possess simple pride in ostentation. But that doesn't mean that luxurious work is not being done now.

The contemporary handmade furniture phenomenon has grown up mostly since World War II, but its roots are in the Arts and Crafts Movement, and for most of its years the aesthetics have been the same: form following function, truth to materials, economy of means and freedom from decoration.

When the art world went crazy in the seventies and prices went out of sight, certain segments of the craft world began to be shopped by collectors. So art-world tendencies began to surface in craft, too, especially the myth of the avant garde, with its premium on innovation. At the same time, a generation of furnituremakers have achieved enough competence with their work that a well-cut dovetail joint is routine. Many sculptors have become furnituremakers, too, since the size and expense of sculpture tend to make commissions scarce for all but a few. As a result, all kinds of ideas are being tried out in furniture: pop imagery, wild decoration, ironic use of classical elements, lots of color, expensive or trash-cheap materials used out of traditional context, various painterly schemes of composition, sybaritic constructions worthy of Ruhlmann.

A client can still order anywhere in the country an understated chest of drawers, well-made, which quietly shows its good construction and well-chosen woods. But in certain galleries, one can buy a chest that looks like a space station, or one that features marquetry veneer trompe-l'oeil effects, or a cabinet so covered with animal carvings it resembles a Dogon granary door. Without question, some of this work is excessive, some poorly built. A lot of it is quite expensive to make and buy, so it represents another round of conspicuous consumption, this time with a self-conscious, slightly defensive "I'm getting mine" attitude. But the sense of a prevailing canon, of an acceptable way of working, is a thing of the past. In this dazzling scene, anything can happen.

—*Fletcher Cox*

Preceding page:
MICHAEL CABANISS
Davenport, CA
*"Trastero" adaptation of a*
*Spanish colonial cupboard*
Japanese ash, American ash,
honey locust
57 in. x 36 in. x 18¾ in.
Photo by Tony Grant

*MIKE McNERNEY*
Ompah, ON Canada
*Corner cabinet*
Cherry, fiddleback cherry
80 in. x 44 in.
Photo by Larry Ostrom

*PETER CHAMBERLAIN*
Broomall, PA
*Television cabinet*
Cherry
72 in. x 20 in. x 34 in.
Photo by Rick Echelmeyer

ROB O'REILLY
Kingsville, OH
*Stereo cabinet*
Air-dried black ash, pecan
64 in. x 20¾ in. x 18¾ in.
Photo by Mark Fainstein

PETER S. DUDLEY
Scottsville, NY
*Courtier cabinet*
Eastern maple,
Brazilian rosewood
13 in. x 13 in. x 41 in.

STEVEN J. HILL
Honolulu, HI
*Headboard with
floating figure*
Philippine mahogany,
wenge, Hawaiian koa,
angico, purpleheart
limba, blue lacquered
maple
70 in. x 15 in. x 10 in.

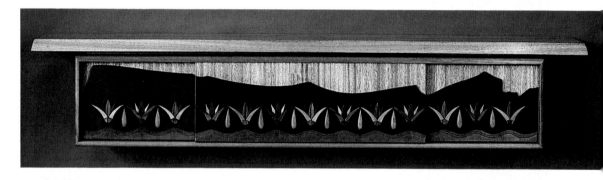

RON CALLARI
Rochester, NY
*Liquor cabinet*
Curly maple, walnut
43 in. x 32 in. x 16 in.
Photo by Woody Packard

5

DENNIS YOUNG
Petaluma, CA
*Bookcase cabinet*
Purpleheart, ebony
72 in. x 18 in.
Photo by Joel Schopplein

JAMES R. JOHNSON
Rochester, NY
*Wine and liquor cabinet*
Cherry, walnut
76 in. x 24 in. x 18 in.
Photo by Jeff Metzger

JOSEPH HASTINGS
San Francisco, CA
*"Kabinett de Stijl"*
Solid maple, curly maple
veneer
90 in. x 80 in. x 24 in.
Photo by Paul Kenny

*"A wall cabinet for books,
objects, stereo (left side),
wine bar (right side) and
television (center)."*

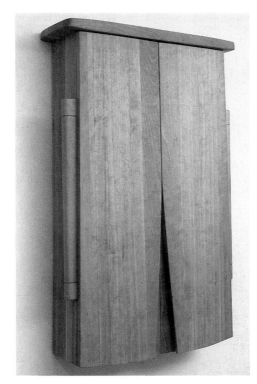

JAMES L. HENKLE
Norman, OK
*Compact-disc wall cabinet*
Cherry
41½ in. x 27½ in. x 8 in.
Photo by Andrew Strout

DAVID B. FOWLER
Albuquerque, NM
*Jewelry chest*
Padauk, curly maple, ebony,
sterling silver, leather, brass
18½ in. x 10 in. x 9¾ in.
Photo by Jonathan Bregman

GERALD PLAIN
Rochester, NY
*Chest of drawers*
Cherry, amaranth, aromatic
red cedar (on
bottom drawers)
54½ in. x 48 in. x 18½ in.
Photo by Jamey Stillings

DUDLEY HARTUNG
and ELLEN MASON
Somerville, MA
*Liquor cabinet*
Curly maple, maple veneer,
sterling silver, German silver,
stainless steel, aniline dye,
lacquer
53 in. x 22 in, x 14 in.
Photo by Tony Scarpetta

VICKI MOSS
New York, NY
*"Plenum" drop-leaf desk*
Curly maple, ebony
18½ in. x 45 in. x 51 in.
Photos by A. Dean Powell

*"Dovetailed case, stack-
laminated legs and turnings,
French polished."*

8

SUSAN PERRY
New York, NY
*Tuscan credenza*
Maple, maple plywood,
bird's-eye maple veneer,
ebony, faux marble, gold leaf
53 in. x 60 in. x 18½ in.

PETER FLANARY
Madison, WI
*Chest of drawers*
Spalted maple, curly maple,
wenge
62 in. x 36 in. x 18 in.

THOMAS J. BECK
Philadelphia, PA
*Tall chest of drawers*
Bubinga, maple,
enamel paint
38 in. x 24 in. x 69 in.

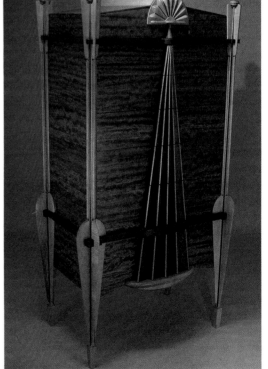

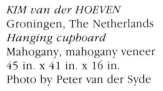

KIM van der HOEVEN
Groningen, The Netherlands
*Hanging cupboard*
Mahogany, mahogany veneer
45 in. x 41 in. x 16 in.
Photo by Peter van der Syde

*ROBERT J. KOPEC*
Longwood, FL
*Cherry blanket chest*
Curly cherry, fiddleback
mahogany, padauk, lined
with aromatic cedar
41 in. x 25 in. x 19 in.
Photo by Paul Jaynes Studios

*DON HARRINGTON*
Billings, MT
*Breakfront stereo/display
cabinet*
Honduras mahogany, bubinga
70¾ in. x 53 in. x 19¾ in.
Photo by Bernie Stefanski

TODD SMITH
Califon, NJ
*Wardrobe*
Eastern white pine
72 in. x 28 in. x 16 in.
Photo by Commercial
Photography

REID H. LEONARD
Pensacola, FL
*Bookcase*
Veneered with Brazilian
rosewood, pau marfim,
angelique and pau ferro onto
hardwood plywood,
mahogany solids, lacquer
50 in. x 21 in. x 11 in.
Photo by Frank Hardy

JOSEPH PIROGOWICZ
and STEPHEN LATTA
Suffield, OH
*Corner cupboard*
Honduras mahogany
88 in. x 43 in. x 24½ in.
Photo by David Base

MARK and NORMAN
GILLESPIE
Toronto, ON Canada
*Television cabinet*
Poplar plywood, mahogany
and crotch mahogany,
veneer, zebrawood,
boxwood inlay
37 in. x 48 in. x 20 in.
Photo by Ian Crysler

*DANIEL PECK*
San Antonio, TX
*Armoire*
Air-dried walnut
44 in. x 84 in. x 24 in.
Photo by Swain Edens Studio

*SVEN HANSON*
Albuquerque, NM
*Library bookcase*
Cherry
102 in. x 90 in. x 20 in.
Photo by Ralph Genter

*"I worked closely with my
clients in this interpretation
of a Chippendale library
bookcase. It was sized for
installation in the large,
viga-ceilinged living room of
their restored adobe home
overlooking the Rio Grande."*

*GORDON R. MERRICK*
Kennebunkport, ME
*Breakfront*
Solid walnut with book-
matched walnut burl veneers
104 in. x 89 in.
Photo by Ed Chappel

ROBERT A. KASNAK
Brownsburg, IN
*Tevis cabinet*
Bird's-eye maple, gaboon
ebony drawer pulls, macassar
ebony veneer back
75 in. x 44 in. x 30¼ in.
Photos by Dick Spahr

DONALD J. GARDNER
Taos, NM
*Jewelry chest*
Cherry, amaranth
42 in. x 22 in. x 15 in.

*"Chest lifts off to expose
leather writing surface."*

JOHN ERICKSON
Lava Hot Springs, ID
*Liquor cabinet*
Curly maple, teak, glass
66 in. x 40 in. x 19 in.
Photo by Dale Olson

*"Frame-and-panel, slumped
glass."*

14

ARNOLD d'EPAGNIER
Colesville, MD
*d'E chiffonier*
Honduras mahogany,
aromatic red cedar, Chinese
cedar, curly maple
22 in. x 42 in. x 72 in.
Photo by Kerins Photography

JON SEEMAN
Laguna Beach, CA
*Buffet*
Hawaiian koa,
Peruvian walnut
20 in. x 50 in. x 34 in.

PETER NARAMORE
Kula, HI
*Hutch*
Chinese black pine with
ebony handles
48 in. x 20 in. x 76 in.
Photo by Steven Minkowski

WILL ORVEDAL
Lecompton, KS
*Halloween piece (secretary)*
Walnut with spalted elm door
panels
64 in. x 32 in. x 16 in.
Photo by Larry Okrend
and Bruce Bandle

SCOTT LEFTON
Melrose, MA
*Drafting tansu*
Bird's-eye maple, mahogany,
padauk, oak, pine, birch
veneer plywood, plywood
37½ in. x 45½ in. x 32 in.
Photo by Dana Groff

16

NANCY HORNE FLADSTOL
Portland, OR
*Teak hutch/china cabinet*
Teak, teak veneer
14 in. x 39 in. x 69 in. (top);
18 in. x 30 in. (bottom)
Photo by Harold Wood
Photographers

ROSS DAY
Seattle, WA
*Pair of night tables*
Claro walnut, maple, ebony
22 in. x 22 in. x 18 in.
Photo by Rocky Salskov

*TERRIE NOLL and
DANIELLE HANRAHAN*
San Francisco, CA
*Art nouveau-style
display case*
Honduras mahogany
30 in. x 16 in. x 78½ in.
Photo by Pablo Mason

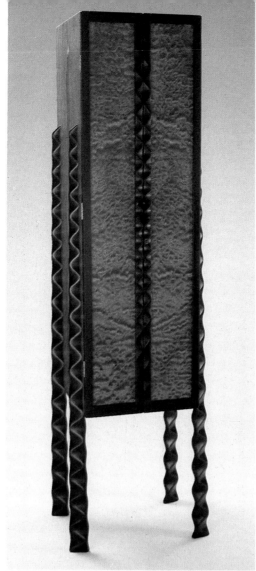

**ALLAN BELL**
Toronto, ON Canada
*Liquor cabinet*
Bubinga, cherry, "pomele"
mahogany veneer with ebony
dots on side; legs and door
stiles are hand-shaped and
finished with black lacquer
15 in. x 15 in. x 66 in.

**ANTHONY GIACHETTI**
East Boothbay, ME
*Display cabinet-on-stand*
Case and stand—East Indian
and Chiquibul rosewood;
doors—curly mahogany,
pearwood; interior—
pearwood
60½ in. x 25 in. x 15¼ in.
Photo by Stretch Tuemmler

*"Pearwood interior lights as
doors open."*

**CHAD VOORHEES**
Saluda, NC
*Freestanding silver chest*
Curly walnut, gaboon ebony,
sterling silver
38½ in. x 17 in. x 15 in.
Photos by Steve Keull

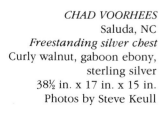

GARY E. DERZINSKI
Leavenworth, KS
*Carving tool chest*
Walnut
53 in. x 24 in. x 15 in.
Photo by Larry Okrend
and Bruce Bandle

DAVID ROWLETTE
Olney, IL
*Shell-top corner cupboard*
Black walnut, basswood,
brass
96 in. x 56 in. x 28 in.
Photo by Brunner Studios

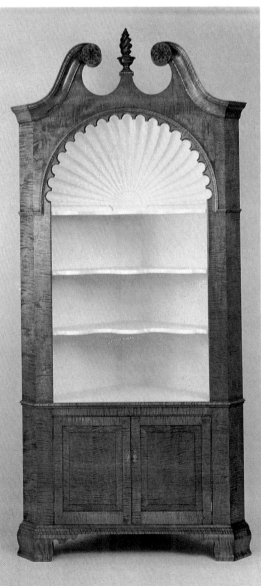

KEVIN R. ARNOLD and
D. DOUGLAS MOOBERRY
Unionville, PA
*Queen Anne highboy*
Walnut, poplar
40½ in. x 20½ in. x 90 in.
Photo by Herb Crossan

JEREMIAH de RHAM
Boston, MA
*Carved-shell corner
cupboard*
Soft curly maple, birch,
basswood
98½ in. x 44½ in.
Photo by Lance K. Patterson

JOHN GOFF
Vista, CA
*Blockfront chest of drawers*
Hawaiian koa, poplar
34½ in. x 36¾ in. x 20 in.
Photo by Melinda Holden
Photography

ROBERT H. EFFINGER
Fryburg, ME
*Massachusetts secretary*
Solid mahogany, maple,
pine back
89 in. x 39 in. x 23 in.
Photo by Bo Parker

GERALD CRAWFORD
Sedona, AZ
*Frothingham high chest*
Black walnut
7⅜ in. x 3½ in. x 1¹³⁄₁₆ in.

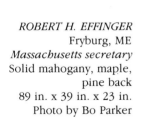

*"Accurately scaled 1 in. to
the ft.; each miniature part
reflects those in the original
displayed at Winterthur
Museum."*

MARK R. WHITE
Boxborough, MA
*Stereo cabinet*
Carcase—medium-density
fiberboard; doors and
drawers—maple
96 in. x 90 in. x 18 in.
Photo by Ted Dillard
Photography; finish by
Peter Feltus

BOB SCHMIDT
St. Augustine, FL
*Armoire*
Red maple, rock maple
76 in. x 88 in. x 20 in.
Photo by Pelican's Eye
Photography

22

*MORGAN REY BENSON*
El Paso, TX
*Entertainment center*
Basswood, birch
76 in. x 34 in. x 25 in.
Photos by Marty Snortum
Studios

*"The main carcase is jointed
solid wood with the top
mitered to the sides. The
doors are laminated, shaped,
then veneered to assure
stability."*

*LEE TRENCH*
Charleston, MA
*Chest of drawers*
Maple, curly maple, glass,
sterling silver
Glass by Harry Bessett

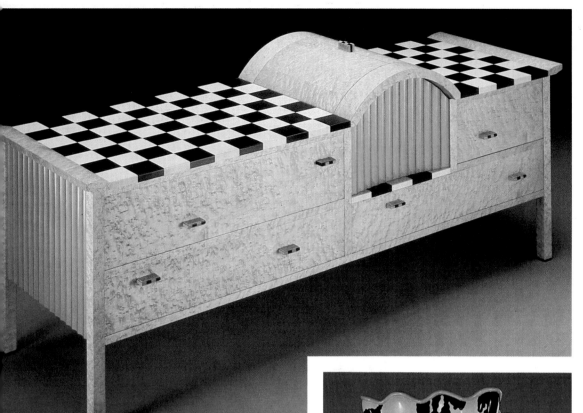

KALLE FAUSET
New York, NY
*Chest and drawers*
Bird's-eye maple, holly,
ebony, color lacquer
60 in. x 20 in. x 22 in.
Photo by A. Dean Powell

MARK E. DEL GUIDICE
Wellesley, MA
*Chiffonier*
Cherry, cherry plywood,
ColorCore, padauk, painted
maple, patinated copper,
mirror, hammered glass
78 in. x 44 in. x 17 in.
Photo by A. Dean Powell

PAUL M. SASSO
Almo, KY
*"Chip 'N Dale Evans"
bookcase*
Poplar (with acrylic paint)
78 in. x 28 in. x 19 in.

24

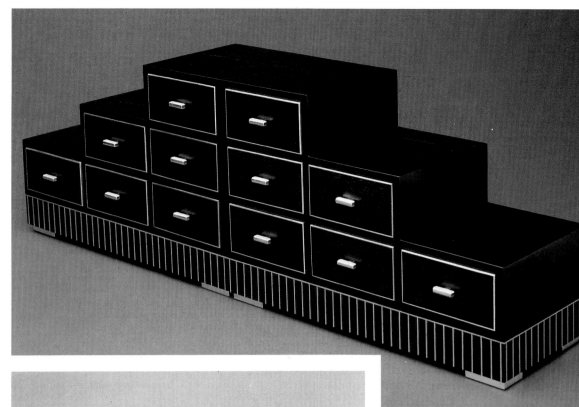

EMMETT E. DAY
Seattle, WA
*Jewelry chest*
Ebony, sterling silver,
mother-of-pearl
6 in. x 11 in. x 33 in.
Photo by Gregg Krogstad

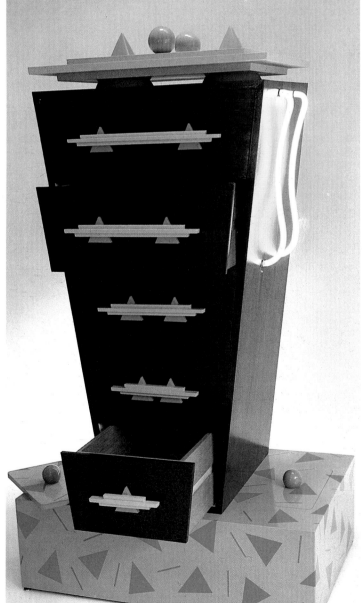

RICHARD ROSE
Yardley, PA
*Chest of drawers*
Plywood, ebony veneer,
MD44, cherry, maple, plastic
laminate, colored lacquer,
neon lights
60 in. high
Photo by Joyce Heisen

*"The carcase is mitered
(seamless) and veneered all
the way around. The base is
lacquered MD44."*

TOM BERRY
Oak Park, IL
*Alchemy chest*
Purpleheart, mahogany,
maple
60 in. x 27 in. x 16 in.
Photo by Joan Harkness
Hantz

25

# Desks

Just talking to itself, the mind can keep a line of patter going, like a comedian, for hours on end. The mind is never at a loss for words until it's time to write a few of them down. As soon as that moment arrives, every word on earth decides to go to lunch. Then, faced with the problem of saying something intelligent, a writer needs all the help he can get. He needs more than a dictionary. He needs a sanctuary. He needs an arsenal. He needs a desk.

Essentially, a desk is a workbench for putting together words, a process that typically consists of making an illegible mess out of a perfectly good piece of paper, cutting out most of it with scissors, and Scotch-taping together whatever's left in the hope that it somehow adds up to a paragraph. What it amounts to is a pitched battle with one's own confusion. You can get by with writing at a table, but it helps to have a desk. There is something to be said for having one place for paper clips and another just for rubber bands—separate— life is already complicated enough. If the written word didn't exist, there would be no desks, but we write, and it appears writing isn't simply a question of where to park the typewriter and a cup of coffee— there also has to be somewhere to squirrel away 2-cent stamps.

Consecrated to the written word, the desk evolved along with writing implements. When we wrote with quills, the quills' curling arabesques influenced the forms of the desks underneath. Then people took to using pens with built-in ink supplies— feathers gave way to fountain pens—and by the time the ballpoint rolled around, desks were streamlined; there were no more inkwells, only puzzling holes on the tops of rows of desks in old brick grammar schools.

Next came the Mighty Wurlitzer of the written word, the typewriter, first the old manual warhorses, then the electrics, and now something called—for lack of a better name—the "word processor." The name suggests a machine that turns words into a kind of cheese spread. People's eyes are starting to turn into fried eggs from gazing into the screens of these things, these word processors, but believers point out that they speed things up. It used to take writers months of chewing on pencils to get a few words to stand up together in a row, but today writers routinely click inspired copy onto TV screens, edit it with a few more clicks, then send it through to "printers" that quickly type it out on paper with rapid squirts of dots of ink.

The mechanization of writing has had its effect on the words themselves—language itself has changed. Technology spits out the words staccato, rather than in the cursive legato of longhand. In general, the antique style of great florid and purple circumlocution—which seemed to flow naturally from the calligraphic flourish of the quill—has been supplanted by a taste for plain, flat statement. . ."just the facts, Ma'am." As fashions in the use of words have changed, so has the look of the place where words are put together—the desk. In modern form, the desk is Action Central, a nerve center all wired and lit up with control panels, phones, buttons, switches and Italian lamps that look like hydroelectric towers. Metaphorically, a desk is a locus of power, a generating station, a transmitter, a refinery, a mill, a small factory all but fitted out with smokestacks.

The word "desk," however, can encompass anything from a "lady's writing table," standing lightly upon toeshoes tipped with ivory, to the mahogany tabernacles of corporate executives, immovable monoliths with writing surfaces of golf-green baize or Morocco tooled with gold. It includes such things as the lap desks of the Shakers—you furnish the legs—and the soan, the low, Korean scholars' desk, hardly ten-inches high and no bigger than a briefcase. Next to these,

there are also tall, statuesque secretaries, not the kind in skirts and high heels, but the kind of desk that is surmounted by a bookcase. A few other types: the rolltop desk—a great invention, one fell swoop and the clutter is out of sight; the L-shaped desk, often with surfaces at different levels—structural compositions that help to choreograph the flow of work; and the stand-up, or "attorneys" desk—Hemingway wrote at one. . .back problems, maybe, from his showdowns with the bulls.

Desks are a challenge to build. The details multiply, and they can get technically complex. The framing, often intricate in itself, is only the beginning. Then there are drawers, where the serious players try for two things: a piston fit of the drawer to the desk, and dovetails crisp as collars with starch. Do these two things, and there will be a bench for you in paradise. Once the desk is more or less structurally complete—fitted out with doors, tambours, panels, pigeonholes and so on—further skills come into play with the veneering, inlay, carving, gilding of the surfaces. It can take as long to build a desk as it does to build a harpsichord. The desk won't make music, but no instrument will— until it's played. That's the writer's job, with a little cooperation from the Muse, if the writer can get it. Sometimes it's hard to get her to smile, but here are some desks that won't leave her any choice. A writer who sits scribbling at one of these has half the battle won.

—*Glenn Gordon*

*DEREK S. DAVIS*
Boulder, CO
*Writing desk and chair*
Cherry, maple burl veneer,
wenge details
39 in. x 30 in. x 51 in.
Photo by George McDonald

28

GREGORY W. GUENTHER
Savannah, GA
*Dressing table with stool,*
*Federal style*
Straight and curly southern
yellow pine from old timbers
36 in. x 18 in. x 56 in.
Photo by Tim Rhoad
& Associates

LANCE PATTERSON
Boston, MA
*Queen Anne writing table*
*(see also p. 27)*
Cherry with Carpathian elm
burl, cherry veneer
22 in. x 36 in. x 28¼ in.

WALTER JAEGER
and CRAIG ERNST
Barboursville, VA
*Ladies secretary*
Curly maple, bird's-eye
maple
39 in. x 25 in. x 18 in.
Photo by Ann Hayes

JONATHAN R. WRIGHT
Cambridge, MA
*Desk*
Mahogany, maple, rosewood,
brass pulls
33 in. x 67 in. x 36 in.
Photo by A. Dean Powell

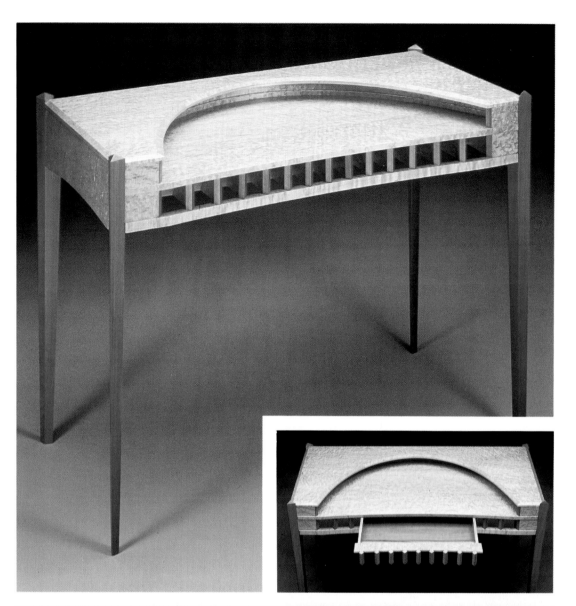

PARKER McCOMAS
New Bedford, MA
*Writing desk*
Curly bird's-eye veneer,
Swiss pearwood
43 in. x 21 in. x 32 in.
Photo by A. Dean Powell

MICHAEL A. GREGORIO
Oceanside, NY
*Writing desk*
Tiger maple, Santo Domingo
rosewood, white oak,
ebony, poplar
48 in. x 29 in. x 30 in.
Photo by Bruce Morgan

*"The desk is completely
veneered. The core is
poplar and plywood."*

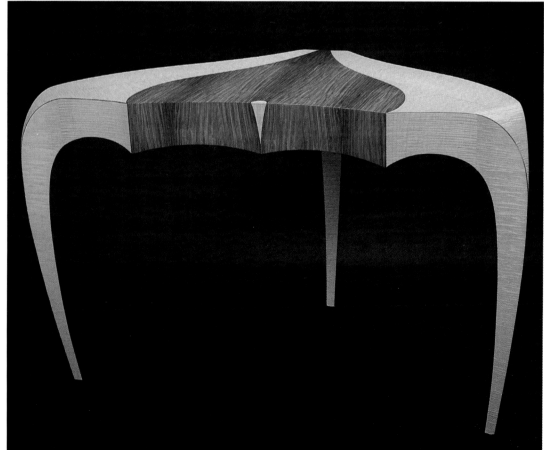

31

THOMAS MERRIMAN
McKeesport, PA
*Calligraphy table*
Redwood, Douglas fir,
sugar pine
30 in. x 46 in. x 36 in.
Photo by Marcy Holquist

*"Mortise-and-tenon frame,
tongue-and-groove work
surfaces."*

MATT HOLTBY
Missoula, MT
*Writing desk and chair*
Cherry, ebony,
sand-cast bronze
60 in. x 27 in. x 31 in.
Photo by Joe Felzman

GERALD D. OTIS
Albuquerque, NM
*Drop-leaf desk*
American black walnut (sawn
veneer and solids),
macassar ebony
20 in. x 36 in. x 45 in.
Photo by Marjorie Cole

*"Case ends are coopered
with tapered slats; inside are
five ebony-fronted drawers
and ten cubbyhole spaces."*

ROBERT (HANK) HOLZER
Seattle, WA
*Walnut writing desk
and chair*
Walnut, fabric, caning
Table—56 in. x 33 in. x
29 in.; chair—17 in. x 39 in.
Photo by Tom Collicott
Photography

33

RAY MULLINEAX, IAN KIRBY
and HOWARD HELENE
North Bennington, VT
*Executive desk*
American black walnut
85 in. x 36 in. x 29¾ in.
Photo by Bernard Hanzel

*"Frame-and-panel, leather
inlay, traditional English
drawer-making."*

DAVID GRAY
Seattle, WA
*Oval office desk*
Hawaiian koa, Nicaraguan
walnut, brass
36 in. x 72 in. x 29½ in.
Photo by Gregg Krogstad

34

JOHN KRIEGSHAUSER
Kansas City, MO
*Writing desk*
Hard maple
29 in. x 28 in. x 52 in.
Photo by Larry Okrend
and Bruce Bandle

HUGH FOSTER
Manitowoc, WI
*Computer desk*
Cherry
28 in. x 60 in. x 29 in.

W.M. ULMER
Arcata, CA
*Dressing table and bench*
Honduras mahogany
74 in. x 20 in. x 30 in.
Photo by Douglas Beck

*"Solid-wood top and
veneered torsion-box legs."*

DON DUPONT
San Ramon, CA
*Ephesus desk*
Alder, Finnish birch plywood,
medium-density fiberboard,
lacquer, faux marble finish
30 in. x 78 in. x 36 in.
Photo by Valerie Massey

*"Autobody technology
(fill, prime)."*

BERT AALBERS
N'Jmegen, Holland
*Writing desk with chair*
European oak, maple
Desk—31 in. x 50 in.
x 24 in.; chair—47 in. high

HENRY BLACK
Botany, NSW Australia
*Desk and chair*
Medium-density fiberboard
(veneered or leather
covered), Tasmanian
blackwood, ebony veneer and
trim
48 in. dia.

WILLIAM TICKEL
Denver, CO
*Self-portrait desk and chair*
Stack-laminated Hawaiian koa
Desk—51 in. x 64 in. x 33 in.
Photo by Mark Archer

STEPHEN STOKESBERRY
Seattle, WA
*Sewing machine cabinet*
Birch, Philippine
mahogany plywood
57 in. x 31 in. x 14 in.
Photo by Howard Giske

TERRY MOORE
Newport, NH
*Fall-front desk*
Honduras mahogany,
Cuban mahogany
49 in. x 36 in. x 13 in.
Photo by Camera Works

*"The Cuban mahogany burl
for the fall-front panel and
drawer fronts was a rare
find."*

KATHLEEN and RION
DUDLEY
Seattle, WA
*Dressing table*
Clear ponderosa pine/white-
wash stain, satin-finish coat
55 in. x 43¼ in. x 20 in.
Custom chrome-plated steel
mirror frames and hinges
by James Garrett

# Tables

A lot of time is spent at a table—eating, drinking, talking...the moments accumulate, and the table is mute witness to them all. After a while, it becomes something like an archeological site, a place dense with evidence of human settlement, the evidence left behind in the Sanskrit of the table's little nicks and dents. You can fall into a reverie and get lost staring into the grain and figure of a tabletop. A table imprints itself, lodges itself in the subconscious, day in, day out.

A table is a thing so central to experience that when philosophers sit down together to try to get to the bottom of things, *it's* the object they usually cite as their *example* of "a thing." They could just as easily choose a shoe, or a pencil, or a coffee cup, but a table is common ground—it's what the philosophers all happen to be sitting around. So perhaps it's easier for them to agree they're all talking about the same thing...for a room full of philosophers, that's not always that easy. Beyond a little agreement on that score, though, there are as many answers to philosophy's classic question, "What is a table?" as there are people making them, and also—as you'll see here—there are more philosophers wondering about the question than those who debate it only with words.

What makes a table a table? First of all, a flat surface—a top. Then, there has to be something underneath to hold it up. How high up depends—higher for dining; lower for in front of a couch. The elevations vary, but the intention is always the same—the idea is to get us up, off the ground. Structurally, there are three main ways to do it: a tabletop can be supported with a trestle, which is bridge-like; with a pedestal, tree-like; or with a set of legs, like a four- (or more) footed creature. A table can also be cantilevered off a wall or a post,

and there is always a wise guy somewhere trying to suspend one from the ceiling, succeeding mainly in turning the problem upside down. Furniture designers have recurring dreams of *levitating* the tabletop—no legs below; no struts above— but gravity, so far, hasn't supported the idea. Until it does, most tables will have to continue to stand on legs, even upon the legs of imaginary animals—the cabriole forms of tradition (the word cabriole alludes to the foreleg of a capering goat). In any case, whatever the table's period or style, the legs are the lone vertical elements of what is, otherwise, a horizontal proposition. And a consideration of the form of the leg, the way it connects to the top, and the sense it gives of the table's footing on the ground is crucial to the harmony of a design.

What follows here is a collection of fifty of the finest tables built in wood in the last few years. In terms of design, no one taste or type of table predominates. "Tables" is the generic heading, but there are all kinds of tables, and every craftsman has his own slant on what a good one ought to look like. So the result here, naturally, is diversity, a mixed collection of different answers to the question of what a table is, let alone what makes one beautiful.

"Beautiful" is a matter of opinion, but the opinion has to do with a feeling that something is elegantly suited to its purpose—not merely an adequate solution, but resoundingly appropriate, to the mood as well as to the function. Not to confuse elegant with "pretty," there are tables here that would hold up if flamenco were danced every night upon their tops...trestles befitting whole roast boars, scenes of stupendous gluttony and riot— greasy drumsticks and wet tankards thumped and slopped all over the planks, producing the finish as the feast wears on. A few pages away are tables for purposes far more delicate...furniture as a form of jewelry...a lacquered hall console, for the repose of a pair of evening gloves. There

are tables here for every occasion, including those that call for an "occasional" table, and coffee tables, for coffee-table books, possibly on the subject of coffee tables. There are little tables for two and the vast expanses of a conference table for twenty, and kitchen tables for conversations that stretch late into the night.... Enough of the table of contents, now for the tables.

*—Glenn Gordon*

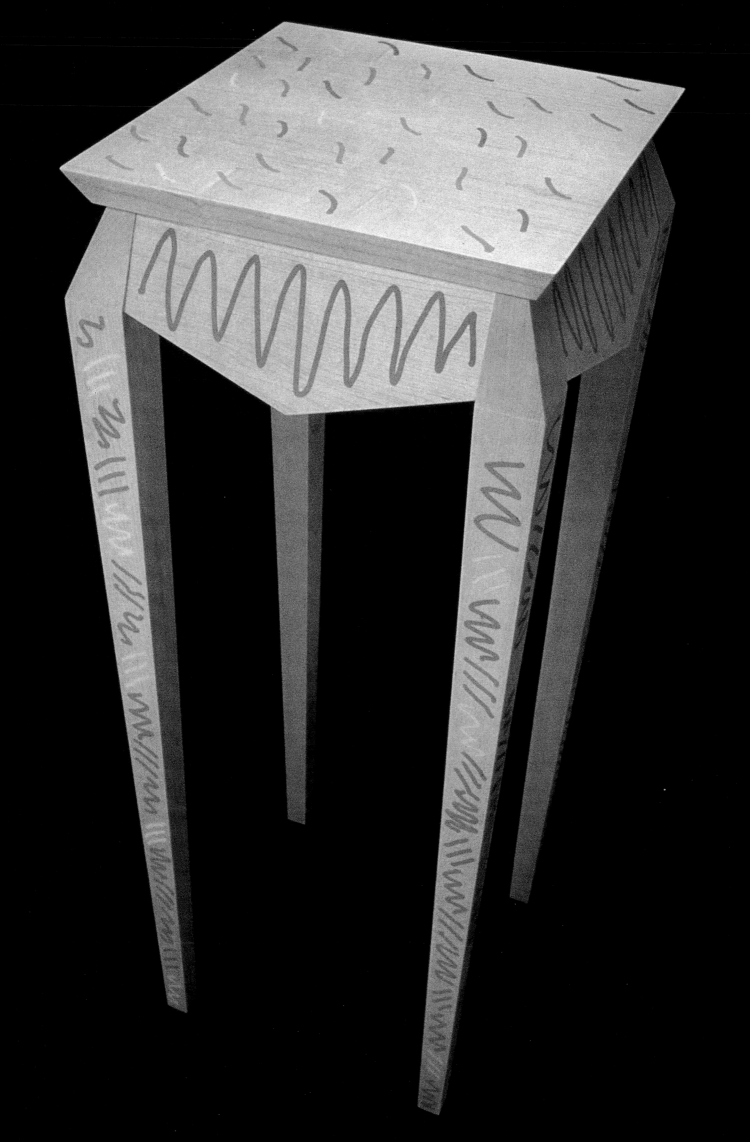

Preceding page:
*PETER FLEMING*
Toronto, ON Canada
*An early Spring table*
Hard maple,
colored epoxy inlay
30 in. x 15 in. x 15 in.
Photo by Peter Hogan

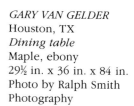

*GARY VAN GELDER*
Houston, TX
*Dining table*
Maple, ebony
29½ in. x 36 in. x 84 in.
Photo by Ralph Smith
Photography

*WILLIAM R. BARTOO*
Fredonia, NY
*Table*
Bird's-eye maple, purpleheart
19 in. x 14 in. x 21 in.
Photo by Paul Pasquarello

*A.J. VanDENBURGH*
Rochester, NY
*Dining table and chairs*
Bleached maple, ebony
48 in. x 64 in. x 30 in.
Photo by Tracey Coletta

*"Table expands to seat six."*

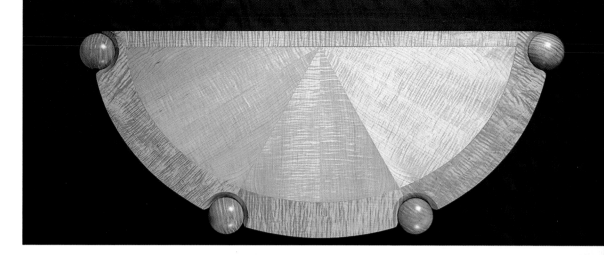

BRYAN SMALLMAN
South Norwalk, CT
*Table*
Curly maple, wenge
43 in. x 30 in. x 18 in.
Photo by Bill West

RICHARD TANNEN
Rochester, NY
*End table*
Black lacquered maple,
curly maple
26 in. x 21 in. x 18 in.
Photo by A. Dean Powell

THOMAS LOESER
Cambridge, MA
*Monopoly table*
Oak and Baltic birch
plywood, enamel paint,
aniline dye
18 in. x 48 in. x 42 in.
Photo by A. Dean Powell

ROBERT J. CHEHAYL
Hoboken, NJ
*Coffee table*
Purpleheart, glass
25 in. x 33 in. x 104 in.
Photo by A. Dean Powell

*JOHN IRELAND*
Toronto, ON Canada
*End table*
Curly maple, purpleheart
16 in. x 16 in. x 24 in.
Photo by Peter Hogan

*MARK GRAVINO*
*and JESSE GOODE*
Scottsville, NY
*G & G tables*
Stained maple, prismacolor
(colored pencils), lacquer
18 in. x 18 in. x 20 in.

*STEVEN HOLMAN*
Dorset, VT
*Hot-mustard table*
Maple, curly maple, walnut,
cherry, aniline dyes, lacquer
29 in. x 26 in. x 10 in.
Photo by Cook Neilson

JOHN MARCOUX
Providence, RI
*Trillium table*
Crab apple with fiber reactive
dye, glass top
29 in. x 21 in.
Photo by A. Dean Powell

*"Assembled with steel cable
at joints, soldered into
retainer washers on the
outside of each joint."*

GLEN D. FULLER
Indianapolis, IN
*Coffee table*
Padauk, Mexican rosewood,
African marble
19 in. x 15 in. x 34 in.
Photo by Spahr Photography

TOM GLEASON
and EDWARD LIPKA
Chicago, IL
*Nightstand*
Rift-cut white oak solid and
veneers, ¾-in. glass top
24 in. x 20 in. x 20 in.
Photo by David Rigg;
designed by Jon Cockrell

*"Legs are solid oak mitered
together. Leg 'tips' are also
mitered to obtain grain
consistency."*

JOHN CLARK
Penland, NC
*Long tall black table (1986)*
Cherry, purpleheart, Formica
74 in. x 20 in. x 34 in.
Photo by A. Dean Powell

JOHN KENNEDY
Philadelphia, PA
*Coffee table*
Curly maple, hard maple,
padauk
52 in. x 28 in. x 17 in
Photo by Gary McKinnis

DAVID A. MUNKITTRICK
River Falls, WI
*Infant's changing table*
Birch, ash, basswood
20 in. x 43 in. x 31 in.
Photo by Philip D. Hinz Set
Designs

MICHEL ARSENEAU
Petit-Rocher, NB Canada
*Table*
Maple, mahogany
38 in. x 12 in. x 29 in.
Photo by Raymond Chiasson

JOHN SIMON
Beaverton, OR
*Cocktail table*
American black walnut,
African padauk
2½ in. x 15½ in. x 48 in.
x 17 in. (table height)
Photo by Jerome Hart

*"The walnut used in the
table came out of one piece
of wood."*

STEVEN G. STAIRS
Prince Edward Island, Canada
*Entrance table*
Ebonized cherry, curly
maple, dyed curly maple
47 in. x 29 in. x 13 in.
Photo by Michael Fortune

KENT JOHNSON
La Mesa, CA
*Tusk table*
South American rosewood,
walrus ivory
52 in. x 24 in. x 30 in.
Photo by Jon Woodward

*"Sight table used by a gem
dealer and clients for
inspecting gems."*

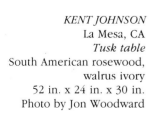

47

JIM WALLACE
Cedar Park, TX
*LF1 table*
Purpleheart, Italian alpiN-iN
veneer, painted ash
29 in. x 48 in.

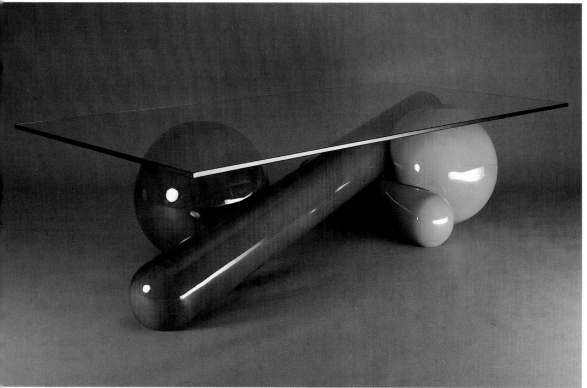

GLENN GAUVRY
Philadelphia, PA
*Low table*
Poplar, acrylic lacquer,
½-in. tempered glass
14½ in. x 32 in. x 63 in.
Photo © 1986 Gary McKinnis

*"All wood parts were turned
on a lathe, hand-shaped to
fit, then finished with 12
coats of tinted clear
lacquer."*

DAVID ORTH
Oak Park, IL
*Coffee table*
Mahogany, plastic laminate,
enamel
15¼ in. x 38½ in. x 16¾ in.
Photo by Aldis Darre

STEVEN EMRICK
Ridgecrest, CA
*Dollar-sign table*
Curly maple on poplar
plywood, black lacquered
maple and mahogany,
annodized aluminum, glass
20 in. x 40 in. x 18 in.
Photo by Beth Largen Emrick

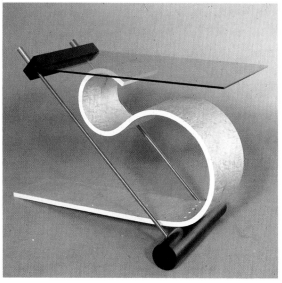

HAL E. DAVIS
Monroe, NC
*Cocktail waitress*
Red oak
45 in. x 20 in. x 20 in.
Photo by Jim Chappell

*"Stack lamination
and carving."*

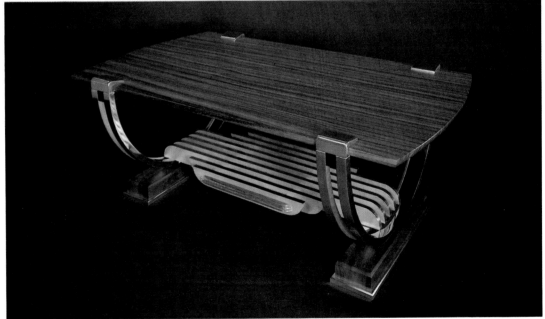

ROGER HEITZMAN
Scotts Valley, CA
*Coffee table*
Guanacosta wood
43 in. x 25 in. x 14 in.

BRUCE WILKINSON
Canoga Park, CA
*Coffee table*
Red oak base; metal laminate
on plywood framework
18 in. x 36 in. x 72 in.
Photo by Laura Wilkinson

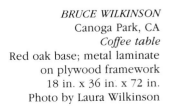

HUGH BELTON
McLean, VA
*Coffee table*
Claro walnut grafted with
English walnut; base is one-
quarter in. steel plate with
black lacquer finish
50 in. x 38 in. x 16 in.
Photo by John Bowden
Studios

MICHAEL P. O'BRIEN
Stillwater, MN
*Coffee table*
Walnut, cherry veneers
21 in. x 54 in. x 16 in.
Photo by Paul Crosby

MICHAEL PENCK
Glenalta, SA Australia
*Boardroom table*
Rimu, jarrah
146 in. x 31-55 in.

*"The two tops are resting on
rubber domes, which are
inserted into the bases."*

BERNARD GOUVEIA
Washington, DC
*Low table*
Western cedar, purpleheart
26 in. x 17 in. x 70 in.
Photo by Paul Kennedy

50

PAUL HARRINGTON
San Francisco, CA
*Buddhist altar*
Purpleheart, ebony
Cabinet—36 in. x 8 in. x 20 in.
table—66 in. x 36 in. x 18 in.
low table—36 in. x 20 in.
x 18 in.
Photo by Peter Donaldson

MICHAEL PUHALSKI
San Luis Obispo, CA
*Office table*
Honduras mahogany, bird's-
eye maple, black walnut,
eastern hard maple
29 in. x 26 in. x 66 in.
Photo © Josef Kasparowitz

JOHN SCHWARTZKOPF
Cedar Rapids, IA
*Serving tables*
Wenge, cordia
11½ in. x 11¼ in. x 32 in.
Photo by Mitchell Benson
Photography

*"These tables (both identical)
were made to be used in a
Japanese-influenced living
room setting (with both
traditional and modern
furniture)."*

51

STEVEN J. HIRSH
New Hope, PA
*Occasional table and stools*
Butternut, mahogany
Table—38 in. x 48 in. x 12
in.; stools—41 in. x 16 in.
Photo by Xenophon A. Beake;
co-designed with Ann Brothers

ANDY WEBSTER
Sumas, WA
*Table and six chairs*
Birch
Table—73 in. x 31 in. x 29 in.
chairs—17 in. x 17 in.
x 32½ in.
Photo by David Scherrer

52

DAN MOSHEIM
Arlington, VT
*Dining table*
Red oak, rosewood
35 in. x 78 in. x 29 in.
Photo by Cook Neilson

SCOTT C. SMITH
Pittsburgh, PA
*Hip end table*
Honduras mahogany, maple,
black-dyed veneer
22½ in. x 31 in. x 25 in.
Photo by David Albrecht

CRAIG E. STEIDLE
Waterford, VA
*Coffee table*
Narra, mango
60 in. x 36 in. x 18 in.
Photo by Charlie Brown

*"Mango from 300-yr.-old tree
toppled by typhoon in the
Philippines."*

LOY D. MARTIN
Palo Alto, CA
*Sideboard*
Steamed pearwood, bubinga,
eucalyptus, maple, ebony
54 in. x 38 in. x 19 in.
Photo by Victor Budnik

*"Sawn veneers."*

JEANNOT BELANGER
Ste.-Foy, PQ Canada
*Center table*
Honduras mahogany
30 in. x 42 in.
Photo by Jean Jolin

RICHARD B. CROWELL
Alexandria, LA
*Sheraton side table*
Louisiana cypress, mahogany
20½ in. x 15¼ in. x 29½ in.
Photo by John C. Guillet

THOMAS WOOD
St. Paul, MN
*Chippendale piecrust table*
Mahogany
30 in. x 30 in.
Photo by Jim Gallop

NEIL LAMENS
and JOHN WALLACE
Lindenhurst, NY
*Table*
South American cedar,
Honduras mahogany,
glass insert
19 in. x 32 in. x 33 in.
Photo by Walter Bredel

*"Hand and Dremel
carving."*

# Chairs

On a quiet day recently, at the Halifax Maritime Museum when the guards weren't looking, I reached inside an open-topped display case and rearranged a wooden deck chair from the Titanic. The chair, skimmed from the otherwise empty swells of the North Atlantic in the days after the unsinkable sank, has been refurbished with a new caned seat. Today it looks, in a spooky kind of way, as sturdy and inviting as those in accompanying photos of the era, where passengers are lounging on deck, sunning, sleeping, smiling at the camera.

The compulsion to crane my arm over the Plexiglas was more than a whim to act out a popular saying about futile gestures. It was mischief in response to the sheer magnetic power of chairs, *any* chairs, and especially *wooden* chairs. It was an impulse related, I'm convinced, to the one which, at some point in their careers, seems to infuse so many designers, sculptors and woodworkers with the energy of true believers—to design, build and plunk down in a chair of their very own creation.

It's hard to say just why we fixate on chairs. Next to the full-length mirror, the chair may be the most narcissistic piece of furniture. Next to the bed, it may be the closest we get, on the slide from vertical to horizontal, to the Tranquility Tank. What's not in doubt is that for users, chairs are intimate and personal, tied for some to the relief of pain and for many to the pursuit of pleasure.

Lightning may have provided the first wooden chair for nomadic hunters, with a storm-felled log grazing a still-erect tree, the two together offering dry seat and backrest. Less speculative is our knowledge of the chairs being made in Egypt in the third millennium B.C., when the privileged elite of the Nile were conscripting craftsmen to create what were literally seats of power. By the mid-14th century B.C., Pharonic thrones and portable wooden folding stools for army commanders had fused forever the notions of chair and authority. The idea of real informal comfort had to wait for the Greeks, for whom by the 6th century B.C. the celebrated *klismos* chair was offering a shallow concave backrest. For the vast majority of Europeans, rude benches remained for centuries rare and coveted possessions.

By the 16th century new forms had emerged. The rear panel of the European storage chest, for example, had been extended to support a sitter's back, while its sides were elongated into arm rests. Chairmaking had matured as a distinct craft, combining the skills of the turner, the joiner and the carver. Chroniclers have long been fond of seeing the essential style of a given period succinctly captured in its finest chairs. What is less often acknowledged is that up until this century, virtually all chairs were made of wood. Today when a maker of chairs looks into his historical rear-view mirror, he sees a long, tree-lined vista.

For the contemporary designer seeking a fresh solution, the task is still daunting, demanding as it does the fully integrated resolution of three separate problems.

The first of these is basic engineering—a structure strong enough to hold the user suspended above the floor in a more or less upright position. The woodworker sketching at the drawing board is suddenly up against the multiple demands of load-bearing, enclosing, connecting, stabilizing and, when all that is done, softening this matrix of applied geometry out of compassion for the human body.

Choices, we learn quickly, lead rapidly in different directions on the design compass: dining vs. lounging, sticks vs. panels, stack-laminated bulk vs. minimal frame, bandsawing vs. steam-bending. Each decision steers the maker in a new direction, and each one has implications for the second major challenge, that of purely visual success. Does the chair look good from all angles? Chairs represent a particularly knotty sculptural problem by virtue of the bundle of constraints placed on form by function. The dilemma is familiar to any lounge-chair designer who has been sorely tempted, at the urging of aesthetics, to chop four inches off the length of arms that were functionally just right to begin with.

The length of chair arms is only one of the aspects of the third major challenge, that of ergonomics. Not only must the chair be strong and beautiful, it has to be *comfortable*—a notoriously subjective attribute which, as Goldilocks taught us all while still kids, is utterly different for Mama Bear, Papa Bear and Baby Bear. One size does *not* fit all, a fact secure in the face of mounting literature that claims to dictate optimal pitch, height, length, contour and density for the seat and the back of the ideal chair. Add to this the conflict that arises when you try to reconcile the spatial needs of the wriggle factor with the unholy urge to cocoon the whole body like a foot in an expanded-polyurethane ski boot, and you can expect to work late and probably lose some sleep.

The very constraints of chairmaking seem to unleash energy and imagination, bringing out the artist in the woodworker and the woodworker in the artist, and offering a signature piece for both. More than any other useful artifact, chairs invite a playfulness on the boundary dividing the functional from the purely expressive.

Perhaps it is because the quest for the perfect chair is an essentially insoluble problem that its contemplation so often shades off into perplexity, humor, even self-parody. Collections of chairs in one place can always be counted on to create a sense of festival, a phenomenon nowhere clearer than in the pages that follow.

*—Tom Hurley*

Preceding page:
*PAUL ST. GERMAIN*
New Lebanon, NY
*Chair*
Cherry
33½ in. x 19 in. x 16¼ in.
Photo by Paul Rocheleau

*KALLE FAUSET*
New York, NY
*Butterfly chair*
Ebonized walnut, madrona
burl veneer, purpleheart,
pau amarelo
30 in. x 30 in. x 29 in.
Photo by A. Dean Powell

*LARRY J. ERPELDING*
Colorado Springs, CO
*Love seat*
Spalted ash
28 in. x 30 in. x 74 in.
Photo by Ed Plank;
upholstery by Mark Lafaye

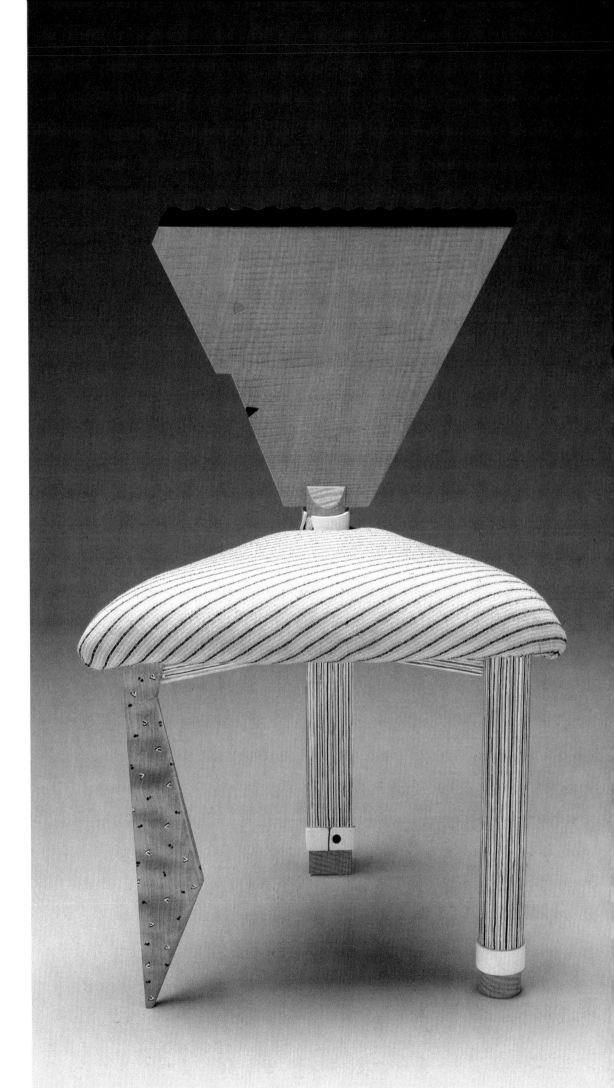

*DUDLEY HARTUNG
and ELLEN MASON*
Somerville, MA
*Marcel chair*
Tasmanian eucalyptus,
ebonized oak, curly birch,
Baltic birch plywood, plastic,
silk upholstery, polychrome
33 in. x 20 in. x 20 in.
Photo by Tony Scarpeta

DAVID L. SMITH
New Bedford, MA
*Tavares love seat*
East Indian rosewood,
ash frame construction
45 in. x 65 in. x 26 in.
Photo by A. Dean Powell

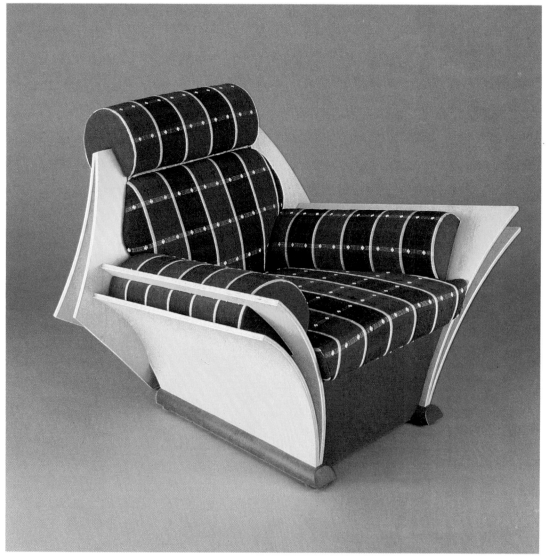

FRED BAIER
Scottsville, NY
*Comfortable chair*
Birch plywood lamination
veneered in English
sycamore, handwoven wool
upholstery
40 in. x 40 in. x 40 in.
Photo by Philip Grey

*"Made from six profiles of the
same curved lamination."*

60

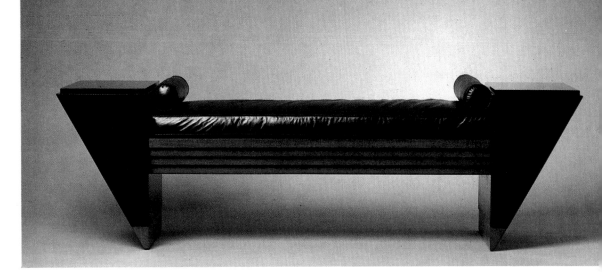

LEE WEITZMAN
Chicago, IL
*Divan*
Dyed mahogany, lacewood,
medium-density fiberboard,
leather upholstery
22 in. x 78 in. x 20 in.
Photo by Joe Davis

NAOMI VOGELFANGER
New York, NY
*Origami chair*
Baltic birch plywood, paint,
upholstery
32 in. x 18 in. x 21 in.

JOHN and CAROLYN
GREW-SHERIDAN
San Francisco, CA
*Chairs*
Cherry
37 in. x 17 in. x 21 in.
Photo by Schopplein Studio;
painting by Patricia Dreher

GRAHAM CAMPBELL
Richmond, VA
*Warped bench*
Birch, plywood, paint
16¼ in. x 32 in. x 12 in.
Photo by Joan Harkness
Hantz

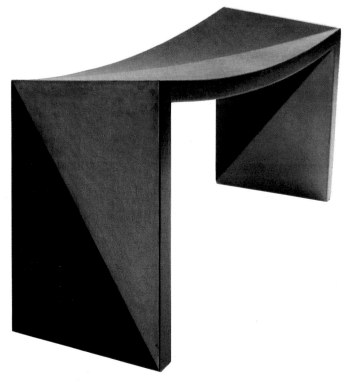

B. RANDOLPH WILKINSON
Richmond, VA
*Miniature Windsor settee
and chair*
Hard maple, poplar, oak
Settee—14½ in. high;
chair—14½ in. high
Photo by Melissa Kimmel

*"These are one-third of the
full-size settees and chairs I
make. Traditional Windsor
construction including
steam-bent pieces."*

WILLIAM TANDY YOUNG
Stow, MA
*Newport Queen Anne side
chair*
Walnut, soft maple
41 in. x 22 in. x 17½ in.
Photo by Susan De Long

RICHARD C. RUPPEL
Randolph, NH
*Continuous-arm chair*
Cherry
37 in. x 22 in. x 17½ in.

*JOHN A. WEISSENBERGER*
Winchester, VA
*Windsor writing armchair*
Curly maple, maple, poplar,
hickory, white oak
43 in. x 36 in. x 30 in.
Photo by Westervelt

*MICHAEL ELKAN*
Silverton, OR
*Rocking chair*
Oregon-grown walnut,
maple burl
42 in. x 20 in. x 23 in.
Photo by Karlis Grants
Photo Arts

*A.B. ACKER*
Cushman, MA
*Chippendale chairs*
Mahogany
20 in. x 20 in. x 40 in.
Photo by Michael Zide

STEPHEN B. CRUMP
Memphis, TN
*Love seat*
Rift-cut white oak,
handwoven cane
45 in. x 64 in. x 28 in.
Photo by Frederick Toma

DAVID D. FLOYD
San Luis Obispo, CA
*Rocking chair*
Oak, padauk
30 in. x 34 in. x 42 in.

MICHAEL GILMARTIN
Atlanta, GA
*Rocking chair*
Marine fir plywood,
Peruvian walnut
37 in. x 24 in. x 31 in.
Photo by Charlie Akers
Photography

CRAIG C. CAMPBELL, Cedar
Rapids, IA
*Rocking chair*
Maple with bird's-eye maple
22 in. x 20 in. x 32 in.
Photo by Larry S. Ferguson;
designed by Priscilla Steele

LEE F. HARVEY
Falmouth, ME
*Maple stool*
Maple, wenge
18 in. x 15 in. x 28 in.
Photo by Dale Olsen

TIM GORKA
Hilton Head, SC
*Jungle rocker*
Mahogany, walnut, bird's-eye
maple, quartersawn white
oak, hickory, ebony, Osage
orange
27½ in. x 25 in. x 16 in.
Photo by Doug Wolfe
Photography

*"Bandsawn and hand-
carved, assembled with
wedged dowels and pinned
tenons."*

TOBIAS DEAN
Trumansburg, NY
*Chair birds*
Poplar, cherry, paint
36 in. x 32 in. x 29 in.
Photo by Jamey Stillings

WEST LOWE
Missoula, MT
*Mistress Anne decorative
stool*
Aspen, lacquer, silk, lace
16 in. x 16 in. x 16 in.
Photo by Jon Schulman

JIM FAWCETT
Highland, NY
*"Shaker breaker" plate
spinning chair*
Cherry, white oak
23 in. x 23 in. x 20 in.
Photo by Ralph Gabringer

67

LOY D. MARTIN
Palo Alto, CA
*Psychiatrist's chair*
Bubinga, ebony
26 in. x 30 in. x 28 in.
Photo by Victor Budnik

DAVID VAN NOSTRAND
Atlanta, GA
*Armchair*
Black walnut
29 in. x 23 in. x 34 in.
Photo by Charlie Akers
Photography

*"Subtractive carving from a single piece of wood, using a chainsaw."*

68

ROBERT C. SOULE
New Haven, CT
*Writing table and chair*
Ebonized mahogany, walnut
with metal inlay
Table—26 in. x 50 in. x 28½ in.
chair—21 in. x 21 in. x 46 in.
Photo by Joseph Szajzfai

JONATHAN COHEN
Seattle, WA
*Mirror-image valets*
Honduras mahogany
17 in. x 17 in. x 54 in.
Photo by John Switten

LARRY and NANCY
BUECHLEY
El Valle, NM
*Armchair*
Maple with padauk
40 in. x 24 in. x 20 in.
Photo by Richard Faller

JOHN M. PIERSON
La Mesa, CA
*Hall bench*
Maple, lacquer finish
17½ in. x 80 in. x 15½ in.
Photo by Stephen Simpson

FREDERICK PUKSTA
Claremont, NH
*Stool*
Ash, ebonized cherry, ebony
24 in. x 24 in. x 30 in.
Photo by Marie Kolchak

MICHAEL PIERSCHALLA
New Bedford, MA
*Tall chair*
White oak, Baltic birch
plywood, Formica ColorCore
66 in. x 20 in. x 20 in.
Photo by A. Dean Powell

DALE BROHOLM
Jamaica Plain, MA
*Side chair*
Curly maple veneer, curly
maple, pearwood, glass
48 in. x 22 in. x 18 in.
Photo by A. Dean Powell

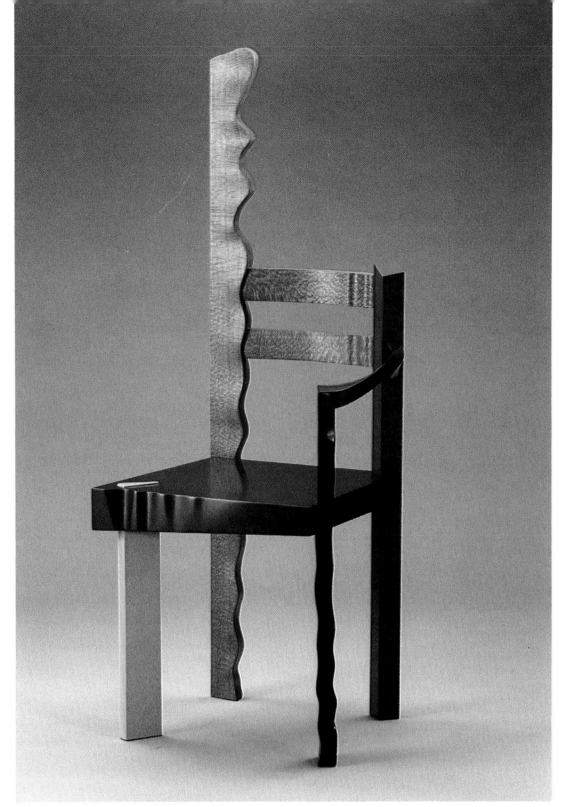

*SVEN PAVEY*
Mississauga, ON Canada
*Asymmetrical side chair*
Australian lacewood,
lacquered hard maple,
medium-density fiberboard
45 cm. x 42 cm. x 122 cm.

*CATHERINE V. SICANGCO*
La Mesa, CA
*Bench*
Maple, padauk
16 in. x 61 in. x 28 in.
Photo by Lawrence Hunter

*"Finish—black aniline dye*
*for maple areas, teak oil for*
*padauk areas."*

71

TONY DEVONALD
Louth, Lincolnshire, England
*Corner chair*
Sycamore maple
17½ in. x 17½ in. x 46 in.

*"A commissioned design as a
memorial to the embroiderer
of the seat cushion."*

THOMAS J. DUFFY
Ogdensburg, NY
*Bench*
Holly veneer, English
harewood, purpleheart legs
and stretchers, dyed wood
inlays, gold leaf
14⅜ in. x 34½ in. x 17 in.
Photo © Museum of Fine Arts,
Boston

PETER BARRETT
Portland, ME
*Conference-table chair*
Black lacquered maple,
bird's-eye maple,
purpleheart, brass

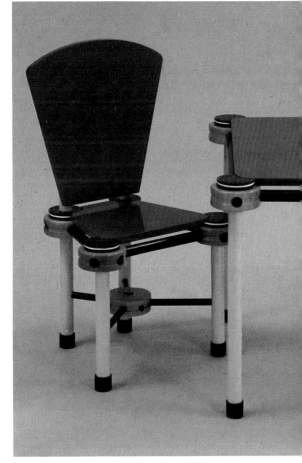

JOHN CHIARA
North Plainfield, NJ
*Child's armchair*
Walnut
28 in. x 16 in. x 13 in.

JOANNE SHIMA
Newtown, PA
*Child's table and chair*
Maple, birch, plywood, paint
Table—24 in. x 24 in. x 17 in.
chair—14 in. x 22 in. x 12 in.

STEPHEN DANIELL
Hartford, CT
*Nemo chairs*
Ash, cherry
34 in. x 24 in. x 18 in.

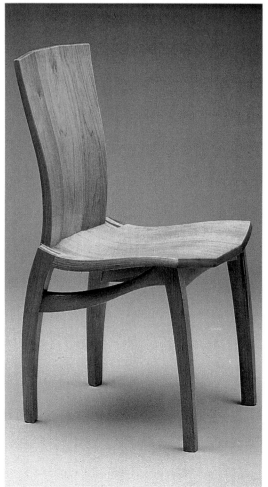

*ROBERT FREEMAN*
Somerville, MA
*Side chair*
Maple
33 in. x 18 in. x 18 in.
Photos by Michael Germer

RALPH PHILLIPS
Sisters, OR
*Chair*
Black walnut
27 in. x 25 in. x 22 in.
Photo by Indivar Sivanathan

RON DIEFENBACHER
St. Louis, MO
*Armchair*
Ash, oak
24 in. x 21 in. x 30 in.
Photo by Randall Hyman

75

BOB INGRAM
Philadelphia, PA
*Settee*
Lacewood, bubinga
32 in. x 28 in. x 60 in.
Photo by Rick Echelmeyer

DAVID B. FOWLER
Albuquerque, NM
*Side chair*
Maple, curly maple, ebony,
cabretta
15 in. x 33 in. x 17 in.
Photo by Ken Riemer

YALE BRUCE BERMAN
Pittsburgh, PA
*Chair from "Mussetta di
Opulence"*
Honduras mahogany, sapele,
Benin, bubinga, lacquer,
plywood core
18 in. x 20 in. x 36 in.
Photo by Michael Ray

76

MICHAEL HELTE STRONG
Bellingham, WA
*Armchair*
East Indian rosewood
30 in. x 23 in. x 24 in.
Photo by Rod Burton

JEFF KELLAR
Portland, ME
*Lounge chair*
East Indian rosewood
31 in. x 24 in. x 28 in.
Photo by Stretch Tuemmler

*"Upholstery is mohair over foam rubber."*

ROBERT DIEMERT DESIGNS
Toronto, ON Canada
*Three leg stool*
Curly maple, Swiss
pearwood, leather
25 in. high
Photo by Peter Hogan

*"Each leg is a lamination of seven pieces of wood (three tapered wedges of curly maple with four slivers of Swiss pearwood for accents)."*

*LARRY OGDEN*
Camarillo, CA
*Doll chair*
Hickory, sassafras
12 in. x 11 in. x 12 in.

*MANIVALDE AESMA*
Burks Falls, ON Canada
*Chair*
Pine, maple rungs
18 in. x 18 in. x 37 in.

*MICHAEL HURWITZ*
Philadelphia, PA
*Bench*
Wenge with paint and
leather seat
55 in. x 16 in. x 19 in.
Photo by Tom Brummett

*JEFFRY MANN*
Aspen, CO
*Rocking chair*
Rosewood
24 in. x 46 in. x 46 in.
Photo by David Marlow

PHILIP WHITCOMBE
Toronto, ON Canada
*Armchairs*
Mahogany, black French
polish, wool upholstery
44 in. x 20 in. x 19 in.
Photo by Oyster Studio

SANDY VOLKMANN
Hamilton, MT
*Armchair*
American walnut, ebony
wedges, upholstered seat
17 in. x 21 in. x 38 in.
Photo by Jon Schulman

PAUL VACCARI
Ridgewood, NJ
*Side chair*
Cherry, raw silk
24 in. x 19 in. x 30 in.
Photo by A. Dean Powell

**MICHAEL FORTUNE**
Toronto, ON Canada
*Dining chairs*
American black walnut,
English holly (inlay),
leather upholstery
22 in. x 20 in. x 34 in.
Photos by David Allen

*"Steam-bent arms and legs,
hot-pipe bent back slats."*

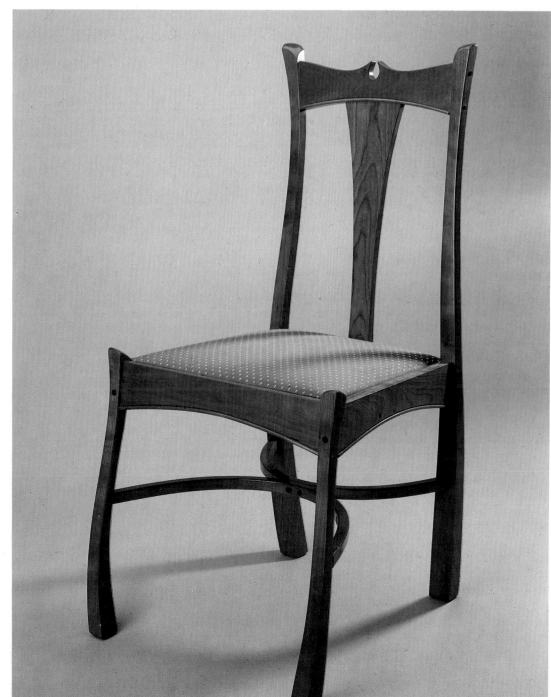

**JOHN RYAN**
**and RAY MULLINEAUX**
North Bennington, VT
*Cherry dining chair*
Cherry, purpleheart, silk,
lacquer
39 in. x 19½ in. x 21 in.
Photo by Cook Neilson

*"Traditional joinery, carved-
and-bent lamination,
upholstery and lacquer."*

# Beds

Our late 20th-century culture pays much attention to bedclothes but, it seems to me, remarkably little to bedsteads. A visit to the bedding section of a department store shows just how fancy our ideas about what we like to lie under and between have become. Comforters and sheets are marketed like haute couture, and we are presented with a range of choices from the wild and trendy through the terribly proper English country look to traditional white.

In contrast to all this splendor, the bed has become a poor thing. Most Americans sleep on a mattress on a box spring on a cheap metal frame, all completely hidden by the bedclothes, and this contraption is likely to have attached to it, at most, a low headboard of indifferent design. If the headboard happens to be covered with a bit of padding, the ensemble is dubbed a Hollywood bed, a name that suggests a kind of glamour that the object itself altogether lacks. Although the movie censors kept double beds off the screen for decades, old movies of the silent era sometimes show us splendid examples of big beds in the Deco and Modern styles that, no doubt, fed a popular craving for the kind of luxury that the Murphy bed back home in the walk-up did not provide. The 1920s, in fact, seem to have been the last great age of bedstead design; but while Art Deco designers were making enormous, elaborate beds, some of which cost as much as a house, the Modern Movement was getting underway in many parts of Europe, and that brought in an era of low-ceilinged rooms and a necessary emphasis on the horizontal in furniture design, since there was so little room for the vertical.

Now the working part of a bed, the surface we lie on, is necessarily horizontal. It follows that design interest is likely to be added by vertical elements, as in four-posters and those remarkable Victorian beds whose great, high, canopied headboards look as though they were intended to double as altarpieces. The Bauhaus-inspired bedroom, with its seven-foot ceiling, and the Modern Movement's industrial aesthetic, with its horror of ornament, combined to finish off the bed as a furniture type worthy of serious design consideration. Although the master designers of the European Modern Movement produced distinguished chaise longues, which are still in production half-a-century later, their bed designs, such as they were, held little interest and have never been popular.

When, after World War II, the Modern Movement captured the fancy of upwardly mobile Americans, low ceilings became standard here, too. There followed a period in which beds became ever lower, until the mattress was on the floor and even, in conversation pits, below it. Mattresses covered entire rooms and living quarters became pads. There was no need at all for headboards, footboards or rails.

It was against this background that the American Crafts Revival got underway in the 1960s. The initial inspiration for much of the early crafts-revival furniture was the Scandinavian Modern style of the 1940s and 1950s. Beds made by our newly emerging craftsmen benefitted from the Scandinavian's frank delight in displaying fine wood—Scandinavian bedrails, for example, are typically not covered by the bedclothes—but Scandinavian Modern headboards and footboards were scarcely more inspiring than their Bauhaus predecessors and, like them, were relentlessly horizontal. To the extent that modern craftsmen in America have addressed the problems of bed design—and this has certainly not been an area on which they have concentrated their attention—they have usually acquiesced to the prevailing horizontal mode.

But a change may be at hand. The younger, upwardly mobile, well-educated household-forming members of our late 20th-century American society (who, I would guess, are the principal buyers of craftsman-made furniture) are, during the 1980s, busily engaged in the rehabilitation of 19th- and early 20th-century houses. These have high-ceilinged bedrooms that cry out for verticals. Unfortunately, of course, the cry is not always heard by the bed buyer—I currently have a commission for a "standard" height, forty-two-inch headboard that is going into a Victorian room with ten-foot ceilings, where it will look like an orphan. Nevertheless, the restoration of such high-ceilinged bedrooms, and the current interest in ornament, open up exciting possibilities of which the designers/craftsmen whose beds are shown in the following pages are clearly very much aware.

—*A.U. Chastain-Chapman*

STEPHEN TURINO
Charlestown, RI
*Bed (queen size)*
Ebonized mahogany
86 in. x 66 in. x 55½ in.
Photo by Paul Ladd

JOHN JEFFERS
Charleston, SC
*Bentwood bed*
Red oak
88 in. x 59 in. x 36 in.
Photo by Terry Richardson

*"Bent lamination."*

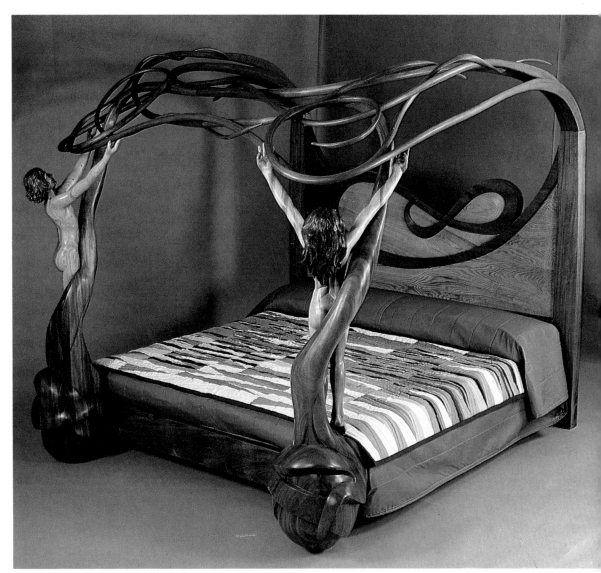

JEFFREY BRIGGS
Newburyport, MA
*Zucker commission*
Mahogany, oak, poplar
144 in. x 144 in. x 100 in.
Photo by Jan Bindas; quilt on
bed by Jude Larzelere

BRUCE KRANZBERG
Boulder, CO
*Bed*
*(see also p. 83)*
African padauk, wenge
40 in. x 70 in. x 92 in.
Photos by Viggio Studios

JUDITH AMES
Seattle, WA
*Shell bed*
White oak
60 in. x 80 in. x 52 in.
Photo by Greggory Krogstad

*"The dowels are steam-bent."*

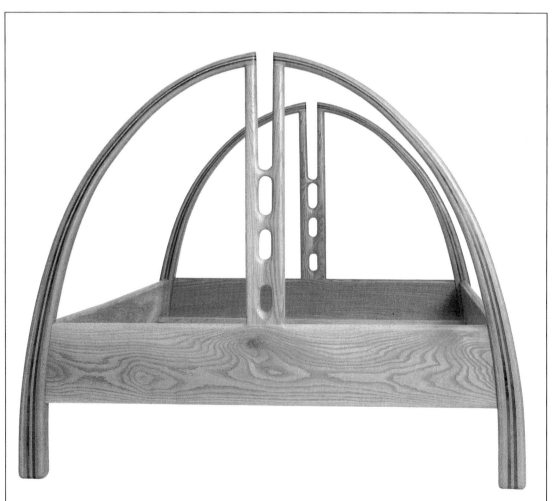

CHRISTOPHER HAUTH
Salem, OR
*Queen bed*
White oak, black walnut
48 in. x 57 in. x 82 in.
Photo by Robert Koval

*"Steam-bent tapered laminations."*

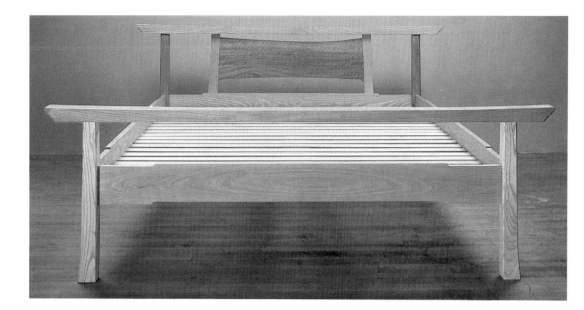

RALF KEELER
Seattle, WA
*Bed frame for futon*
Ash, pauldao
69 in. x 85 in. x 39 in.
Photo by Roger Schreiber

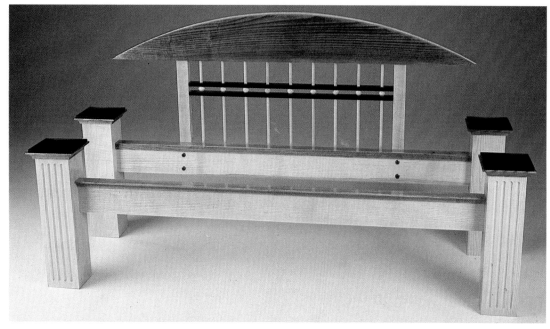

TOM FREEDMAN
Portland, OR
*Bed*
Ash, dye, acrylic enamel,
clear lacquer finish

TOM WHITLOW
Ithaca, NY
*Bed "Aurora Borealis"*
Curly maple, plain sugar
maple, black walnut wedges
89 in. x 68½ in. x 57 in.
Photo by Harvey
Ferdschneider

87

PAUL BIEHLER
Berkeley, CA
*Mono bed*
Bubinga, wenge, oak (slats)
80 in. x 60 in. x 37 in.

*"Stack laminated and carved."*

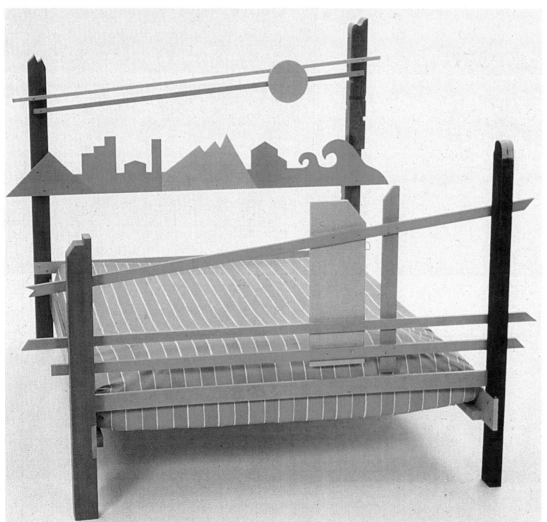

JAN BELL
Nashville, TN
*The bed that couldn't decide*
Redwood, poplar, pine
92 in. x 79 in. x 64 in.
Photo by Beth Odle

*"I let myself make the bed every way that I wanted. The footboard is a visualization of Hawaii and the guest house I hope to own one day."*

RICHARD CHALMERS
Providence, RI
*Child's lofted bed with*
*shelving and desk*
Maple, plywood, maple-
veneered plywood
48 in. x 96 in. x 78 in.
Photo by Gene Dwiggins

*"Knockdown construction:*
*the loft disassembles for*
*ease of moving."*

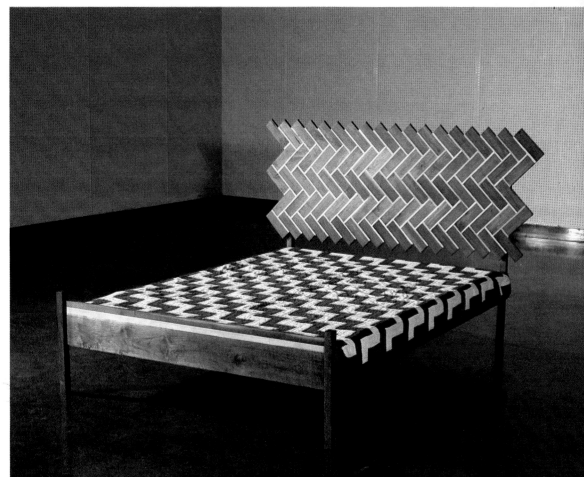

DAVID HALL
Brentwood, TN
*Z bed*
Walnut, poplar
84 in. x 72 in. x 48 in.

*"Herringbone pattern,*
*designed after a quilt made*
*by my grandmother."*

*OSCAR MORENO*
Fredricktown, MO
*Cradle*
Black walnut
48 in. x 72 in.
Photo by Jabr Dumit

*BARRIE GRAHAM*
Arundel, PQ Canada
*Baby's swinging cradle*
Mahogany
24 in. x 46 in. x 45 in.
Photo by Vincent Provost
Studio

*"All sides of cradle and the
end supports are coopered,
sequential pieces. It can be
disassembled in one minute
to six principle parts. The
joining mechanisms are
tapered, sliding dovetails."*

*JAMES D. ROOT*
Evanston, IL
*Crib/love seat/youth bed*
Cherry, red oak, walnut
60½ in. x 38½ in. x 56½ in.
Photo by Michael Baldi

*"Crib sides attach with
spring-loaded wooden latches
to come on and off quickly;
front removes to become love
seat (with cushions); taking
back off creates youth bed
with headboard and
footboard."*

90

BEN duPONT, JR.
Branford, CT
*Chase's crib*
Quartersawn white oak,
purpleheart
51 in. x 45 in. x 31 in.
Photo by Phillip Fortune

JEFF SCHALL
Milan, NH
*Cradle for Stephen*
Red oak, black walnut
48 in. x 36 in. x 27 in.
Photo by Andruskevich
Photography

BELA B. HACKMAN
Memphis, TN
*Will's cradle*
Ash, padauk
30 in. x 18 in. x 14 in.
Photo by Crocker
Photography

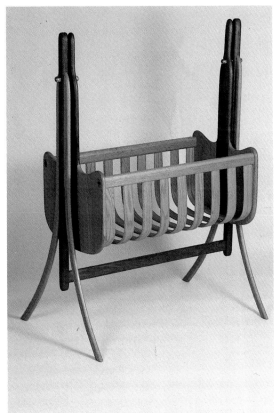

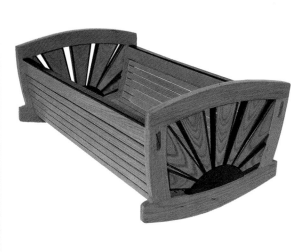

91

# Accessories

Duane and James, a couple of woodworkers, were in the middle of a run of plastic laminate business and not feeling that great about it.

There had been two kitchens, twenty-four feet of bank teller stations, and thirty-two feet of commercial display cases. The shop bills were getting paid, the installations looked great, the customers were happy, but something was missing—wood. There weren't any maple scraps to throw in the shop stove. There weren't any oak splinters in James' fingers. There were no pine planer shavings for Duane's friends who keep farm animals.

Around that time, Duane and James had put together some all-plywood carcases for a woodworker friend who found plywood spiritually beneath him. While they did that job, the shop walls heard some far-ranging discussions about woodworking, values and spirituality.

So when a carpenter friend asked the pair how they felt about making so many things with particleboard, James looked at Duane and said, "Tell him."

"Mark," Duane began, "this may come as something of a surprise to you, but particleboard is the very essence of trees. Boards that are cut from the body of a tree are full of the gross imperfections that plague all flesh. These boards twist and warp, demonstrating their lack of in-tuneness with the Cosmic One. But particleboard is made of the finest dust that floats up when the tree's body is killed, as though the escaping soul of wood were caught and held in each four-by-eight sheet. Particleboard embodies trees' highest consciousness, and to seal it in plastic laminate is to preserve it forever."

"Bull," said Mark. "You guys have been sucking the fumes of too much contact cement."

This story illustrates several things, one of which is that carpenters are not as stupid as cabinetmakers think they are. More to the point, it suggests how we woodworkers, a group of people who manipulate objects to make objects, get remarkably verbose talking about what it is we're doing, why we're doing it, and just what it all means.

We make things. We intend them to be useful, wish them to be appropriate and perhaps even beautiful. We do it to give a tree another life, to keep a business afloat, to express something of ourselves and the state of our work. We live with the object, invest it with our efforts, and then let it go. We are left with what the making of it has made of us. The things we make ultimately must stand free of us and all our words and feelings about them. They take on their own life in the world, as on these pages.

The work that follows is the most diverse category in this book. Some of these objects are free to come and go, light travelers seeking welcome. Others are deeply rooted in the one place for which they were intended. No two were born under the same constellation of need, method and motive.

But what leads a woodworker to build a mirror or lamp rather than, say, a table or chair? Why a door or spiral staircase instead of a cabinet? For some, like George Nakashima, the inspiration to make a piece may arrive in a dream. For most of us, the origin is more likely to come from outside ourselves in the form of a telephone call, a friend or potential customer walking through the door. "Can you make this?" they ask, and a job or a career is set in motion.

As problem-solvers, we find a proper challenge in perfecting the adjusting mechanism on a music stand, or finding a comfortable stride—as well as meeting a mandated standard—in the rise and run of a staircase. But I suspect that many of the pieces in this section may be the result of woodworkers being drawn to objects that resonate ineluctably with richly metaphorical lives that go beyond mere function. The unseen behind a screen, the door that is an emblem of the life behind it, the light shed by a lamp and the darkness it defines, a mirror that insists we look into ourselves, the sound of woodwinds waiting to be freed from sheet music on a stand made of trees, the context of use and space in features built into a home—there are coronas of charged meanings that surround these simple objects.

There is a danger, however, of so heavily investing an object with meaning, the weight of inexpressible personal longings, that our work becomes too self-conscious, the object overwrought, and the entire process too wordy and too precious. We may become paralyzed with fear of failure, afraid to ruin the piece, unaccepting of our own and wood's limitations, and unable to let the thing go.

The opposite pitfall—at the bottom of which we saw Duane and James struggling morally and professionally with a material whose usefulness depends on its being uniformly barren of individual character—is making objects devoid of personal feeling, or which we debase through lack of attention. They can only remain lifeless, and the process by which we make them can only diminish us.

So we search out where our talents are hiding, hope for a commission to do what we like doing most, and dream of the client who will pay for and accept no less than our very best work. We make things, and if we make them well, we may accept what the making of them makes of us.

It may be as though we have opened a door into this profession, climbed a stairway of skills and techniques, switched on the light of understanding, and looked in a mirror to see ourselves suddenly wooden, wordless and whole.

—*Richard Ewald*

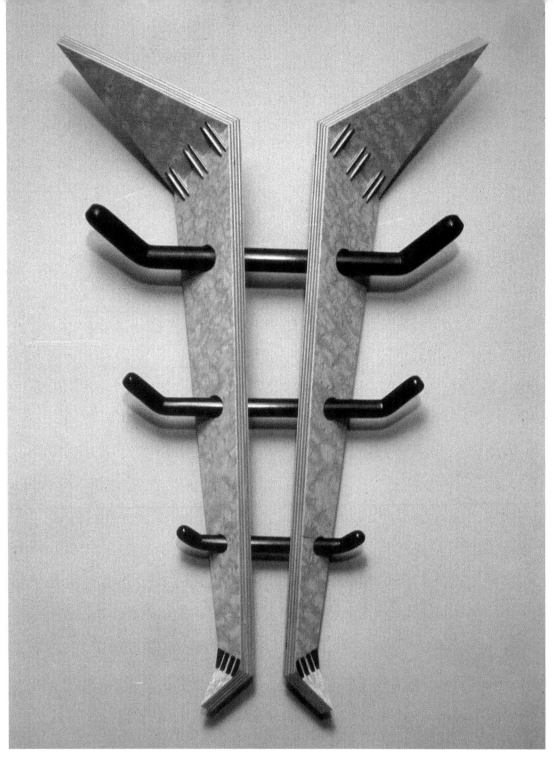

SEAN LEDOUX
Vancouver, BC Canada
*Tie/scarf tree a.k.a. wall
sculpture*
Bird's-eye maple veneer on
Baltic birch substrate, dyed
pearwood veneer, black
lacquered maple (dowel)
21 in. x 14 in. x 3 in.

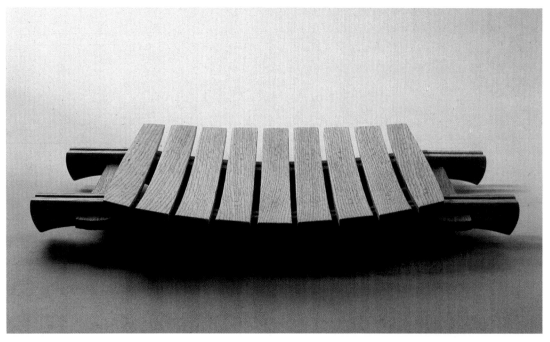

EDWIN RUPERT
Newtown, PA
*Ritual tray*
Oak bent and joined with
brass pins
18 in. x 11½ in. x 2 in.
Photo by Stefano Merlini

*JIM McGILL*
Seattle, WA
*Music stands*
Philippine mahogany,
western maple
21 in. x 42 in. x 61 in.; music
support—15 in. x 18½ in.
Photo by Skip Howard

*WILLIAM KEYSER*
Honeoye Falls, NY
*Music stand*
*(see also p. 93)*
Rosewood, ash
56 in. high
Photo by David J. Leveille

*JEFFREY WEBSTER*
Chicago, IL
*Adjustable music stand*
Ash, brass, plastic, ebony
58½ in. x 12 in. x 22 in.

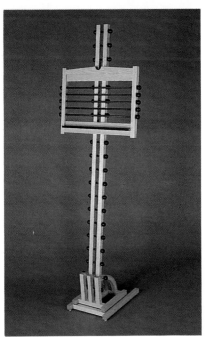

JEFFREY COOPER
Portsmouth, NH
*Folding screen #3*
Cherry, red oak, walnut,
imported rice paper with
inlaid ferns
70 in. x 88 in.
Photo by Pirini-Howe
Photography

CHRISTOPHER WEILAND
Penn Run, PA
*Screen*
Bird's-eye maple, red elm,
ebony
71 in. x 60 in.
Photo by Cesar Paredes

*ROBIN PARKINSON*
New York, NY
*Folding screen*
Mahogany
70 in. x 70 in.

*KIM FLEMING*
Grauenhurst, ON Canada
*Room-dividing screen*
Black walnut, white ash
72 in. x 108 in. x 1 in.
Photo by Dave Gregan

*MALCOLM SUTTLES*
Seattle, WA
*Folding screen*
Fir, fiberglass
84 in. x 28½ in.
(each section)
Photo by Tom Collicott

97

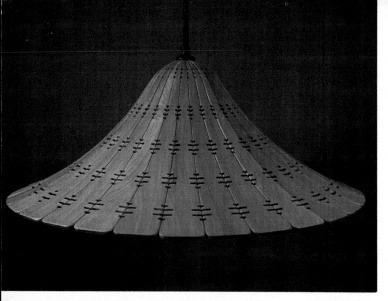

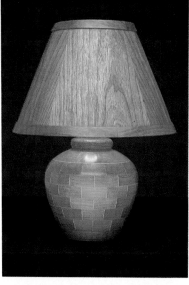

*BERT LUSTIG*
Berkeley Springs, WV
*Hanging lamp*
Hard maple pierced
24 in. x 10½ in.

*ROBERT LEACH*
Clinton, NY
*Table lamp*
Base—cherry segments
separated by maple strips;
shade—butternut, cherry
15 in. x 12 in.
Photo by Klineberg, Inc.
Commercial Photography

*TOM FREEDMAN
and BETH YOE*
Portland, OR
*Lamp*
Satinwood, ebonized ash,
etched glass
24 in. x 24 in. x 30 in.
Photo by David Brown

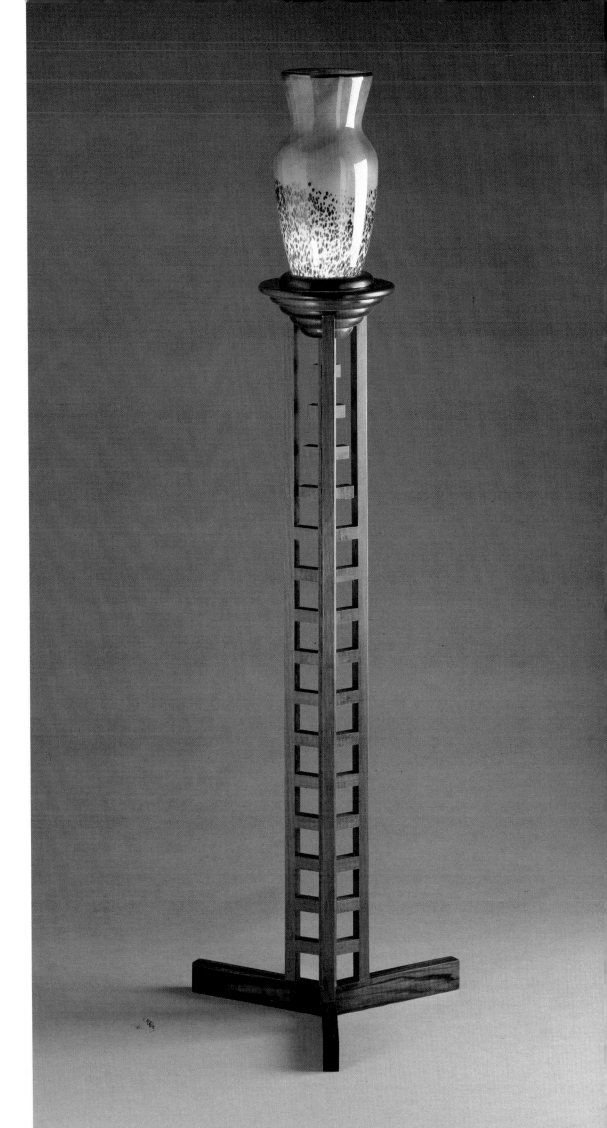

*BRUCE DECKER*
Slocum, RI
*Floor lamp*
Purpleheart, ebony,
blown glass
60 in. high
Photo by Marty Doyle; blown
glass by Mark McKonnell

99

WINFIELD AUSTIN
Mt. Prospect, IL
*Wall shelf with light*
Quilted mahogany veneer
60 in. x 24 in. x 24 in.

*"Torsion-box construction, vacuum molding and veneering."*

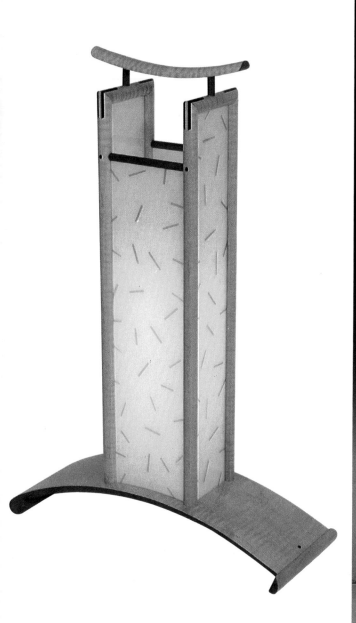

GEOFFREY WARNER
Exeter, RI
*Floor lamp*
Curly maple, ebony,
red lacquer, glass
20 in. x 16 in. x 7 in.
Photo by Paul Ladd

LEE TRENCH
Charleston, MA
*Lamp*
Ebonized ash, brass hinges
60 in. x 15 in. x 15 in.

*DAVID S. MARK*
San Francisco, CA
*Double-helix bookcase*
Natural birch plywood, solid
birch molding with
lauan-base laminate
80 in. x 38 in.
Photo by Moulin Gabriel
Studios

*"This piece can function as a
bookcase or as a display
fixture for artwork."*

101

TED HUNTER
Toronto, ON Canada
*Once upon a sandbank*
Cherry
64 in. x 44 in. x 30 in.
Photo by Jeremy Jones

*"Lathe-turned with texture transferred via carving machine from a sand casting of the beach."*

JOEL BENDER
Hamilton, MT
*Set of three utility spoons*
White oak, Oregon myrtle
2½ in. x 13½ in.; 2½ in. x 11 in.

*HOWARD WERNER*
Mt. Tremper, NY
*Hollow disc*
Elm
41 in. x 8 in.
Photo by Woody Packard

103

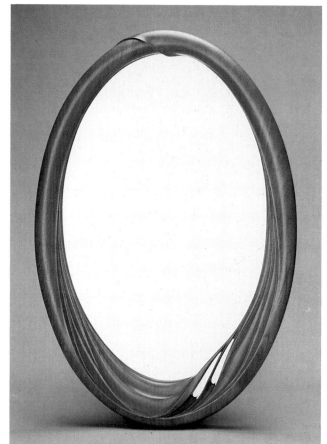

*GREGG LIPTON*
Portland, ME
*Standing mirror*
Brazilian satinwood,
purpleheart
17½ in. x 54 in.
Photo by John Tanabe

*GRANT VAUGHN*
Lismore, NSW Australia
*Carved oval mirror*
Australian red cedar, lacquer
32 in. x 21 in.

*"Initially shaped with power tools, then conventional carving chisels."*

*TONY CLARKE*
W. Hatfield, MA
*Shell mirror*
Cherry, padauk
18 in. x 40 in.
Photo by David Levy

*CHRIS KUNKLE*
Witter, AR
*Wall mirror*
Hand-carved cherry
32 in. x 30 in.
Photo by Bob White

*TIMOTHY SUTHERLAND*
Atlanta, GA
*Summer screen*
Mahogany
34 in. x 75 in.
Photo by Bill Fibben

104

*TONY LA MORTICELLA*
Coburg, OR
*Entry door*
Honduras mahogany with
ebony pins, port orford cedar,
western red cedar
34 in. x 78 in.
Art glass by Gayle Marquess

*"The construction of the door
is conventional mortise-and-
tenon; the ebony pins are
functional."*

*DANIEL BOUDREAU*
Clearwater, BC Canada
*Main entrance door to
dental clinic*
Cedar burl, walnut, oak,
Douglas fir, birch, poplar,
pine
Door—88 in. x 70 in.;
casing—4 in. x 10 in.
Photo by Terry Richmond

*"Sandwich construction with
insulated core, marquetry is
fastened to plywood backing
and applied to frame."*

*JOHN MARTINEZ,
PHIL MARTINEZ
and DAVID SAMORA*
Santa Fe, NM
*Arched doorway with etched
glass*
Philippine mahogany;
lumber, veneer
96 in. x 60 in. x 12 in.
Etched glass by Mary Kanda

*SHERMAN E. LaBARGE*
Conway, NH
*Carved entry door*
Mahogany, stained glass
80 in. x 36 in. x 1¾ in.
Photo by Andrew Haltof

*" 'Spring,' family name goes
on banner (one-of-a-kind)."*

WAYNE L. WESTPHALE
Steamboat Springs, CO
*Mantel clock*
Padauk, Bolivian rosewood
18 in. x 12 in. x 6 in.
Photo by Bobby Hansson

PAT GURESKI
Nashville, IN
*Spice rack*
Red oak, black walnut
2¼ in. x 2¼ in. x 3¾ in. (each
container)
Photo by Dave McCrary

106

JAMES ADAMS
Leverett, MA
*Photographic camera*
Philippine mahogany, brass
60 in. x 60 in.
Photo by Peter Jones

*"This photographic camera
produces 20-in. x 24-in.
negatives."*

KENT BAILEY
Annapolis, MD
*Luxury liner sculpture*
Oak, walnut, mahogany, teak
34 in. x 3½ in. x 29 in.

*"Has four drawers for
drawing instruments plus
inkwell hatch for India ink.
The smokestacks are brass,
the funnels copper, and the
whistles, anchor and diving
boards are sterling silver. The
smoke clouds are ivory,
and the flags are fired
vitreous enamel."*

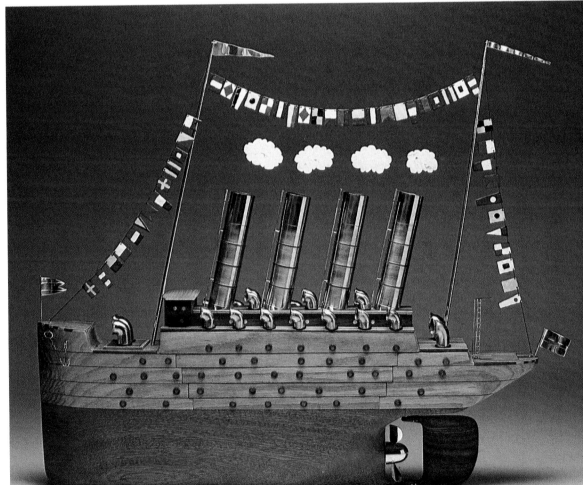

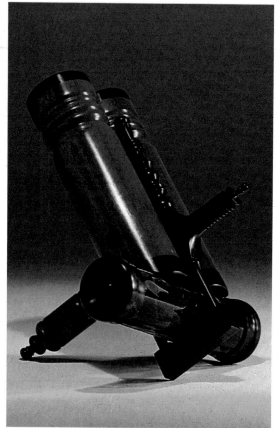

JOHN GOODMAN
Cambridge, MA
*Grandfather's clock*
Cherry, walnut
90 in. x 22 in. x 12 in.
Photo by Robert Schoen

*"In the collection of
Dan Quatrella."*

STEVEN J. GRAY
Bozeman, MT
*Double-barrel kaleidoscope*
Bloodwood, macassar ebony
7½ in. x 10½ in. x 11 in.

HARRY WILHELM
Groton, NY
*Television set*
Cherry, oak, padauk,
wenge, maple
46 in. x 22 in. x 17 in.

*DARRYL PFAU*
Kalamazoo, MI
*Wall relief*
Basswood; walnut;
wenge with gessoed,
lacquered wood
36 in. x 36 in. x 1½ in.

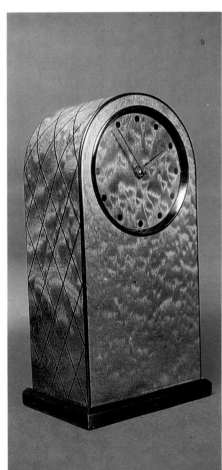

*JON FROST*
St. Paul, MN
*Mantel clock*
Quilted mahogany veneer,
ebony, brass
14 in. x 7 in. x 5 in.
Photo by John Gregor

*TERRY JOHNSTON*
Hamilton, ON Canada
*Hall table*
Bird's-eye maple, bubinga
30 in. x 16 in. x 14 in.

DARRYL KEIL
Portland, ME
*Lounge bar*
Honduras mahogany, African
ribbon-stripe veneer
204 in. x 228 in.
Photo by Geoffrey C. Parker

WALTER HUBER
Clackamas, OR
*Walnut mantelpiece with
applied carvings*
Walnut
82 in. x 49 in. x 10½ in.
Photo by Harold Wood;
designed by Sam Bush

**WILLIAM J. SCHNUTE**
Carmel Valley, CA
*River otters*
Cherrywood, agate,
stained glass
96 in. x 54 in. x 7 in.
Photo by Rob Bradley
Photography

111

# Bowls

When I decided to turn wood for a livelihood, I had seen a lathe in action for less than ten seconds (and eight years before, at that). I recalled, only vaguely, long-handled tools and the speed with which the squared blank became round. The speed—that's where the fascination lies. The facility to reduce the rough to symmetry in seconds, further satisfying our constant urge to create order in place of nature's rude chaos.

A wonderfully simple tool, the wood lathe. Difficult to master, but a skilled turner can reduce any irregular lump of wood to round very quickly. . .and to just about the sort of round you might want. The lathe was one of the earliest human inventions that enabled mass production, and it remains the tool upon which millions of chair or ladder rungs, door knobs, handles and the like are made, though many of the lathes are now automatic.

In the affluent Western world, hand turning is now largely the preserve of the amateur, an iceberg of a craft. Above the waterline are the high-profile professional virtuosos of the international seminar circuit, and a few of the more productive and skilled amateurs who, between them, stock the craft galleries formerly called gift stores. These men (incredibly few women appear to turn wood) mostly have a fixation about bowls and their bastard cousins, the "bowl forms," to the exclusion of all the other wonderful possibilities of the lathe. Below the waterline, the mass are more creative and wide-ranging in their application of techniques; the amateur has no need to be cost effective in earning a living, and so he can indulge in long or complicated jobs any professional might find uncommercial, even at the most pretentious gallery level.

Why this obsession with bowls? Apart from the fact that most bowl forms are quick and easy to create, wood is often a spectacular material and undoubtedly turners can display this better on the surface of a bowl or platter, rather than of a box, scoop, bangle or spindle. It is a sad fact (to me, anyway) that most bowl turners still seem preoccupied with the grain, color and figure of the wood—and with technique—at the expense of form. Thin is beautiful, and don't worry too much about the shape! Thin plus dramatic grain is sublime, it seems. A bowl of spectacular grain and color will always draw gasps of admiration, regardless of its shape, but this should never be taken as an indication of how good the bowl is. It is the wood that is being praised, not the bowl. Not all bowls have a form strong enough to ensure that, once the wood has oxidized and mellowed, it will be treasured through generations. There are a lot of dull bowls riding along on the material purporting or aspiring to be Art (with a capital A), but more than a high price tag and pretty wood should be required to justify that accolade.

I continue to make bowls. But for me, wood is a convenient material and not the object of a sustained love affair. What I chase are those illusive proportions and curves that combine only very occasionally to a homogeneous whole, creating a usable, everyday sort of bowl that looks good and *feels* even better. The joy of turning wood is that I can create an object with greater speed and fewer hassles than is possible in almost any other medium, and so explore many forms over a relatively short period. And, I find the constant practice breeds fluency and finesse, which aids and encourages me to maintain the search. Away from bowls, the material rarely overwhelms the object. The challenges are concerned more with proportions and controlling the desire to display the trivia of turning virtuosity in the form of excessive beads and coves, especially while making spindles or boxes; the search for a box lid that fits perfectly should keep most of us quiet for a lifetime.

Among the finest work emanating from lathes recently are those quieter, less-flamboyant pieces that require great attention to detail and that frequently are more demanding of skills and technique (though not obviously so) than bowls. Small-scale boxes with exquisite detailing, interesting and surprising interiors, and lids that slide nicely—not too tight and not too loose. Others have screw lids with the grain still running through from base to lid, apparently unbroken. Or, sets of spindles featured in furniture or buildings, or again some of the wonderful laminated bowls immaculately made and of sound traditional form. It is such objects as these that should now be considered state of the art; not the ultra-thin bowls, no matter how large or spectacular. Most of this work never goes on sale, though a good deal is exhibited. But, unlike most bowls, practically all earn the right to be, and should become, the cherished heirlooms of generations.

—*Richard Raffan*

Preceding page:
*TED HODGETTS*
Millbrook, ON Canada
*Hollow vessel*
Walnut, holly, ebony,
red epoxy
9 in. x 9½ in.
Photo by Jack Ramsdale

*JAY HOSTETLER*
Athens, OH
*Free-edge bowl*
Catalpa
8 in. x 10½ in.
Photo by Chris Eaton/2c
Studios

*"Collection of
Mrs. Earl Seigfred."*

*ROD CRONKITE*
Racine, WI
*Decorative bowl*
Maple burl
6 in. x 8 in.

*WILLIAM FOLGER*
Crested Butte, CO
*Bowl*
Green-bark ceanothus burl,
also called wild lilac
7½ in. x 5 in.
Photo by Patrick Hickey

114

CLAY FOSTER
Krum, TX
*Turned vessel*
Live oak
16 in. x 9 in.

G.A. GOFF
Athens, GA
*Antlers*
Turned mountain-laurel root
13 in. x 7 in.

115

PETER M. PETROCHKO
Oxford, CT
*Butternut bowl with
bark exterior*
12½ in. x 11½ in. x 10 in.
Photo by Frank Poole

BRUCE MITCHELL
Point Reyes, CA
*Wishing well*
Yellow stringybark eucalyptus
10¾ in. x 21 in.

*"Outside rim is hand
chiseled."*

*STEVE LOAR*
Rochester, NY
*Bowl for the coastal tribes*
Spalted maple, dyed veneer,
plywood, paints
13 in. x 16 in. x 12 in.
Photo by Jamey Stillings

*"Turning, veneering,
sandblasting, painting."*

*JOSEPH KAZIMIERCZYK*
Trenton, NJ
*Carved bowl*
Basswood
9½ in. x 7½ in. x 3 in.

117

*MICHELLE HOLZAPFEL*
Marlboro, VT
*Woven vase*
Burled red maple
11 in. x 18 in.
Photo by Ralph Gabringer

118

*LOTTIE KWAI LIN WOLFF*
Norwalk, CT
*Ammonite bowl*
Maple
6¼ in. x 2¾ in.
Photo by Ted Wolff

*"Turned and carved."*

*PETER SZYMKOWICZ*
Shoreham, VT
*Untitled bowl*
Eastern hemlock burl
10 in. x 5¾ in. x 7½ in.

*"Chainsawn, carved,
scraped and sanded."*

*GEORGE VAN DYKE*
Alexandria, VA
*Bowl*
American holly
9 in. x 1½ in.
Photo by Chip Clark

119

STEVEN B. LEVINE
Dayton, NJ
*Balloon vessel*
Yellow poplar, bubinga
10 in. x 16 in.
Photo by Grant Peterson

ROBERT FRY
Covington, KY
*Wood vase*
Curly maple, mahogany
9 in. x 3 in.
Photo by Jay Bachemin

120

*MAX KRIMMEL*
Boulder, CO
*Turned-wood plate
(Makowenaplege)*
Maple, Hawaiian koa, wenge
37 in.

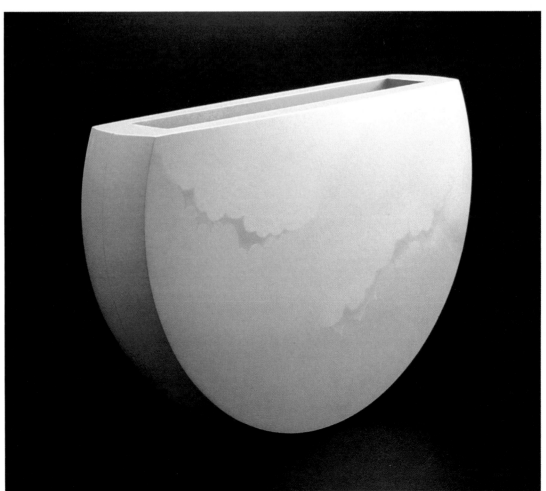

*WAYNE RAAB*
Waynesville, NC
*Cloud vase*
Maple, acrylic lacquer
16 in. x 3½ in.

*"Faceplate turned
and spray painted."*

121

WAYNE HAYES
Fredericton, NB Canada
*Bowl*
Walnut, padauk, rosewood,
ash
7 in. x 3½ in.
Photo by Don Johnson

GRANT VAUGHAN
Lismore, NSW Australia
*Carved bowl form*
Australian red cedar
11¾ in. x 6 in.
Photo by John W. McCormick

*"Carved, not turned. Power
tools were used for initial
roughing out, then carving
chisels were used for
shaping."*

*R.E. RENNER*
Vancouver, WA
*Flexible platter*
Myrtlewood burl
15 in. x 1 in.
Photo by Jim Piper

*JAY HOSTETLER*
Athens, OH
*Bowl*
Quilted maple, wenge
3½ in. x 12 in.
Photo by Chris Eaton/2c
Studios

123

ADDIE DRAPER
Tajique, NM
Bloodwood, ebony, holly,
black-dyed birch veneer
4¾ in. diam.
Photo by Bud Latven

*"Complex segmented
construction, build-turn-
build process."*

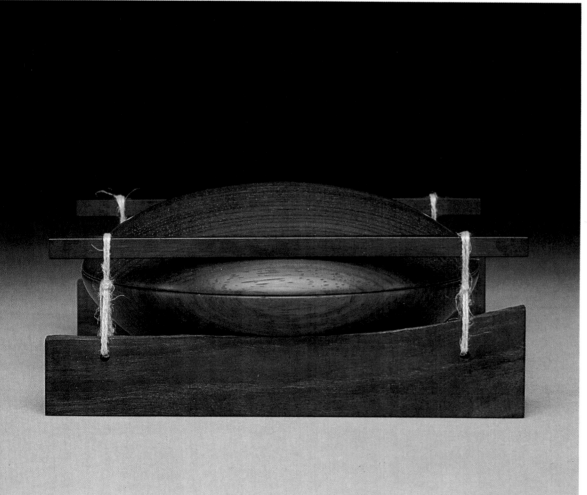

WAYNE HAYES
Fredericton, NB Canada
*Round-bottom container
and stand*
Padauk, ebony, linen cord
7 in. x 3 in.
Photo by Don Johnson

124

*BUD LATVEN*
Tajique, NM
*Pheus no. 3 in pau cetim*
Pau cetim (satinwood),
African blackwood, yellow
and black-dyed birch veneer
4½ in.

*"Stave construction, disk
and segmented lower
elements, build-turn-
build process."*

125

TODD CAMPBELL
Wailuku, Maui, HI
*Translucent closed form*
Norfolk pine
16 in. x 9 in. x ³⁄₁₆ in.
Photo by Eric T. Sato

*R.W. (BOB) KRAUSS, JR.*
Dinosaur, CO
*Lidded container*
Chittam burl
5 in. x 3 in.

*NIGEL B. BRIGGS*
Falls Church, VA
*Cherry bowl*
Cherry
7 in. x 4½ in.
Photo by Andrew Bradtke
Photography

*JOSEPH POLLAK*
Scarborough, ME
*Two bowls*
Cocobolo
6 in. x 2 in.; 6 in. x 1⅝ in.
Photo by Tom Pollack

126

ROLAND SHICK
Bethlehem, NH
*Goblets*
Curly maple, ebony, bocote
4½ in. x 3 in.
Photo by Andrew Haltof

KIP CHRISTENSEN
Plano, TX
*Lidded box*
Spalted maple
2 in. x 3½ in.
Photos by Robert Kuski

JOHN SERINO
Sugar Hill, NH
*Tree box*
Rock maple, purpleheart
10 in. x 2½ in.
Photo by Sue Drinder Garvan

*"Used for jewelry or other
precious things; purpleheart
is a free panel held in place
by a half-dovetail
turned ring."*

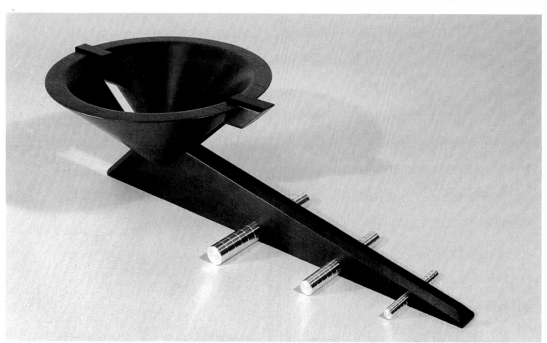

MICHAEL S. CHINN
Ames, IA
*Tri-1000 vessel*
Purpleheart, Indian ebony,
aluminum
4 in. x 12 in. x 6 in.

**PETER MURAD**
Marina Del Rey, CA
*Vases and bowl*
Baltic birch, padauk,
East Indian rosewood,
macassar ebony, walnut
Bowl—9½ in. x 4 in.; vases—
11 in. x 14 in., 6 in. x 9 in.,
8½ in. x 8 in.
Photo by Beverly Elam

**BARRY T. MacDONALD**
Grosse Pointe Park, MI
*Canister*
White ash, amaranth,
maple veneer
4½ in. x 8½ in.

*"Stave construction and
hand-rubbed lacquer."*

**MICHAEL D. MODE**
Zionsville, PA
*Chalice*
Cherry, Indian rosewood
9 in.
Photo by David Haas

129

DAN KVITKA
Corvallis, OR
*Vera-node form*
Verawood
13½ in. x 13 in.
Photo by Peter Krupp

DON MITCHELL
Glendale, AZ
*Vase*
Western maple burl
6 in. x 5 in.
Photo by Steven Burger

JASON MARLOW
Abbotsford, BC Canada
*Cherry bowl*
Bing cherry
7½ in. x 9½ in.
Photo by Dale Klippenstein

130

*THOMAS DAVIN*
Slocum, RI
*Two canisters*
Claro walnut, ebony
Pitcher—22 in. x 12 in. x 9 in.
vase—18 in. x 8 in. x 8 in.
Photo by Morgan Rockhill

131

# Boxes

A box is a private matter. "People never give boxes for wedding presents," says Carol, and she's right. A vessel would be much more appropriate— a bowl, say, for holding the shared food, thereby symbolizing how a marriage holds the lives of the couple. But something happens when you put a lid on a vessel: the interior becomes dark, a little secretive.

The box segregates its contents from the world. We put something in a box because it is too precious for the rough-and-tumble of everyday life. It might be lost, become worn, dirty, broken—become an everyday piece of stuff. Instead, the box functions like our skin, which protects us from the agents of entropy and allows us to persist through time.

Even if the box remains unused, it expresses this function of containing something. An empty box awaits use, implies a future. And something in a box, movable, has a life outside the box, a past. This narrative quality brings the contents into our human world, domesticates them as our stories and language itself do.

Thus the box is more than itself: it is both a real object in the world and a potential. In this way it is like a human being: an object but also a changing set of associations. The box's characteristics of a public exterior hiding a private interior, and of a skin protecting a delicate being, intensify our feeling that a box is extremely personal.

In recent years boxes have become more idiosyncratic. Traditional rectangular and cylindrical shapes are still being made, but many woodworkers have enjoyed using bandsawing and stack-laminating techniques to achieve all kinds of forms, from biomorphic suggestions of seedpods or shells to wild fantasy creations. In fact, "box" may no longer be the appropriate name, since it connotes squareness. Many makers prefer the less prejudicial "container."

How did boxes become rectangles to begin with? The earliest box was surely two hands cupped around something. Later models must have been natural objects like gourds or shells. The will to a regular form seems to matter at least as much as practicality. American plains Indians, for example, folded animal skins into containers called parfleches; they were rectangular. And trees, which are anything but square, are elaborately formed at great cost into rectangular lumber and thus rectangular boxes.

"Rectangle" means the *right* angle: the sense of moral judgment still clings. Upright sides express strength and balance; the horizontal top and bottom suggest the earth's stability and endurance. The six sides correspond to the six directions: four cardinal points plus up and down. Looking at the shape from one side, one knows what the other side looks like. Carl G. Jung, the Swiss psychologist, points out that along with circles, squares are used worldwide as symbols of harmony and wholeness.

Our experience of gravity gets transposed to our structures. Upright is balanced and stable; any other angle but 90° is dynamic: leaning, moving, propped up, falling. So only cylinders and rectangles give us this feeling of stasis. This is why they have a timeless feeling. This is also why cylinders and rectangles can take all the varied kinds of decoration: because the form itself is inherently restrained, and will restrain exuberance in pattern. Other shapes tend to succeed according to how simply they are worked; here clean surfaces provide the restraint the form lacks. So in this way, the rectangular form both confines and liberates the maker of boxes.

If you decided to make a freer-shaped box, you would be confronting the problem of shaping the interior: should it be the same as the exterior? In the world of vessels, the best walls are of consistent thickness, so the shape the vessel offers for use is the same (but a little smaller) as the shape of the space it occupies. Inner equals outer, for short. Partly this is a technical question: it is easier to make vessels with heavy bottoms and thin rims, so such a pot feels amateurish. Likewise, it is easy to drill press a cylindrical hole in a lump of wood and confine your attentions to sculpting the outside. This diminishes the box, illustrating clearly the maker's lack of care. But what of the deliberate alteration of the space, the pleasant surprise of denied expectations, perhaps even secret compartments? Such a box embodies a theory of personality: that all is not knowable, that the inner self will never conform to the outer, that mystery will always invade reform.

*—Fletcher Cox*

Preceding page:
*LEE J. HEROLD*
Salt Lake City, UT
*Jewelry box*
Pink ivory, purpleheart,
beveled mirror, brass hinges
4¼ in. x 9 in. x 11 in.
Photo by Rick McClain

KEN ALTMAN
Silverton, OR
*Jewel box*
Cocobolo, ebony, 14-kt. gold
2¾ in. x 2⅞ in. x 1⅞ in.

JEFFREY T. McCAFFREY
Portland, OR
*Cassette box*
Rosewood
12 in. x 4 in. x 24 in.
Photo by Jim Piper

*"Hexagonal cylinders
constructed, turned and split
to form rounded parts."*

*ERNIE IVES*
Ipswich, SU England
*Memories box*
Avodire, makore, rosewood
veneers
14 in. x 10 in. x 6 in.

*"Parquetry. There are
approximately 3,500 pieces
and the whole box took 350
hours. It won the special
award for parquetry at the
1985 British Marquetry
Society Exhibition."*

*GARY PYE*
Lismore, NSW Australia
*Kidney box*
Huon pine, tung oil finish
11 in. x 5½ in. x 2 in.
Photo by John McCormick

*DAVID BAYNE*
Northfield, VT
*Box for four chopsticks*
Spruce
3¾ in. x 3¾ in. x 14 in.
Photo by A. Dean Powell

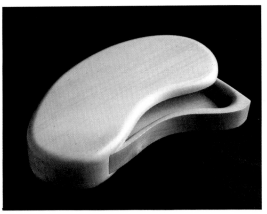

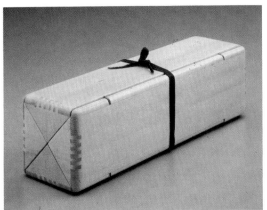

*CRAIG NUTT*
Northport, AL
*One small step for mankind*
Pecan, ebony, padauk,
satinwood, Plexiglas,
electronics
Size 7½ B

*"One of a series of
'shoeboxes'; the ankle swivels
to reveal a compartment,
when picked up, the
toenails flash."*

*PAUL and JOANNE ROCHON*
Hoboken, NJ
*Jewelry box*
Australian walnut, bird's-eye
maple, bubinga, cocobolo,
ebony, holly, mahogany,
padauk, purpleheart,
rosewood
14 in. x 15 in. x 13 in.
Photo by Stephen Mark
Needham

*"Designed for a client's fifth
wedding anniversary."*

*IAN FORSBERG*
Berkeley, CA
*Chest # 1*
Amazon yellowwood,
purpleheart, maple
13 in. x 18 in. x 20 in.
Photos by Aaron Jones

*"Veneering, laminating,
plywood construction,
traditional joinery, turning
and tambour."*

*JOHN NESSET*
Minneapolis, MN
*Jewelry box*
White holly, cherry, butternut
(bottom), black walnut (tray)
18 in. x 6¾ in. x 2⅜ in.
Photo by Robert Friedman

*DAVID LILIENTHAL*
Barnstable, MA
*Plane box*
Cherry, mahogany
6 in. x 24¼ in. x 12 in.
Photo by William R. Thauer

CAPT. JON O. GRONDAHL
Staten Island, NY
*Norwegian hope chest*
Birch, pine
34 in. x 18 in. x 23 in.
Photo by Dennis Gottlieb
Studio

*"Painted in the Norwegian 'rosepainting' style in oil colors."*

PAULA COOPERRIDER
Scottsdale, AZ
*Ribbed chest*
Honduras mahogany,
polished bone
20 in. x 42 in. x 18 in.
Photo by Russ Good

138

**JAMES SCHRIBER**
New Milford, CT
*Box*
Cherry, bird's-eye
maple, poplar
18 in. x 18 in. x 7 in.
Photo by John Kane

*"This box was an award
given to James Merrill by the
Connecticut Commission on
the Arts as Connecticut's Poet
Laureate. Box bottom is an
Ouija board."*

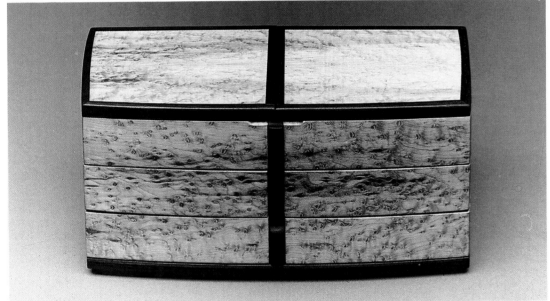

**CURT MINIER**
Seattle, WA
*Jewelry box*
Bird's-eye maple,
rosewood trim
16 in. x 8 in. x 7 in.
Photo by Gregg Krogstad

*"Lid is resawn, book-matched
veneer."*

**JOSEPH DelNOSTRO**
Los Angeles, CA
*Hope chest with drawers*
Black walnut, solid and burl
veneer, French walnut
veneer, eastern cedar,
ebony veining
23 in. x 24 in. x 34 in.
Photo by Don Milici

139

# Musical Instruments

Here I am, standing in my spray booth, gun in hand, staring at hundreds of little red-orange spots that just sputtered out of said spray gun. Mockingly, they return my stare from their new home on this guitar neck—where there should now have been an even coat of color. This is a brand new trick of my playful (and expensive) spray gun. Over the years it has produced, for my entertainment, every other possible variation on how not to spray a proper, even pattern or a correct fluid/air mixture. But this is one it overlooked. Until now.

Why this had to happen on a day already written off as a disaster, I can only guess.

First thing this morning, a long overdue shipment of guitar cases arrives and, I should've known, they were the wrong model. One hour later a hairline crack magically appears in the top of a new guitar not two hours shy of completion. Inopportune timing? The customer was already on her way, by train, to take delivery! To cap the morning off, there is still no sign of that past-due payment from my overseas dealer. Hello overdraft!

On days like this it's an effort to recall why I chose to be a guitarmaker. At the same time, I wonder whether contemporary society truly has a need for craftsmen like me. Could it be that I am an anachronism?

It is a sobering moment when such a thought presents itself. Still, I feel very much a part of contemporary life and truly believe I am helping the modern guitar develop its unrealized potential. But if what I do for a living could be better done by a modern factory production line, I would cease working at it.

Luckily, all evidence considered, that doesn't appear to be the case. Musicians and listeners seem both able and anxious to recognize and seek out the qualities that place the expertly made, hand-built instrument above others. In fact, the reality is that the talented luthier can rise to the challenge and, indeed, surpass the factory product. That truth is what answers my own need for relevancy. Furthermore, it seems apparent that as long as humans have need for music, there will be a demand for the sounds of the original instruments despite the popularity of synthesizers, emulators and other computer-enhanced electronic instruments.

So why is it that I chose to be one of the people filling that demand? The Challenge, capital C intended, is the only possible answer. The challenge to make not only the most wonderful-sounding instrument, but also to have it be perfectly playable and of flawless craftsmanship and design. It's no easy task reaching these goals. I've been at it more than fifteen years, yet only now have I begun to feel I'm any good.

There is a job in stringed instrument making called purfling—another case where a noun, the wooden strips of purfling that surround the body, has evolved into a verb. The luthier has the choice of either butt-joining these tiny multilayered strips as they are glued in place or taking twice the time to miter each joint. I love doing mitered purfling. If I could but convey the delight of watching minute layers of dyed softwood fall accurately into angled place after one well-aimed cut with a sharp chisel, then you would understand my pleasure.

Greater satisfaction, though, lies in achieving sought-after qualities of sound. After all, musical instruments are in their functions more than objects, surpassing craft and becoming vehicles for creative expression. It is a heartwarming moment for a maker to witness demanding players seeking, and receiving from one of your instruments, the musical responses that they want and need.

I recall one incident when a certain classical guitarist, an excellent concert-level player, arrived at my shop to try out a recently completed guitar. I will never forget watching his eyes open wide in astonishment at the "mature, round sweetness of note" that was definitely not as prominent in the last instruments he'd played. "What did you do?" he questioned. "Was it the wood or just a fluke?" Happily, I knew exactly what it was. I also knew for certain it was the construction change I had made that was responsible for the improvement in sound.

Probably, for a luthier, the most wonderful pleasure of all is to be stirred by the music emanating from an instrument of your making. You silently wonder..."Did I really just take pieces of trees and build something that can do so much; make me laugh, make me cry, bathe me in such a satisfying warmth?" Hundreds of instruments have come into being in my shop, yet, to me, it's still a marvel.

Then again, on days when your spray gun is sputtering, your bank manager is phoning, and who knows what else might happen if you dare put tool to wood, philosophical musings provide about as much solace as congealed coffee.

I confess that on days when the universe doesn't seem to be unfolding as I feel it should, and the idealized greener grass of a more lucrative job is a recurring vision, I look around my workshop, and gradually, with dwindling reluctance, am reminded of how lucky I am. This shop, in every sense, is my own. The tools, the Plexiglas jigs, the stacked wood, the crammed file drawers, the workbenches, the hundreds of hanging objects concealing the walls, even the multihued mounds of wood dust growing ever higher in hard to reach corners; all were designed, constructed, sought, selected, purchased and created by me.

Surrounded by such tangible satisfactions, gloomy defenses crumble. I'm left with little choice but to concede, in all honesty, how well and truly hooked I am to this business.

*—William Laskin*

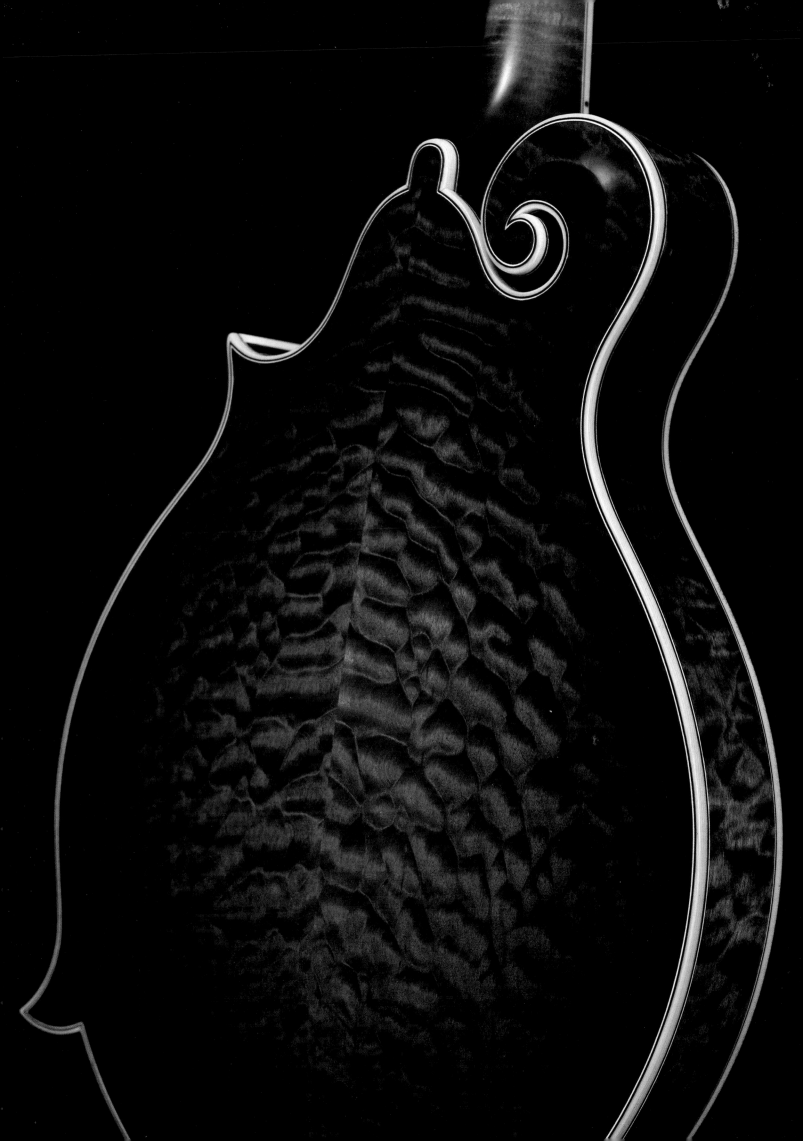

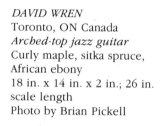

DAVID WREN
Toronto, ON Canada
*Arched-top jazz guitar*
Curly maple, sitka spruce,
African ebony
18 in. x 14 in. x 2 in.; 26 in.
scale length
Photo by Brian Pickell

KENT EVERETT
Atlanta, GA
*Guitar*
Quilted maple, ebony,
mahogany
39¼ in. x 16 in. x 2¾ in.
(16 in. at lower bout)
Photos by Billy Howard

*"Inlay—mother-of-pearl and
abalone."*

142

RICHARD B. WALKER
Irvine, CA
*Small steel-string guitar*
Rosewood, cedar, Honduras
mahogany
36 in. high; 19 in. x 14 in. x 4
in. (lower bout); 9 in. (upper
bout)

TOM H. ELLIS
Austin, TX
*Mandolin*
*(see also p. 141)*
German spruce, quilted
maple, ebony
27¼ in. x 10 in.
Photo by Reagan Bradshaw

*"Hand-rubbed aniline stain,
clear lacquer finish."*

143

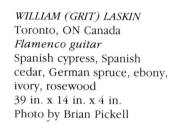

WILLIAM (GRIT) LASKIN
Toronto, ON Canada
*Flamenco guitar*
Spanish cypress, Spanish
cedar, German spruce, ebony,
ivory, rosewood
39 in. x 14 in. x 4 in.
Photo by Brian Pickell

RION DUDLEY
Seattle, WA
*Small-bodied steel-string
guitar*
Hawaiian koa (back and
sides), ebony (bridge and
fingerboard), sitka spruce
(top), curly walnut and holly
(head, rosette)
38 in. x 13 in. x 4½ in.

ROBERT GIRDIS
Guemes Island, WA
*Cutaway dreadnaught guitar*
German spruce, ebony, red
and green abalone, mother-
of-pearl, mastodon ivory,
Brazilian rosewood,
Honduras mahogany, padauk
42 in. x 16 in. x 4¾ in.
Photo by Larry Hartford

144

*RICHARD SCHNEIDER*
Sequim, WA
*Schneider long-model
concert guitar 1984 (with
Kasha soundboard
and bridge)*
Redwood, Brazilian
rosewood, Honduras
mahogany, ebony
40¼ in. x 4 in. x 14½ in.
Photo by Dennis Crawford

145

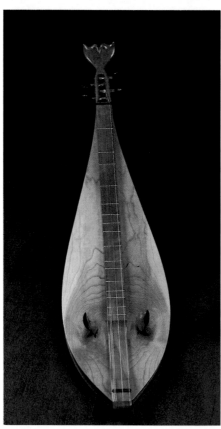

RALPH ASHMEAD
Inverness, CA
*Viola d'amore*
Hawaiian koa, sitka spruce,
mountain mahogany, ebony
veneer, bow of snakewood
32¼ in. x 9¼ in. (lower bout)
x 7¼ in. (upper bout) x 2 in.
(rib height); 14½ in. (string
length)
Photo by Jean Spraque

H.F. GRABENSTEIN
Duxbury, VT
*Bass viola da Gamba bows
and Renaissance violin bow*
Snakewood, boxwood, horse
hair, gaboon ebony, ivory
1½ in. x 28 in. (each bow)

WARREN A. MAY
Berea, KY
*Whale of a dulcimer*
© 1984
Cherry, Indian rosewood,
tuning pegs
37 in. x 8½ in. x 2½ in.
Photo by Albert Mooney

*"The sound holes are natural
knotholes which determine
the unique proportion of
each instrument."*

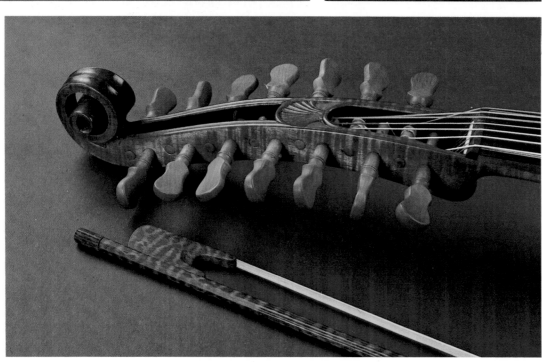

CHARLES R. ERVIN
Austin, TX
*Viola after Amati*
Spruce, curly maple,
ebony, boxwood
17 in. x 8 in. (top bout)
x 10 in. (bottom bout)
Photo by David Glover
and Charles Ervin

JAMES WOODS
Washington Island, WI
*Hammered dulcimer*
Cherry, maple,
black walnut, redwood
36 in. x 15½ in.
Photo by Steve Mofle

147

CHARLES M. RUGGLES
Olmsted Falls, OH
*Pipe organ*
Primarily oak, poplar,
grenadilla, red cedar, ebony,
sugar pine
102 in. x 60 in. x 36 in.
Photo by Keith Berr

*"Organ made for*
*Baldwin-Wallace College,*
*Berea, Ohio."*

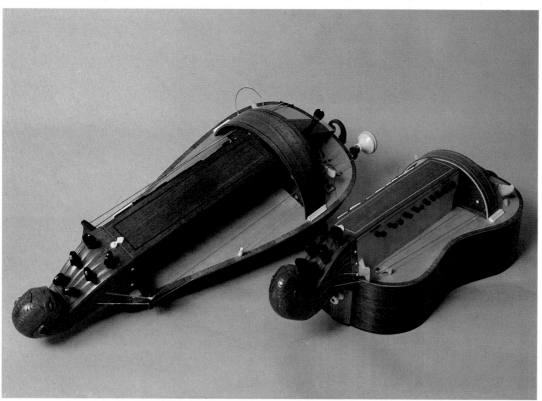

BERNARD RAMSDALE
Ashton-in-Makerfield,
England
*Hurdy gurdies*
Walnut, boxwood, maple,
spruce, ebony, ivory
24 in. x 9 in. x 8 in.
29 in. x 11 in. x 9 in.
Photo by John Morris

*"Both are played regularly*
*by professional musicians."*

*R.J. REGIER*
Freeport, ME
*Single-manual harpsichord*
Tulip poplar, spruce, maple,
walnut, ebony, cherry, cow
bone, sheepskin parchment
76 in. x 31 in. x 34 in.
Photo by Kip Brundage

*STEVEN M. LASH*
Birmingham, MI
*Bentside spinet*
Pine, oak, mahogany and
mahogany veneers, cherry,
spruce, birch, maple,
pearwood, holly, brass
hinges, natural ivory keys
33 in. x 73 in. x 30½ in.
Photo by Joni T. Strickfaden

*"The Queen Anne-styled
spinet was designed after the
John Harris bentside spinet,
which is in the Metropolitan
Museum of Art in New York."*

149

# Directory

## Alabama

**Theodore A. Bowen,** Route 3 Box 585, Cottondale 35453 (205) 553-3034 *Original and custom woodworking and design.*

**Glenn Crocker,** PO Box 4815, Huntsville 35815

**Margaret de Gruy, de Gruy Woodworks,** 11630 Jeff Hamilton Rd., Mobile 36609 (205) 633-5765

**Victor Doumar, Jr.,** 102 Angela Rd., Madison 35758 (205) 895-0895 *One-of-a-kind, specialty items, turnings.*

**Ben Erickson, Erickson Woodworks,** 158 Myrdledian Ave., Eutaw 35462 (205) 372-9727 *Quality handcrafted furniture, cabinets and millwork. Traditional to contemporary.*

**Tom Hagood,** 612 East Main St., Albertville 35950 (205) 878-0222

**Jim Iwerks, The Bowlworks,** 1414 Marguerite Ave. Apt. #2, Anniston 36201 (205) 236-3236 *Antique reproduction, lathework.*

**Bobby Michelson, Ramwood Furniture,** 2127 1st Ave. S., Birmingham 35233 (205) 323-5070

**(135) Craig Nutt,** 2014 Fifth St., Northport 35476 (205) 752-6535 *Fine furniture design and construction, sculpture.*

## Alaska

**Beth Antonsen, Etc.,** 305 Austin, Ketchikan 99901 (907) 225-3738

**Frances Brann, Woodworking,** PO Box 298, Delta Junction 99737 (907) 895-4231 *Exquisite inlay and carved hardwood furniture styled for individuals.*

**John E. Carlson, Custom Furniture & Cabinetry,** PO Box 95, Haines 99827 *Roccoco-style furniture.*

**Steve Gingrich, Taxodium Studio,** 211 West Cook Ave., Anchorage 99501 (907) 277-3862 *The creation of fine objects of wood and other precious materials: calligraphy and illustration.*

**Jeffrey R. Patrick, The Dovetail,** 1820 Toklat St., Anchorage 99508 (907) 279-0395 *Custom woodwork: furniture, cabinets and woodturning.*

**James E. Talley, Custom Cabinet Shop,** 4109 Old Seward Highway, Anchorage 99503 (907) 561-1874 *Custom furniture and high-quality cabinetry. Traditional and contemporary designs.*

## Arizona

**Richard J. Barrett, Barrett Environmental Artworks,** 543 West 16th St., Tempe 85281 (602) 966-4911 *Original-design and execution in all media. Hand-carving, bending, exotic finishes, etc.*

**Philip Brennion,** PO Box 360, Chino Valley 86323 (602) 636-2692 *Sculpture and furnishings from natural forms.*

**William J. Burke, Woodworker,** 2124 N. Izabel, Flagstaff 86001 (602) 774-3822

**Peter A. Chrisman,** 1126 E. Fort Lowell Rd., Tucson 85719 (602) 624-1313 *Fine furniture for the house and office, custom cabinetry.*

**Dimitri Cilione, Designer/Craftsman,** 19 E. Toole, Tucson 85701 (602) 623-2871 *Unique, highly crafted custom works and originals.*

**(138) Paula Cooperrider, Lone Mountain Designs,** 28755 N. 78th St., Scottsdale 85262 (602) 585-4137 *Functional sculpture, one-of-a-kind containers.*

**(21) Gerald Crawford,** 51 Remuda Rd., Sedona 86336 (602) 282-5285 *Museum approved authentic recreations of 18th-century furniture in miniature.*

**Paul and Boksun Darnell, Woodworks,** 4045 E. Yawepe, Phoenix 85044 *Custom cabinetry, wood or lamination.*

**Frank DeGrazia, Furniture Design and Construction,** 311½ S. Marina, Prescott 86301 (602) 778-0238 *Hardwoods and traditional wood joinery.*

**Susan Eisenberg,** 4854 E. Turquoise Ave., Paradise Valley 85253 (602) 483-8879

**Todd Hoyer,** Box 1451, Bisbee 85603 (602) 432-4893

**Terry Israelson, Quartersawn Architectural Woodworks,** Box 412, 2160 Shelby Dr., Sedona 86336 (602) 282-3106 *Design and construction of custom furniture, doors and kitchen cabinets.*

**(130) Don Mitchell, Heartwood Designs,** 17831 N. 55th Dr., Glendale 85308 (602) 938-9566 *Fine furniture, cabinetry and turnings.*

**Steve Peck,** 20 S. San Francisco St., Flagstaff 86001 (602) 774-2362 *Custom, one-off furniture and stringed instruments.*

**Phil Sawyer,** 4793 E. Hop St., Phoenix 85044 (602) 893-9628

**Linda Schmitz,** PO Box 1743, Prescott 86301 (602) 445-9735 *Folding divider screens, custom designing and limited editions.*

**David P. Vogel,** PO Box 153, Jerome 86331 (602) 634-7497 *Sculpture, design and custom woodworking.*

**Wildwood,** 3216 E. Jefferson, Phoenix 85034 (602) 267-8269 *Designers and builders of signature curved staircases, specializing in freestanding.*

**Woodesign, A Corp.,** 13 S. 32nd St., Phoenix 85034 (602) 267-1939 *Designers/builders of signature furniture specializing in curves and veneers.*

## Arkansas

**James Cottey, Furniture Design,** Box 311 HC 63, Clinton 72031 (501) 723-4694 *One-of-a-kind functional sculpture.*

**Robyn Horn, Sentinel Press & Studio,** 7801 Westwood, Little Rock 72204 (501) 568-4743 *One-of-a-kind, lathe-turned bowls, vases and plates.*

**(104) Chris and Anne Kunkle, Deep Woods,** HCR 63 Box 42, Witter 72776 (501) 677-2787 *Carved wall mirrors, boxes, hand mirrors and bowls.*

**Richard Massey, Fine Woodwork,** Route 2 Box 69, Eureka Springs 72632 (501) 253-9094 *Contemporary furniture, accessories, doors, stairways and cabinetry.*

**Douglas Stowe Woodworking,** PO Box 247, Eureka Springs 72632 (501) 253-7387 *Custom furniture and display cabinets, small cabinets in limited editions.*

**Dennis R. Wilson, The Wood Tic,** 54 Morningside Dr., Wynne 72396 (501) 238-7780 *Unique clocks, woodturning and accessories.*

## California

**Kevin Ben Abe,** 5622 Surf Way, Sacramento 95822 (916) 441-3321

**Gary Adkins, Foothill Woodworks,** 5550 Casitas Pass Rd., Carpinteria 93013 (805) 684-4868 *Cabinetry, furniture, doors, windows and millwork.*

**Bob Agnew,** 7148 Grovewood La., Orange 92669 (714) 538-5726 *Sculpture (abstract, intertwined Moebius strip, lifeform, castle) and wildlife carvings.*

**Muneef Alwan,** PO Box 862, Meadow Vista 95722 (916) 637-4236 *One-of-a-kind custom furniture in mahogany, walnut and teak.*

**Jim Amberg, Marc Garfinkel, Amber-Barc Contemporary Hardwood Puzzles,** 2062 Cima Ct., La Costa 92008 (619) 753-9030 *Hardwood puzzles, domestic and exotics, custom orders welcome.*

**Timothy A. Anderson,** 3387 Reliez Highland Rd., Lafayette 94549 (415) 935-4624

**P.A. Arenskov, A&S Development Co.,** 2311 Huntington Ave., Anaheim 92801 (714) 774-2010 *Designing and handcrafting of decorative turnings.*

**(146) Ralph Ashmead, Historical Instrument & Bowmaker,** PO Box 208, Inverness 94937 (415) 669-1647 *Viols, lutes, viola d'amores, pre-Tourte and modern bows.*

**Peter Axtell, Custom Woodworking,** 5276 Bennet Valley Rd., Santa Rosa 95404 (707) 523-2533 *Custom furniture and display cabinets.*

**P.J. Barlow,** PO Box 26, Jenner 95450 (707) 865-1686 *Finish carpentry, custom cabinetmaker, furniture.*

**Terry Beaudet,** 624 Redmond Rd., Eureka 95501 (707) 443-1072 *Woodturnings, tables, stands, large bowls and trays.*

**Douglas C. Beck, Beck's Kaleidoscope Design,** 2340 Fairfield St., Eureka 95501 (707) 443-2639 *Artist—sculpture—woodworking.*

**D.S. Beckstead, Functional Art,** 139 Burke La., Kneeland 95549 (707) 442-5925 *Harpsichords, music stands, music accessories and related furniture.*

**William Bell, Wood Designs,** 8000 B East Side Rd., Ukiah 95482 (707) 962-0263 *Furniture and cabinets made to please.*

**Noel D. Belsky, Noel's Creative Woodworking,** 3575 Princeton Ave., San Diego 92117 (619) 274-9921 *Custom wall units and stereo cabinets.*

**(88) Paul Biehler,** 1525 Arch #4, Berkeley 94708 (415) 843-6005 *Beds, art floors and tables.*

**Kirk Bonds,** 3100 Luna Ct., Santa Rosa 95405 (707) 578-8853 *Studio workshop for furniture and architectural interiors.*

**S.J. Booth, Woodcarving,** PO Box 5892, Napa 94581 (707) 252-7029 *Hand-carving, designed especially for you.*

**Gary Boudreaux Fine Woodwork,** 184 Grove St., Nevada City 95959 (916) 272-7037

**Joseph H. Bowley,** Mt. San Antonio College, 1100 North Grand Ave., Walnut 91789 (714) 594-5611 *Work mostly with hardwoods for beginner, intermediate and advanced woodworking students.*

**Lawrence D. Box,** 311 Orcas St., Morro Bay 93442 (805) 772-2475

**Robert Brady Design,** PO Box 523, La Honda 94020 (415) 747-0364 *Integrity in form and function, custom commissions.*

**Larry C. Breedlove,** 4821 Pine St., La Mesa 92041 (619) 698-3693 *Custom furniture and woodturnings.*

**Robert Hoben Brown, Furniture/Fine Wood Furnishings,** 3545 Alabama, San Diego 92104 (619) 291-0974 *Furniture design, fine wood interiors, architectural detailing.*

**John Brzovic, John Brzovic Woodworking,** 294 S. "D" St., San Bernardino 92401 (714) 885-3951 *Cabinets, doors and fine furniture.*

**Ted A. Bunge, Cabinets,** PO Box 53, Avery 95224 (209) 795-1329

**Mike Burruss,** Kelseyville High School Woodworking Club, PO Box 308, Kelseyville 95451 (707) 279-4923 *Custom wine racks and local-interest trinkets.*

**(3) Michael Cabaniss,** PO Box 142, Davenport 95017 (408) 426-9418 *Custom furniture design and manufacture.*

**Cameron Carr,** 5224 El Carro, Carpinteria 93013 (805) 684-9533

**Bill Chappelow,** PO Box 327, Descanso 92016 (619) 445-2802 *Wooden spoons, toys, bowls, balances and scales.*

**David Chilcott, Nexus Woodshop,** 2707 8th St., Berkeley 94710 (415) 849-3599 *Custom furniture, cabinets, fixtures, restorations, remodeling, refinishing.*

**Charles B. Cobb,** 1042 Gloria Dr., Santa Rosa 95407 (707) 527-8348

**Mike Craven,** 323 Beemer Ave., Sunnyvale 94086 (408) 245-8193 *Custom abstract furniture and sculpture using wood and other media.*

**George Crezee, Unreal Furnishings,** PO Box 2021, Big Bear City 92314 (714) 866-4100 *Custom cabinetry, chainsaw carvings, commercial signs, novelties and raw slabs.*

**Tom Custer, Debra Weisheimer, Backwoods,** 18441 Rainbow's End Rd., Nevada City 95959 (916) 265-5490 *Exotic wood accessories: inlays, furniture, cabinets, boxes. Custom and production.*

**Chuck Davis Cabinets,** 5060 Fallen Oak Dr., Morgan Hill 95037 (408) 779-3822 *Built-ins of furniture quality, requiring a custom approach for customer satisfaction.*

**Michael Davis,** 3501 51st Ave., Sacramento 95823 (916) 427-8191 *Custom furniture for homes or offices.*

**Ron Day, Designer/Craftsman,** 2030 Avy Ave., Menlo Park 94025 (415) 854-0380 *Custom furniture, solid-wood cabinetwork and unique casework.*

**Louis Debret Woodworking,** PO Box 390, Coloma 95613 (916) 622-6330 *Custom cabinetry, one-of-a-kind furniture.*

**(139) Joseph DelNostro,** 917 Hilldale Ave., Los Angeles 90069 (213) 652-7608 *Custom-design furniture and cabinetry in all styles.*

**Larry Dern, Furniture and Cabinetmaker,** PO Box 906, 324 Mill Creek La., Trinidad 95570 (707) 677-3956

**Tom Diedrich, Ben Thomas, Tom Diedrich Carpentry,** 540 Cole St. #1, San Francisco 94117 (415) 861-8426 *Cabinets, furniture and original-design beds.*

**Ivy Dixon,** 4116 E. 5th, Long Beach 90814 (213) 438-5864

**Gary Donefer, Custom Guitars,** Box 251, Albion 95410 (707) 937-1372

**Tom D'Onofrio, D'Onofrio Fine Woodworks,** Box 326, Bolinas 94924 (415) 868-1070 *Hand-carved sculptures and fine furniture.*

**Leo G. Doyle, Doyle & Sons,** 378 W. 53rd St., San Bernardino 92407 (714) 886-2301

**William Dudley,** 1040 Round Hill Circle, Napa 94558

**(36) Don Dupont, Joinery Custom Woodworking,** 38 Beta Ct. B-6, San Ramon 94583 (415) 831-9754 *Custom furniture.*

**Richard Eisner,** 4749¾ Baverly Blvd., Los Angeles 90004 (213) 384-4358 *Traditional and custom fine furniture, antique restoration.*

**Christopher Emhardt,** PO Box 5541, Santa Monica 90405 (213) 396-7906

**(48) Steven Emrick,** 1012 East California Ave., Ridgecrest 93555 (619) 375-0369 *One-of-a-kind custom sculptural furniture.*

**Chuck Engberg, Engberg Wood Sculptures,** 2217 Clinton Ave. Apt. B, Alameda 94501 (415) 865-6933

**George S. Evans,** PO Box 981, Del Mar 92014 (619) 775-0149 *Custom-design, one-of-a-kind and all general woodworking.*

**Richard Farwell, Furniture and Cabinetry,** 1551 Palm St., San Luis Obispo 93401 (805) 544-5209 *Handcrafted residential and office furniture. Contemporary design, traditional quality.*

**Dave Fischer,** PO Box 65602, Los Angeles 90065 (213) 227-8121

**(64) David D. Floyd, Woods By Design,** 6464 Via Venado, San Luis Obispo 93401 (805) 595-2935 *Custom furniture to production woodwork, custom homes.*

**David Fobes, Designer/Craftsman,** 519 Island Ave., San Diego 92101 (619) 231-6607 *Innovative prototype design for production and one-off furniture/sculpture commissions.*

**Fred Formel, D.F. Woodworking,** 23313 S. Caldwell Ave., Ontario 91761 (714) 947-6553

**(137) Ian Forsberg,** 2042 Vine St., Berkeley 94709 (415) 548-4032 *One-of-a-kind design, traditional joinery, veneering.*

**Eric Anton Fredsti, Sculptor & Decorative Carver,** PO Box 890, Escondido 92025 (619) 745-5527 *Wildlife sculpture, decorative picture frames and boxes.*

**Peter W. Fries,** 10200 DeSoto Ave. #208, Chatsworth 91311

**Dewey N. Garrett,** 2647 Wellingham Dr., Livermore 94550 (415) 447-9364 *Cabinetwork and faceplate turning.*

**Steve Gellman,** PO Box 4348, Arcata 95521 (707) 826-2100 *Turnings, spiral staircases, doors and steam-bent furniture.*

**Michael Gerber,** PO Box 669, Mt. Shasta 96067 (916) 938-3092

**Frank Giammona, Giammona Woodworking,** PO Box 1547, Healdsbury 95448 (707) 433-5849 *Furniture, cabinets and screen doors.*

**David K. Gill, Rothwood Products,** 2260C Canoas Garden Rd., San Jose 95125

**Carl M. Glowienke,** 2316 Bancroft St., San Diego 92104 (619) 280-3315 *Realistic and abstract hardwood sculpture.*

**(21) John Goff,** 1078 Oak Dr., Vista 92084 (619) 724-0638 *Antique copies and contemporary furniture.*

**Andy Goldman, ADG Woodcrafting,** PO Box 2, Placentia 92670 (714) 524-1946

**Manuel Albert Gomez,** 530 46th St., Oakland 94609 (415) 654-3830 *One-of-a-kind accessories for the home and office.*

**(61) John and Carolyn Grew-Sheridan, Grew-Sheridan Studio,** 500 Treat Ave., San Francisco 94110 (415) 824-6161

**Erik Gronborg,** 424 Dell Ct., Solana Beach 92075 (619) 481-9105 *Any commission compatible with my style.*

**Ruben Guajardo, Woodworker,** 2623 G St., LaVerne 91750 (714) 596-7294

**Joe Guida, Guida's Woodworks,** 7347 Deering Ave., Canoga Park 91303 (818) 716-8915

**Russ Hall,** Ca. State U. San Bernardino, 5500 State College Pkwy., San Bernardino 92407 (714) 887-7201 *Woodturning and original one-of-a-kind contemporary furniture.*

**Jonny Hamilton,** 8694 Lenon Ave. #16, La Mesa 92044 (619) 469-6663

**Kathy Harper,** 12454 16th St., Yucaipa 92399 (714) 787-4223

**(51) Paul Harrington, Custom Cabinets & Fine Furniture,** 1439 20th Ave., San Francisco 94122 (415) 661-8986

**Cliff Harris, Harris' Woodworking,** 121 Segre Pl., Santa Cruz 95060 (408) 423-6458 *Stylized Louis XIV design, specialty desks and cabinets.*

**Tim Harrison,** 1048 Miramar St., Laguna Beach 92651 (714) 497-3650

**J.A. Hassberger, Plane Crafts,** 348 Turnstone Dr., Livermore 94550 (415) 422-1025 *Naturally finished, contemporary hardwood furniture using traditional woodworking techniques.*

**David Haxton, Wood for Touch Designs,** 2350 16th St., Eureka 95501 (707) 445-1810

**(49) Roger Heitzman, Heitzman Woodworking,** 750 Whispering Pines, Scotts Valley 95066 (408) 353-2464 *Custom woodworking of all varieties: furniture, boat building, cabinetry and architectural.*

**Katherine Heller, K.H. Furniture Maker,** PO Box 3, Pacific Grove 93950 (408) 625-0252

**Guy Helmuth, Eureka Hardwood Supply,** 3346 D. St., Eureka 95501 (707) 445-3371 *Sales of figured redwood, western hardwoods, burls, unusual or exotic woods.*

**Ed Holzmann, Woodwork by Holzmann,** 19242-1 Hamlin St., Reseda 91335 (818) 708-7759 *Custom wood objects: large and small, furniture, cabinets, boxes and bowls.*

**Patrick Huglin Design,** 1261 Ferrelo Rd., Santa Barbara 93103 (805) 967-3282 *Contemporary furniture with Scandinavian/Oriental flair.*

**Charles Jacobs, Hand-carved Furniture,** 672 Rockford, Claremont 91711 (714) 624-5425

**Andrew Jacobson,** PO Box 723, Point Reyes St. 94956 (415) 663-1775 *Designer/craftsman of high-quality contemporary furniture.*

**Ted L. Jacox,** 230 Neil Terrace, Vista 92084 (619) 726-3452 *Cabinetmaking and wood sculpting.*

**Francine Johns, Furniture Designer,** PO Box 15013, San Diego 92115 (619) 265-2855 *Lumbar-support chairs, tables, segmented lamination, mail-order.*

**Dennis and Janice Johnson,** 1186 Hanchett Ave., San Jose 95126 *Custom furniture and cabinetry.*

**Jeff Johnson,** PO Box 151045, San Diego 92115 (619) 277-4671

**(47) Kent Johnson, Dimensional Graphics,** 8107 Commercial St., La Mesa 92041 (619) 469-5034 *Signs, commission furniture and commercial fixtures.*

**L.C. (Bud) Johnson, The Woodsmith,** 2 Rose Ct., Novato 94947 (415) 892-2028 *Handmade hardwood furniture, custom-design work, fine cabinetry.*

**Royce H. Johnson,** PO Box 1212, 8384 Speckled St., Kings Beach 95719 (916) 546-3275

**Leon W. Jones,** 7704 Woodchuck Way, Citrus Heights 95610 (916) 726-6509 *Carved mantels, doors, beds, etc., by commission to your specifications.*

**Ray Jones Woodcrafts,** 17619 Tulsa St., Granada Hills 91344 (818) 368-6796 *Specialize in boxes and desk accessories.*

**Anthony Kahn Furniture,** PO Box 178, Arcata 95521 (707) 822-6722 *Designers of one-of-a-kind and limited-production furniture.*

**John Karpinski, Karpinski Woodworking,** 22600 Meadow La., Sonora 95370 (209) 532-0218

**Michael & Pat Kelley,** PO Box 3584, La Habra 90631 (714) 526-0276 *Original-design furniture and accessories.*

**Kimberly A. Kelzer,** 1424 Little Orchard St., San Jose 95110 (408) 286-8949

**Louis Kern, Functional Art,** 519 Castro, San Francisco 94114 (415) 553-3841

**Paul Kinsey, Cabinetmaker,** 7881 Valley Dr., Eureka 95501 (707) 445-9120

**Steve Klein, Klein Custom Guitars,** 22522 Burndale Rd., Sonoma 95476 (707) 938-4189 *Guitars, inlay, other stringed instruments, design and manufacture.*

**Mark Kobe, Kobe Woodworks,** 643 Blackberry La., San Rafael 94903 (415) 479-0348 *Period reproductions with contemporary functions.*

**Larry Lawlor Furniture,** Box 119, Gualala 95445 (707) 884-1125 *Chairs —including custom-fitted chairs.*

**Po Shun Leong, Design Studio,** 8546 Oso Ave., Canoga Park 91306 (818) 341-1559 *Design and production of prototype models for mass production.*

**Bruce Levenstein,** 3081 Knob Dr., Los Angeles 90065 (213) 222-9030 *Contemporary, innovative furniture.*

**Michael Levy,** 26472 Evergreen Rd., San Juan Capistrano 92675 (714) 364-3495

**William H. Livingston, Livingston's Wood Creations,** 12309 E. Los Altos, Clovis 93612 (209) 299-0538 *One-of-a-kind desks, bowls, clocks and home accessories.*

**William Loehr,** 1580 Garst La., Ojai 93023 (805) 646-4122 *Custom hardwood furniture, chairs, tables and desks.*

**Rolf Lygren, Rolf's Furniture Design,** 122 Monterey Ave., Pacific Grove 93950 (408) 372-6223 *Fine furniture from tables to boxes.*

**Thomas C. MacMichael,** 7815 Normal Ave., La Mesa 92041 (619) 589-8453 *Functional art and custom furniture.*

**(101) David S. Mark, Space Age Design Furniture,** 194 Sagamore St., San Francisco 94112 (415) 239-0230 *Furniture displaying mathematical and natural forms by combining curved-laminate structures.*

**David J. Marks, Designer/Craftsman,** 2128 Marsh Rd., Santa Rosa 95401 (707) 526-2763 *Individually designed, handcrafted hardwood furniture and accessories, meticulous craftsmanship.*

**Ed Marsh,** 11264 White Oak Ave., Granada Hills 91344 (818) 360-5066

**(54, 68) Loy D. Martin, Furniture,** 820 Ramona St., Palo Alto 94301 (415) 329-0533 *One-of-a-kind, handmade furniture.*

**Gerald B. McCauley,** 163 Caymus Ct., Sunnyvale 94086 (408) 736-6094

**Ric McCurdy, McCurdy Guitars,** 630 W. Micheltorena St., Santa Barbara 93101 (805) 962-2254 *Custom electric instruments featuring exotic hardwoods and modern design.*

**Tom McFadden, Furniture,** 1901 Guntly Rd., Philo 95466 (707) 895-3627

**Ron Medlock, Applewood Studio,** PO Box 2576, Apple Valley 92307 (619) 242-4387 *Fine arts woodwork, custom-design furniture and accessories.*

**Don Milici, Carpentry,** 235 Churchill Rd., Sierra Madre 91024 (818) 355-4511

**James Minges,** 2898 Lindaloa La., Pasadena 91107 (818) 356-6269

**(116) Bruce Mitchell,** PO Box 966, Point Reyes 94956 (415) 663-1819/ 663-9343 *Sculptural woodturning.*

**Charles Mitchell, Mitchell Mountain Woodworking,** 14505 West Park Ave., Boulder Creek 95006 (408) 338-9855 *Custom-designed cabinetry and furniture.*

**Lanny Mitchell, Sulan Woodworks,** 1775 S. 1st St. #14, San Jose 95112 (408) 297-9663 *Furniture guaranteed for 100 years.*

**(129) Peter Murad, Murad Designs,** 4111 Lincoln Blvd. #318, Marina Del Rey 90292 (213) 396-4471 *Custom contemporary furniture. Woodturning and light sculpture.*

**Eric Nanson,** 9546 Janell La., Redding 96001 (916) 246-1224 *Almost anything that is crazy or weird and wood.*

**Emmor Nile,** 825 West Ream Ave., Mount Shasta 96067 (916) 926-4846

**(18) Terrie Noll,** 519 Frederick St., San Francisco 94117 (415) 759-1066

**(78) Larry Ogden, Coppice Woodcrafts,** 2084 N. Herron Ct., Camarillo 93010 *Furniture made from local small trees.*

**Omananda,** 610 May Ave., Santa Cruz 95060 (408) 429-6875 *Quality custom furniture and casework for treasured items.*

**Todd Ouwehand,** 924 Belmont Ave., Long Beach 90804 (213) 439-7374 *Design and construction of custom furniture.*

**Mark C. Petherbridge, Artist/Craftsman,** 1475 E. Date St. #105, San Bernardino 92404 (714) 882-4058 *Custom furniture, art objects, limited-production runs and colored finishes.*

**Karen Phillips-DiBartolomeo,** Route 1 Box 86, Crowley Lake 93546 (619) 935-4810

**Kathy S. Pierce,** 2408 Teresa Ct., Bakersfield 93304

**Michael Pierceall,** PO Box 6214, Burbank 91510

**(70) John M. Pierson, J.M.P. Furniture,** 8107 Commercial St., La Mesa 92041 (619) 469-5034 *High-end custom furniture.*

**Stuart Polack,** 924 Patricia La., Modesto 95354 (209) 576-2561

**John Pollard, The Turning Point Gallery,** 208 N. Myrtle #C, Monrovia 91016 (818) 359-2339 *Decorative, sculptural turnings.*

**Bob Pugh,** 4758 N. Harrison, Fresno 93704 (209) 227-4308 *Custom, one-of-a-kind furniture and cabinetry.*

**(51) Michael Puhalski,** 3036 McMillian Rd., San Luis Obispo 93401 (805) 543-4301 *Contemporary furniture in the craftsman tradition.*

**David Ramirez, Mt. Sac. Woodshop,** 1100 N. Grand Ave., Walnut 91789 (714) 594-5611

**George H. Rathmell, Rathmell's Antiques,** 324 Rodman Dr., Los Osos 93402 (805) 528-1222

**Paul Reiber, Furniture Maker,** 543 S. Franklin St., Fort Bragg 95437 (707) 964-7151 *Carved doors and windows, architectural details, mirror frames, furniture and mantels.*

**Karl H. Reuss, Specialty Woodworking,** 1407 Kingsmill, Rowland Heights 91748 (714) 595-8655 *One-of-a-kind tables, bowls, jewel boxes, etc.*

**Bruce Riche, Carver,** 6341 Colgate Ave., Los Angeles 90048 (213) 937-7921 *Hand-carved art—sculptural and functional.*

**Norman Ridenour, Ridenour's Studio,** 1060 17th St., San Diego 92101 (619) 239-0588 *Sculptural pieces achieved through bent or stave-lamination.*

**Todd R. Ritchie, Ritchie Fine Furniture,** 27034 Spring Creek Rd., Rancho Palos Verdes 90274 *Fine handcrafted furniture, antique furniture reproductions.*

**Ed Rizzardi,** 1049 W. Pine #C, Upland 91786 (714) 985-9365 *Freestanding custom pieces of furniture.*

**Monroe Robinson,** 31200 Cedar St., Ft. Bragg 95437 (707) 946-1685

**Saul Rosenfield, Sawdust Ink,** 128 Precita Ave., San Francisco 94110 (415) 648-1339 *Architecture and furniture designed and crafted.*

**Kenneth C. Ross,** 973 Madrone Way, Livermore 94550 (415) 443-5623

**Thomas Ruvolo, Romas Designs,** 1012 Northpark Blvd., San Bernardino 92407 (714) 886-9181 *Custom and one-of-a-kind furniture and accessories.*

**Jon Sauer,** PO Box 803, Daly City 94017 (415) 355-8424 *Hand and ornamental turnery in exotic woods.*

**Steven Savitch, Limited Editions,** 171 Staples Ave., San Francisco 94112 (415) 239-2999

**Tom Schargitz,** 13392 Anawood Way, Westminster 92683 (714) 846-0550

**Brenda Schlegel, Joseph Hastings, Holiday For Plywood,** 323 Divisadero St., San Francisco 94177 (415) 861-1876

**(111) William J. Schnute, Oak Leaves Studio,** 41 Poppy Rd., Carmel Valley 93924 (408) 659-0652 *Sculpture and decorative architectural accoutrements, entryways, room dividers, signage and wall reliefs.*

**Mel and Jan Schockner,** Box 467, 16 Sylvan Way, Woodacre 94973

**Bradford Schwartz,** 2247 S. Parton St., Santa Ana 92707 (714) 850-0777 *Quality furniture design and construction.*

**Jeffrey Seaton, Seaton Wood Design,** 5 Orange Ave. #D, Goleta 93117 (805) 964-5352 *One-of-a-kind decorative and functional accent containers.*

**(15) Jon Seeman, Designs In Wood,** 1901 Laguna Canyon Rd. #6, Laguna Beach 92651 *Art furniture.*

**Mona A. Selnick-Doshay, Doshay Designs,** 5241 Bishop St., Cypress 90630 (714) 527-6890 *Lathe-turned objects, cabinet and furnituremaking and Judaic art.*

**Shea Woodworks,** 619 85th Ave., Oakland 94621 (415) 632-2854 *Architectural woodwork and furnishings, curved work, including spiral stairs.*

**(71) Catherine V. Sicangco,** 5417-7 Lane Murray Blvd., La Mesa 92042 (619) 589-5529 *One-of-a-kind and limited-edition furniture pieces.*

**Richard Silvera, Fine Wood Interiors and Furnishings,** 13139 Centerville Rd., Chico 95928 (916) 342-7748 *Architectural finishwork, custom furniture, design and manufacturing.*

**John W. Slawinski,** 255 N. Burnaby, Glendora 91740 (818) 963-3441

**Ann E. Rohloff Smith, Furnituremaker,** 12195 Winter Gardens Dr., Lakeside 92040 (619) 390-9154 *Design and construction of one-of-a-kind and limited-production functional furniture.*

**Andrew Stauss,** Paradise High School, 5911 Maxwell Dr., Paradise 95969 (916) 872-6451

**Michael Sterling, Sterling Woodworking,** PO Box 4374, Chico 95927 (916) 894-3206 *Custom, one-of-a-kind furniture, doors and architectural woodworking.*

**Ross Stockwell, Carver,** 1419 Chalcedony St., San Diego 92109 (619) 272-4696

**David Stohl, Fine Art Furniture,** 962 Dorthel St., Sebastopol 95472 (707) 829-2015

**Rick Sugarek,** 323 Byxbee St., San Francisco 94132

**Peter Tarbox,** 1090 Atchison St., Pasadena 91104 (818) 794-8318 *Sculpted vessels and turned bowls.*

**Thomas C. Tencza,** 7605 Oxbon La., Dublin 94568 (415) 828-9741

**Steven Tenglesen, Woodworker,** Box 1510451, San Diego 92115 (619) 277-4671

**Tom Thompson, Unlimited,** PO Box 41012, Santa Barbara 93140 (805) 962-6699 *Furniture designer and builder specializing in custom kitchens, stairs and mantels.*

**Brian Tinius,** 12335 Califa St., N. Hollywood 91607 (818) 761-2329 *One-off designs.*

**Calvin E. Titus, Original Woodcraft,** 450 Wilson Rd., Sebastopol 95472 (707) 823-5600 *One-of-a-kind and limited-production furniture—solid-panel cabinetry.*

**Donald S. Tower,** 1830 Woodland Ave., Santa Clara 95050 (415) 296-2854

**Michael Turi,** 413 I St., Arcata 95521 (707) 826-1794 *Artistic and architectural woodturning.*

**Elliot Tyson,** 3142 Hollycrest Dr., Los Angeles 90068 (213) 876-0436

**(35) W.M. Ulmer, Woodworks & St. Michael's Harps,** P.O. Box 687, Arcata 95521 (707) 822-Wood *Sculptured and traditional furniture, Shoji, cabinetry, Windsor chairs and harps.*

**Richard Vest, Rising Tide Wood Sculpture,** Box 2884, Castro Valley 94546 *Original sculpture in fine woods, sea/animal life.*

**Will Vinet, Oakholm Studios,** 6233 Woodlawn Ave., Bell 90201 (213) 562-0188

**Dale W. Vollmer, Maderas Finas,** 1023 Bellview, San Bernardino 92410 (714) 884-9582 *Rolltop desks and classic guitars.*

**David Von Kohorn, Von Kohorn Design,** 79 Homer Ave., Palo Alto 94301 (415) 326-9003 *Architectural signage and custom cabinetry.*

**David Wade,** 15320 Ocaso Ave., DD 202, La Mirada 90638 (714) 522-4769

**Patrick Warner,** 1427 Kenora St., Escondido 92027 (619) 747-2623 *Furniture in wood in shapes of bent steel tubing.*

**Gregory Watson,** 2697 House Ave., Durham 95938 (916) 891-5502 *Cabinets, millwork and doorways.*

**Mark R. Webster,** 670 North G. St., Porterville 93257 (209) 781-4074

**Richard Wedler Cabinetry,** 11100 Cumpston Ave. #35, No. Hollywood 91601 (818) 761-1433 *One-of-a-kind benchmade furniture and cabinets.*

**Barry R. Weiss, Furniture,** 3542 Lincoln Ave., Oakland 94602 (415) 531-7496

**C. Stuart Welch & Associates,** PO Box 776, Marshall 94940 (415) 663-1775 *Furnituremaking, turning and prototype work.*

**Jeni Sue Wilburn, Cabinetmaker,** PO Box 2046, Trinidad 95570 (707) 677-0194 *Custom commission work, mostly cabinets, bookcases, desks and tables.*

**(49) Bruce Wilkinson, Furnituremaker,** 22216 Tioga Pl., Canoga Park 91304 (818) 716-6348 *Wide variety of furniture design to fit the client's needs.*

**Richard Willits, Willits Fine Furniture,** 1298 Anvick Rd., Arcata 95521 (707) 826-0591 *Custom-built furniture for the home and office.*

**Donald S. Wilson,** 407 Lotus La., Mountain View 94043 (415) 968-2876

**Sherry Wolf,** PO Box 333, Agoura Hills 91301 (818) 991-1136 *Sculpture, sculptural wall pieces and decorative items.*

**Matt E. Womack, Womack Enterprises,** 914 San Antonio, Alameda 94501 (415) 521-9083 *Furniture; Victorian and craftsman-style architectural reproduction woodwork.*

**David E. Worfolk, Design Woodworking,** 709 N. Sacramento St., Lodi 95240 (209) 334-6674 *European casework, commercial and residential furnishings.*

**(6) Dennis Young, Handmade Furniture,** 1814 Skillman La., Petaluma 94952 (707) 763-4666 *Handmade furniture of diverse design. Specialist in utilizing local hardwoods.*

## Colorado

**Steven K. Barnhill, Black Canyon Woodworks,** PO Box 421, Gunnison 81230 (303) 641-3645 *Distinctive woodturning and custom work.*

**Dave Boykin, Woodworking and Furniture Design,** 3943 Blake St., Denver 80205 (303) 294-0703 *Custom furniture and specialty woodworking.*

**Terry Boyle,** 73 Blackfoot Trail, Gunnison 81230 (303) 641-0855 *Handmade cabinet and furniture work.*

**Doug Christie, Doormaker,** 98C Everett, Durango 81301 (303) 247-4985

**Ron Christie,** 4665 South Jason, Englewood 80110 (303) 789-0683

**Steve Covert, Against the Grain,** 4217 S. Ann, Ft. Collins 80526 (303) 226-2806

**Craig A. Cox, Silverthorn Clock and Furniture Works,** 29320 Thunderbolt Circle, Conifer 80433 (303) 838-2026 *Variety of clocks, tables and turnings.*

**Bryan A. Coxey, Classic Creations,** 3603 Mead St., Ft. Collins 80526 (303) 226-0927

**Mark Darlington, Darlington Designs,** PO Box 774064, Steamboat Springs 80477 (303) 879-8046 *Hand-carved veneers, inlays, bent-laminations and exotic woods.*

**(28) Derek S. Davis,** Box 7405, Boulder 80306 (303) 440-9485 *Custom furniture.*

**Mike Dziekan,** Box 271, Erie 80516

**Murray Eaton, Sawtooth Woodworks,** Salina Star Rte., Boulder 80302 (303) 447-9155 *Custom cabinets, furniture and commercial fixtures.*

**(58) Larry J. Erpelding,** 3441 N. Prospect, Colorado Springs 80907 (303) 635-9979

**(114) William Folger, Contemporary Turnings,** Box 262, 309 Third St., Crested Butte 81224 (303) 349-5328 *Functional and artistic wood and stone turnings.*

**C.J. Grimes,** 2645 Vrain, Denver 80212 (303) 477-6050 *Commissioned and noncommissioned artworks in wood-sculpture and bas-relief.*

**Cyn Hales, What-Knots in Wood,** 10650 Irma Dr. #22, Northglenn 80233 (303) 452-7049 *Custom designs, commercial and residential furnishings.*

**Jay Hatfield, Masonville Custom Woodworking,** PO Box 61, Masonville 80541 (303) 669-6952 *Custom furniture and cabinetry, done as artistically as possible.*

**David Y. Hill, McKenzie Co.,** 3850 Spring Valley Rd., Boulder 80302 (303) 443-0304

**Pat Kraker, Quality Woodworking,** PO Box 15215, Lakewood 80215 (303) 238-2107 *Clocks, scientific instruments and tools, jigs and fixtures for craftsmen.*

**(83, 85) Bruce Kranzberg, Design Studio,** 2962 4th St., Boulder 80302 (303) 440-7199 *Commercial and residential furnishings individually designed; complete interior design services.*

**(126) R.W. (Bob) Krauss, Jr., Wood Nuances,** PO Box 96, Dinosaur 81610 (303) 374-2443 *Woodturning, quality art and craft items. Furniture restoration and spindle replacement.*

**(121) Max Krimmel,** Salina Star Rte., Boulder 80302 (303) 442-3924 *Gallery turning, guitars.*

**Scott LeCocq, LeCocq Woodworks,** 8919 Field St. #123, Westminster 80020 (303) 423-2163 *Custom woodworking and furniture restoration.*

**J.H. Lewis, Custom Woodwork,** 918 N. Royer St., Colorado Springs 80903 (303) 632-8548

**(79) Jeffry Mann, Unique Custom Furniture,** Box 3420, Aspen 81612 (303) 925-8651 *Rocking chairs, dining chairs and tables, stools.*

**Harv Mastalir,** 2231 Columbine, Boulder 80302 (303) 440-4924 *Custom woodworking, commissions.*

**Mike Newbold, Newbold Woodworking,** 27550 Route 14, Oak Creek 80467 *One-of-a-kind chairs, vases and boxes.*

**Mike Norby, Acacia Woodworking,** 16015 W. 4th Ave. #1, Golden 80401 (303) 278-4606 *Original pieces that go with and complement fine antiques.*

**Jerry Patrasso, Summerwood,** 660 North St., Boulder 80302 (303) 449-0705 *One-of-a-kind sculptural exotic wooden jewelry boxes and furniture. Commissions accepted.*

**Tom Pearce, Woodworker,** 3943 Blake, Denver 80205 (303) 294-0703 *Custom furniture, sensitively designed and carefully crafted.*

**Jack Peeso, Jr., Piseau Woodworks,** 1345 Elm Ave., Grand Junction 81501 (303) 245-5886 *Custom woodworking.*

**D. Schenk & Associates,** 5763 Arapahoe Ave. #16, Boulder 80303 (303) 444-5551 *Interior space and furniture design and fabrication.*

**Jeffrey Simon, Whitewood Designs,** 30355 Jacob Cir., Box 1980, Steamboat Springs 80477 (303) 879-7543 *Furniture: tables, chairs, beds, dressers. Bent-laminations, doors.*

**Dennis Sohocki, Sculptor,** 947 S. Williams, Denver 80209 (303) 777-2028 *Sculpture commissions and wood sculpture.*

**Ken Thoman, Thoman Productions,** Whale Rock Rd., Bellvue 80512 (303) 493-2109 *Limited-production items, specialty boxes, woodcarving, signmaking and custom furniture.*

**(37) William Tickel, Wood,** PO Box 2367, Denver 80201 (303) 296-6451 *Commissions and limited-edition production in American and exotic hardwoods.*

**Brian Tormey, Tormey's Furniture,** 437 N. Mesa Ave., 81401 (303) 249-6875 *Fine furniture and cabinetry made to order.*

**(106) Wayne L. Westphale, Contemporary Time,** 33536 R.C.R. 43A, Steamboat Springs 80487 (303) 879-4142 *Wooden works clocks from exotic hardwoods.*

**R.G. Wolff, Miracle Shop,** 7245 S. Quebec Ct., Englewood 80112 (303) 770-7882 *Accessories and lathe products.*

**Bob and Bill Wood, Fine Materials,** 547 Kalamath St., Denver 80204 (303) 623-5924

## Connecticut

**Brian Art,** 326 Winthrop St., Torrington 06790 (203) 4807 *Custom furniture—designed and constructed.*

**Herbert O. Bergdahl II,** Box 501, Canaan 06018 (203) 824-7528 *Cabinetmaking, carving, marquetry, interior restoration.*

**Nancy Blowers,** 50 Walnut St. Stratford 06497 (203) 377-6109 *One-of-a-kind hand-carved sculptures specializing in animals.*

**Kevin J. Bulwidas, Kevy's Toy Works,** PO Box 257, Sandy Hook 06482 (203) 426-5789 *Toys, hobby and rocking horses, wooden boxes and woodcarving.*

**Steve Chisholm,** 96 Lee Farm Dr., Niantic 06357 (203) 739-2018

**Ron Curtis, Woodworks,** 91 Tunxis Ave., Bloomfield 06002 (203) 242-4285

**(74) Stephen Daniell,** 204 Sargeant St., Hartford 06105 (203) 246-3891 *Chair work, electronic display (LED) furniture.*

**Jesse Good Design and Demolition,** 27 Whisconier Hill Rd., Brookfield 06805 (203) 775-1959

**Edger Downs, Design in Wood,** 437 Chestnutland Rd., New Milford 066776 (203) 354-3507 *Furniture, architectural woodworking.*

**(91) Ben Dupont, Jr., Interwood Designs,** 151 Stony Creek Rd., Branford 06405 (203) 633-3766 *Custom woodworking, furniture, casework and sweater chests.*

**Bob Friedman,** 116 Mile Common, Easton 06612 (203) 968-0763

**Fred M. Gardner, Woodworker,** 111 Stockade Rd., S. Glastonbury 06073 (203) 633-5184 *Custom-designed fine furniture.*

**Darel Gustafson, Gustafson Woodworking,** 58 Poplar Dr., Shelton 06484 (203) 926-1120 *Toys, boxes, bowls and small cabinets.*

**Kenneth V. Johnson,** Box 43, North Stonington 06359 (203) 535-1076

**David H. Meiklem, Meiklem Co.,** PO Box 106, Yantic 06389 (203) 889-1494 *Design and construct all types of furniture and cabinets on commission.*

**Mark Peterson, Michael Price, Full Moon Studios,** 74 Hoyts Hill, Bethel 06801 (203) 792-9254 *One-of-a-kind work, architectural stained glass.*

**Louis J. Morin, Novelty Crafts,** 6 Rentschler St., East Hartford 06118 (203) 568-5168 *Clocks, music boxes, windmills, bowls, mugs, etc.*

**Paul Perras,** 25 Terry's Plain Rd., Simsbury, 06070 (203) 651-8515 *Barrel-stave furniture, hand-carved humorous toys, sculpture.*

**(116) Peter M. Petrochko,** 370 Quaker Farms Rd., Oxford 06483 (203) 888-9835

**Don Rich, G.S.T. Designs,** 3 Rull Rd., Stratford 06497 (203) 375-3807 *Custom turnings and gift items.*

**(139) James Schriber,** 57 West St. Box 1145, New Milford 06776 (203) 354-6452 *Furniture, cabinets, architectural accessories.*

**Larry Sherman, Bebop Wood Shop,** 1 Reed St., Vernon 06066 (203) 872-7530 *Contemporary furniture and built-ins that squeeze out the hatchway.*

**(41) Bryan Smallman, Architectural Furniture,** 59½ South Main St., South Norwalk 06854 (203) 854-1719 *Designing and manufacturing of fine furniture.*

**(69) Robert C. Soule, Maker Fine Furniture and Cabinetry,** 835 Elm St., New Haven 06511 (203) 787-3335 *Limited-edition furniture and cabinetry of original design, traditional adaptations, reproductions.*

**Stefan Tabak,** 466 Mansfield Ave., Darien 06820 (203) 655-0840

**Harry Wunsch,** 24 Compo Pkwy., Westport 06880

**Edward Zucca,** Route 1 Box 24A, Woodstock 06281 (203) 974-2704 *One-of-a-kind furniture, lights, eclectic styles, fancy hardwoods or paint.*

## Delaware

**Vincent Clarke,** 2402 Landon Dr. Chalfonte, Wilmington 19810 (302) 478-4473

## District of Columbia

**(50) Bernard Gouveia,** 3906 Ingomar St. NW, Washington 20015 (202) 966-0960 *Custom-designed furniture on a commission basis.*

**Thomas and Barbara Wolf, Instrument Makers,** 931 R St. NW, Washington 20001 (202) 332-3341 *Harpsichords, forte-pianos, virginals, clavichords, restoration of fine antique keyboard instruments.*

## Florida

**Garrett A. Bouvier, House Of Bouvier, Inc.,** 420 12th Ave., Indialantic 32903 (305) 725-0187 *Custom furniture, cases, jewelry boxes, accent pieces for the home or office.*

**George L. Carter, The Wood Emporium, Inc.,** 307 North Main St., Havana 32333 (904) 539-9848 *Antique restoration, custom furniture and cabinets.*

**Richard W. Choyvette, Americana Woodcrafters,** 5901 Jetport Ind. Blvd., Tampa 33614 (813) 886-6423 *Epoxy plaques and boat tillers, furniture, etc.*

**Donald Esterberg,** 3375 Shannon Pl., Pensacola 32503

**Richard Fadil,** 8123 SW 82 Pl., Miami 33143

**Steve J. Fox,** 27 Neuchatel Dr., Tallahassee 32303 (904) 562-5216

**David Freundlich,** 26080 SW 192 Ave., Homestead 33031 (305) 245-2057 *Turned objects in tropical fruit woods.*

**Russell Ginsberg,** 9500 SW 60 Ct., Miami 33156 (305) 666-0185

**Cas Grabowski,** 19705 SW 134th Ave., Miami 33177 (305) 253-3863

**Keith Hanson, Bezalel Woodworks,** 202 107th St. Gulf, Marathon 33050 (305) 743-9246 *Custom furniture, built-in cabinetry and kitchen cabinetry.*

**Jeffrey Harris, Harris Furniture,** 1663 11th St., Sarasota 33577 (813) 365-3669 *One-of-a-kind fine furniture for residential and executive clients.*

**Dean Hight,** 3725 Bowden Circle, Jacksonville 32216 (904) 737-6745

**Tiffany Hopkinson,** PO Box 208, Nokomis 33555 (813) 485-4423 *Everyday items recreated in wood.*

**Doug Jewell,** PO Box EG24, Melbourne 32936 (305) 984-7183 *Custom design and construction of wood furniture.*

**Larry Kellam, Craftworks,** 4425 SW 71 Ave., Miami 33155 (305) 667-9913 *Architectural woodworking, fine cabinetry, specialty fabrications.*

**Kenneth Keusch, Wood 'N Weave,** 6201 SW 112 St., Miami 33155 (305) 665-0370 *Woodturning: custom, one-off objects.*

**(10) Robert J. Kopec, Woodworker,** 715 Raven Ave., Longwood 32750 (305) 830-9353 *Handcrafted fine furniture and design by commission.*

**Thomas Krauss,** 1965 Henderson Rd., Ormond Beach 32074 (904) 672-9664 *Custom woodfinishing and artistic turnings.*

**Mark Krenz, Custom Furniture,** 18665 SW 191 St., Miami 33157 (305) 252-1469 *Furniture created with quality as a forethought. Exotic hardwoods, lacquer.*

**(11) Reid H. Leonard, Leonard Furniture,** 537 Brent La., Pensacola 32503 (904) 476-4616 *Hardwood furniture and fine art woodwork.*

**Stuart A. and Joyce R. Lilie,** 200 Reading Way E., Winter Park 32789 (305) 644-4697

**Bill Long, The Turnery,** 605 22nd St. North Beach, St. Augustine 32084 (904) 824-6924 *Functional sculptural objects—small to furniture.*

**Robert D. Patterson,** 1896 40th Ave., Apt. 8, Vero Beach 32960

**Patricia Pettit,** 2626 Oakmere La., Sarasota 33581 (813) 924-6112 *Special, one-of-a-kind hardwood furniture and accessories.*

**Ray Pirello, Woodworking,** 2025 NW 139th St., Miami 33054 (305) 681-2999 *Custom-design furniture and cabinetry, millwork design consultants.*

**W.H. Powers,** 1020 49th Ave., Bradenton 34203

**Primary Wood,** 1735 Blitz Ave., Palm Bay 32905 (305) 729-8944 *Custom furniture in solid wood and fine veneers.*

**Judy Gale Roberts,** PO Box 3346, St. Augustine 32084 (904) 824-0682 *Intarsia: inlaid wood-relief sculpture, custom designs up to 400 sq. ft.*

**(22) Bob Schmidt, Signature Furniture,** 56 San Marco Ave., St. Augustine 32084 (904) 824-7860 *Custom hardwood furniture.*

**Allen Stone, Wood Shop,** 4487 NE 6th Terrace, Fort Lauderdale 33334 (305) 771-1740

**Russell Thornton, Touch of Wood,** 588 Citrus Ave., Oviedo 32765 (305) 365-3508 *Custom furniture, rocking horses.*

**Richard vom Saal, Sculpture Limited,** 701 NW 8 Ct., Boynton Beach 33435 (305) 734-2916 *One-of-a-kind sculpture and furniture.*

**Jim West,** Route 3 Box 910, Gainesville 32606 (904) 377-5370

**Larry Williams, Artist,** PO Box 4633, Ft. Walton Beach 32549 (904) 243-5216 *Sculpture, original-design fine furniture and stained glass.*

## Georgia

**Fred Allen,** 1464 White Circle Rd., Marietta 30060 (404) 427-4053 *Mechanical toys and kinetic sculpture.*

**George Archer,** 18 Black Forest Dr., Savannah 31410 (912) 897-5319 *Tables, chairs, casework and desks.*

**Michael Brubaker,** 1330 E. 54th St., Savannah 31404 (912) 352-7161

**Peter Bull Woodworks,** Box 1129, Cleveland 30528 *Contemporary designs and cabinetwork.*

**Greg Davidson,** 1713 Council Bluff Dr., Atlanta 30345

**George de Alth,** 262 Old Holcomb Bridge Way, Roswell 30076 (404) 587-3691

**Robert Erwin,** Route 16 Box 11, Cumming 30130 (404) 889-0445

**Vincent Eugenio, Works With Wood,** 431 Duchess Dr., Marietta 30066 (404) 394-4804 *Fine cabinets, boxes and tables.*

**(143) Kent Everett, Everett Guitars, c/o Atlanta Guitar Works,** 3701 Clairmont Rd., Atlanta 30341 (404) 451-2485 *Construction of musical instruments.*

**(65) Michael Gilmartin, Interpreta Woodworking,** 1260 Foster St., Atlanta 30318 (404) 351-2590 *Design and manufacture of furniture and fixtures.*

**(115) G.A. Goff, G.A. Goff Wood Turning,** PO Box 6893, Athens 30604 (404) 549-9675 *Lathe-turned art objects of unique and original styles.*

**(29) Gregory W. Guenther, Furnituremaker,** 418 E. State St., Savannah 31401 (912) 233-5238 *Furniture and design by commission.*

**Jack Harich,** 1209 N. Highland Ave., Atlanta 30306 (404) 876-6732 *Cedar chests of all shapes and sizes.*

**John P. Harris, Harris Design,** 667 Roxbury Dr., Riverdale 30274 (404) 478-7201 *Turning combined with metal work.*

**Heather Hilton,** 548 Linwood Ave., Atlanta 30306 (404) 688-4075 *Sculpture making—nonfunctional and functional sculpture in wood.*

**Joel Katzowitz,** 2570 Chimney Springs Dr., Marietta 30062 (404) 641-9718

**John McGee, Woodworks,** 101 Alice La., Carrollton 30117 (404) 834-7373 *Original and custom-designed furniture and accessories.*

**Chip Mochel,** 150 S. Atlanta St. 32K, Roswell 30075 (404) 992-7232

**Michael Murrell,** 1415 Midview Dr., Decatur 30032 (404) 658-2257 *Bentwood, carving and sculpture.*

**Ayokunle Odeleye, Odeleye Studios,** 1427 Metropolitan Ave. SE, Atlanta 30316 (404) 373-8063 *Hand-carved sculpture and fine wooden objects.*

**Jim Schulz, Creative Contours,** 1742 Moores Mill Rd. NW, Atlanta 30318 (404) 355-0143 *Custom-design/built furniture and architectural woodwork.*

**(104) Timothy Sutherland, Sutherland Studios,** PO Box 7086, Atlanta 30357 (404) 688-9089 *Furniture consultant, designers, fine art manufacturer.*

**Donald Tarr, Emmons-Tarr Co. Product Design,** 8155H Colquitt Rd., Dunwoody 30338 (404) 395-1141 *Modeling, mockups and prototypes.*

**Gerard van Lier, Furniture Design Alternatives,** 1079 Brittney Way, Norcross 30093 (404) 381-0756 *Design, execution and restoration of fine furniture.*

**(68) David Van Nostrand,** 1260 Foster St. NW, Atlanta 30318 (404) 351-2590 *Commission work from harvested native woods.*

**Thomas H. Williams,** 3502 Cold Spring La., Atlanta 30341

## Hawaii

**(126) Todd Campbell,** 1993 E. Main St., Wailuku, Maui 96793 (808) 242-8063 *Woodturning.*

**Marcus Castaing, Heartwood,** PO Box 483, Naalehu 96772 (808) 929-9275 *Custom and one-of-a-kind furniture and architectural finishwork.*

**Wayne J. Jacintho, The Kauai Cabinet Works,** PO Box 38, Kilauea 96754 (808) 828-1214 *Custom furniture, woodworking in native and introduced island woods.*

**Ron Kent,** 5329 Kalanianaole Hwy., Honolulu 96821 (808) 536-4511 *Translucent bowls: very thin, diameter to 24 in.*

**(16) Peter Naramore, The Kingswood Shop,** 214 Kula Hwy., Kula 96790 (808) 878-6209

**Wayne N. Omura,** RR 1 Box 691, Kula 96790 (808) 878-2855

**Steven J. Hill, Stephen Meder, Meder Hill Designs,** 1615 Silva St., Honolulu 96819 (808) 845-6811

**Roger Wordlie, Furnituremaker,** 525 A Cummins St., Honolulu 96814 (808) 537-2642

**Robb Young,** 867 Robello La., Honolulu 96817 (808) 841-5532 *Fine custom furniture designed for the home and office.*

## Idaho

**Paul Barks, Tinker Bells,** 2672A S. 1050 E., Hagerman 83332 (208) 837-4488

**Nicholas Cavagnaro, Cavagnaro Woodworking,** PO Box 2052, Orofino 83544 (208) 476-3456 *Very high-quality original furniture pieces.*

**Chuck Ekenrode, Idaho Fine Joinery,** 1109⅓ Longmont, Boise 83706 (208) 343-3495

**Kevin Gray, Trail Creek Woodworks,** Box 34, Glendale Rd., Fruitvale 83620 (208) 253-4765 *Rockers, chairs, stools, small tables, hand-tool oriented.*

**Michael Hamilton, Heartwood,** 2012 N. 19th St., Boise 83702 (208) 345-6384 *Boxes, special cabinets and restoration.*

**Myles W. Hougen, Sculptor,** 10-405 Hwy. 95 N., Sandpoint 83864 (208) 263-1778 *Sculpture and architectural—personal.*

**Bill Petersen, Petersen Woodworks,** 6898 W. Belhaven, Boise 83703 (208) 343-9860 *Tables, china cabinets and desks.*

**Ivan Phelps, The Lathe Shop,** RR 1 Box 73, McCall 83638 (208) 325-8886

**Bill Sargent,** Route 1, Murtaugh 83344 (208) 432-5207

**Mark Smith, White Cloud Studio,** Star Route #3325, New Meadows 83654 (208) 347-2149 *Finely carved furniture, architectural features and accessories, commissioned.*

**John Studebaker, Furniture,** 2102 Harrison Blvd., Boise 83702 (208) 345-7139 *Furniture and custom woodworking.*

**John Taye,** 1412 E. Jefferson St., Boise 83712 (208) 344-6321 *Realistic sculpture of still life and figure subjects.*

**David L. Trapp,** Box 182, Victor 83455 (208) 787-2752

**Will Venard, Alpine Woodworks,** Route 1 Box 495, Bonner's Ferry 83805 (208) 267-3815 *Sculpture, custom wood products, wood trader.*

**Wesley Wadsworth, Wacky Wood Works,** HC 63 Box 2360, Monteview 83435 (208) 657-2217 *Handcrafted furniture, custom products, cabinetmaking and turnings in exotic and domestic woods.*

**James R. Wilson, Wilson's Planing Mill & Cabinet Shop,** 1623 Eldridge Ave., Twin Falls 83301 (208) 733-2329 *Custom fine woodwork: furniture, cabinets, doors, windows, moldings, custom millwork.*

**Timothy J. Zikratch, In The Woods,** 335 East Lewis, Pocatello 83201 (208) 233-4003

## Illinois

**(100) Winfield Austin,** 567 Franklin Dr. #116, Mt. Prospect 60056 (312) 228-9512

**Don and Melva Beeler, Hearthside Heritage,** RR 1, Irving 62051 (217) 594-2208 *Handcrafted, carved and painted furniture and accessories. Custom-orders welcome.*

**(25) Tom Berry,** 915 Augusta, Oak Park 60302 (312) 386-0874 *Custom furniture.*

**R.D. Brown, Woodworks,** RR 1 Box 224, Genoa 60135 (815) 784-5885 *Tables, chests and art woodwork.*

**James Q. Buffenmyer,** 19W12Y Rochdale, Lombard 60148 (312) 627-8444 *Musical instruments, clocks, wall hangings and wooden greeting cards.*

**(45) Bailey & Gleason Cabinetmakers,** 1750 North Wolcott Ave., Chicago 60622 (312) 486-2260 *Furniture, entertainment centers, architectural woodwork primarily through architects and designers.*

**Steve Case,** 3847 N. Lincoln Ave., Chicago 60613 (312) 327-6348 *Custom-design furniture, custom-woodworking service.*

**Robert James Clemens, Clemens Violins,** 3753 West Grace St., Chicago 60618 (312) 583-9382 *Handcrafted instruments of the violin family.*

**Arthur E. Dameron,** 1248 Beecher Ave., Galesburg 61401 (309) 342-3252

**Loren Diehl, Wildwood Crafts,** 2134 Running Deer La., Freeport 61032 (815) 232-2373 *Gift items, laminated woods, jewelry, boxes, rolling pins, etc.*

**Brian Donnelly, Donnelly Design Associates, Inc.,** 506 W. Walnut St., Carbondale 62901 (618) 549-0544

**John Fezi,** 2100 W. Algonquin Rd., Mt. Prospect 60056 (312) 956-0289

**Richard D. Frank,** 1713 Briarcliff, Urbana 61801 (217) 367-1223

**Eugene Geinzer,** 6525 N. Sheridan Rd., Chicago 60626 (312) 508-2177 *Original designs—custom cabinetry.*

**Richard M. George,** 1558 Columbia Ct., Elk Grove Village 60007 (312) 399-4778

**Roger L. Harshman,** RR 3 Box 79, Sullivan 61951 (217) 797-6913 *Furniture repair and woodworking.*

**Leo Hellmer, Woodworking,** 904 Goldenview, Champaign 61821 (217) 356-8357

**Don Hintz,** 1532 Chapel Ct., Northbrook 60062

**Patrick Holley,** 6830 N. Ashland #2, Chicago 60626 (312) 939-0550

**Scott Jaster,** 6803 N. Keeler, Lincolnwood 60646 (312) 675-5926

**John F. Klemundt,** 3313 Irving Park Rd., Chicago 60618 (312) 478-1212

**Mark S. Levin, Levin Inc.,** 1611 Simpson St., Evanston 60201 (312) 328-6541

**Dan Levit, Wood Design,** 861 Fairfield, Elmhurst 60126 (312) 941-7658 *Hand-carved craft and sculpture.*

**Nick Lipousky,** 315 Michigan Ave., Westville 61883 (217) 267-2213

**Gregory Mader,** 4733 North Troy St., Chicago 60625

**Richard Malacek, Weathertop Woodcraft,** 26 W. 282 MacArthur, Wheaton 60188 (312) 668-3324 *Decorative carving/custom-carved wood signs.*

**Daniel J. McCarthy, Woodlines,** 1400 Linden, Park Ridge 60068 (312) 698-6466 *Useful objects made with a playful blend of visual and tactile surprise.*

**Tom McCue Interiors,** 2708 Arrowhead Dr., Springfield 62702 (217) 523-2546 *Custom-designed and built wood casework and accessories.*

**Leonard B. Mellinger,** 1205 E. 16th St., Sterling 61081 (815) 625-9145

**Paul J. Meyer,** 915 Augusta, Oak Park 60302 (312) 386-0874

**Jeff Miller, Handcrafted Furniture,** 1768 W. Greenleaf Ave., Chicago 60626 (312) 761-3311

**Mark D. Miller,** 746 Euclid Ave., Glen Ellyn 60137 (312) 858-0907 *Lathework, furniture and antique repair.*

**Jim Newbury, Newbury Wooden Toys,** PO Box 47, Bethalto 62010 (618) 377-8544

**H.M. Orloff,** 1181 Lincoln Ave. S., Highland Park 60035 (312) 432-5956 *Custom furniture for beauty and use, contemporary design.*

**(48) David Orth,** 1107 Chicago Ave., Oak Park 60302 (312) 383-4399 *Art furniture and sculpture for your home and church.*

**Don E. Paule,** 43 W. 310 Hawkeye Dr., Elburn 60119

**John P. Reichling,** 413 Orchard, Oswego 60543 (312) 554-1037

**(20) David Rowlette,** Cabinetmaking Instructor, Olney Central College, Olney 62450 (618) 395-4351 ext. 2224 *Craftsman of fine furniture.*

**Henry Royer,** 224 S. Humphrey Ave., Oak Park 60302 (312) 383-4945 *Fine wood furniture and turnings with metal work.*

**Peter Smith, The Woodsmith,** 296 Williams Pl., East Dundee 60118 (312) 426-7266 *Furnishing design and construction.*

**Robert L. Sutton,** 816 W. Ridgemont Rd., Peoria 61614 (309) 686-0383

**Patrick F. Tanner, Tanner Carousel,** 4 Hickory Rd., Oakwood Hills 60013 (312) 639-0328 *Merry-go-rounds and carousel animals.*

**John Tomczyk, Woodworker,** 3514 N. Lakewood, Chicago 60657 (312) 525-4121 *Fine furniture, accessories and wooden boats.*

**Preston V. Wakeland, Omni Craft Inc.,** Route 4 Box 40, Lockport 60441 (815) 838-1285 *Custom hardwood furniture in all styles.*

**Sidney R. Ward,** 4147 North Richmond, Chicago 60618

**(95) Jeffrey Webster,** 1418 North Milwaukee Ave., Chicago 60622 (312) 252-8045

**(61) Lee Weitzman,** 1524 S. Peoria, Chicago 60608 (312) 243-3009 *Design and fabrication of one-of-a-kind or limited editions.*

**Charles Wilkin,** 329 S. 7th Ave., La Grange 60525 (312) 354-1561

**Peter Zaluzec,** 25134 Columbia Bay Dr., Lake Villa 60046 (312) 356-8381 *Traditional and contemporary furniture.*

## Indiana

**David Bellamy,** 111 E. Sixteenth Apt. 410, Indianapolis 46202 (317) 631-2262

**Sharon L. Calhoon,** 8525 Eagle Crest La., Indianapolis 46234 (317) 299-4409

**Valerie Eickmeier,** 1836 N. Delaware, Indianapolis 46202 (317) 925-7647 *Bent and stack-lamination (painted sculpture).*

**(45) Glen D. Fuller, FullerAllen Furniture LTD.,** 4033 North Industrial Blvd., Indianapolis 46254 (317) 293-0291 *Art-quality furniture pieces to full-scale hotel-room furniture.*

**A.J. Gouichowski,** 58029 Grumstown Rd., South Bend 46619 (219) 287-9582

**Mike Hamilton,** 517 Brentwood Dr. W., Plainfield 46168 (317) 839-5445 *One-of-a-kind pieces in native hardwoods.*

**Frank D. Hart, Hart Furniture,** 875 Avon Rd., Plainfield 46168 (317) 839-0637 *Custom-built hardwood furniture, repairs, antique restoration.*

**George Huffman,** 12 Maple Crest Dr., Carmel 46032 (317) 846-1866

**Millard Huffman,** RR 1 Box 103, Troy 47588 (812) 547-6153

**Bob Humphrey, Wood Designs,** 9601 Southeastern Ave., Indianapolis 46239 (317) 862-5693 *Tables, cabinets and customized pieces.*

**Mike Kahlert,** RR 1 Box 52D, Berne 46711 (219) 692-6438 *One-off custom pieces made of solid wood only.*

**(14) Robert A. Kasnak, Kasnak Designs,** 5505 N. 1000 E., Brownsburg 46112 (317) 852-9770

**David Kastner, Cabinetmaker,** 1410 3 Rivers E., Fort Wayne 46802 (219) 424-3486 *Fine custom furniture, internationally recognized, classic modern design.*

**Verlin Miller—Woodworker, The Dovetail Joint,** 513 W. Garfield Ave., Elkhart 46516 (219) 295-4315 *Custom furniture, cabinetry and other woodworking.*

**Gary Prater, Maranatha Woodmen,** RR 6 Box 529, Muncie 47304 (317) 759-6898 *Sculptural hardwood and woodcarving embodied in furniture of the highest order.*

**Larry Ramsbey, Timber Guild,** RR 1 Box 40B, Walkerton 46574 (219) 586-3081 *Large one-piece bowls to 36 in.+.*

**George R. Sarris, South Bend Millwork and Manufacturing,** PO Box 3717, South Bend 46619 (219) 289-2132 *Architectural millwork and commissions using domestic and imported hardwoods.*

**Eric Schlesinger,** 2305 Crawford St., Terre Haute 47803 (812) 232-6050

**Harold R. Sharpe,** 576 S. Century Oaks Ct., Zionsville 46077 (317) 873-4927

**Gene Short, Artist in Wood,** 315 N. Indiana, Goshen 46526 (219) 533-1566 *Woodturning and one-of-a-kind pieces.*

## Iowa

**Mary Ann Beecher,** 3014 Woodland St., Ames 50010 (515) 292-1313

**(65) Craig C. Campbell,** 117 21st NE, Cedar Rapids 52402

**Jim Carpenter, Carpenter's Woodwright Shop,** 2003 Main, Emmetsburg 50536 (712) 852-2506

**Dan Demmer, Demmer Clocks and Cabinet Shop,** RR 1 Box 156, Fairfax 52228 (319) 446-7218 *Custom-made cabinets, clocks and art pieces.*

**Vernon L. Devore, Devore Wood Shop,** RR 2, Wapello 52653 (319) 523-2634 *Furniture, including antique reproductions.*

**Jeff Easley,** Box 248, Oxford 52322 (319) 628-4515/4766 *Design, durability, integrity and satisfaction.*

**Walter Elder, Elder's Mfg. Co.,** PO Box 65322, West Des Moines 50265 (515) 223-4653 *Custom-made furniture and cabinets, wood specialties, toys and clock cases.*

**Dale F. Goldthorpe, Woodworker,** 1008 N. 4th St., Ames 50010 (515) 232-9273 *Custom woodworking, design and construction of fine furniture.*

**Bruce E. Greene, Cedars of Lebanon, Makers of Fine Furniture,** 117 Main St., Randall 50231 (515) 328-3420/3670 *Period reproduction and custom furniture, custom woodturning and furniture repair.*

**Walter E. Greenley,** 1203 Broadway, Webster City 50595 (515) 832-3621

**Jeffrey T. Hayes,** 3217 88th St., Urbandale 50322 (515) 276-4198

**Jeff Life, Life Enterprise,** 472 Loma, Waterloo 50703 (319) 233-7173 *One-of-a-kind, limited-production handmade furniture.*

**Don Mostrom, Sculptor/Woodcraftsman,** 3216 4th St., Des Moines 50313 (515) 280-3065 *Custom furniture, specialty woodworking and carving.*

**David Naso, Communia Woods,** 700 S. Dubuque St., Iowa City 52240 (319) 338-0497

**Larry Nordin,** 259 N. Hyland #2, Ames 50010 (515) 296-2026

**R. Kirby Poole,** 1125 8th, Nevada 50201 (515) 382-5255

**Mike Roths, Bear Paw Custom Cabinets,** 603 F. Ave., Vinton 52349 (319) 472-5169 *Custom kitchen cabinets and furniture.*

**(51) John Schwartzkopf Cabinetry,** 1113 19th St. SE, Cedar Rapids 52403 (319) 363-5836 *Custom furniture design and fabrication.*

**Robert A. Spangler,** 1807 Stevens Dr., Iowa City 52240 (319) 337-6415 *Contemporary furniture design, 18th-century Chippendale and Queen Anne reproductions.*

**John Thoe, Ralston Creek Woodworker,** 700 S. Dubuque St., Iowa City 52240 (319) 338-0497 *Acanthus and Victorian carving wood sculpture.*

**Kirk Vandecar, Vandecar Woodworking,** 1232 W. 4th St., Davenport 52802 (319) 323-2303

## Kansas

**Robert S. Brown, Artist in Wood,** 9726 Cedar Dr., Overland Park 66207 (913) 648-1753 *Shelves and cabinets with hand-carved decoration.*

**(20) Gary E. Derzinski, Period Furniture,** RR 1 Box 34 A, Leavenworth 66048 (913) 682-8857 *Hand-carved Queen Anne and Chippendale furniture.*

**Neal L. George, Ditto's Woodwork,** Box 206, Logan 67646 (913) 689-7437 *Lathe turning, furniture designing and construction, wooden spiral staircases.*

**John Hachmeister, Sculptor/Craftsman,** Route 1 Box 97, Oskaloosa 66066 (913) 863-2982 *Sculpture in wood and one-of-a-kind furniture.*

**Matthew Kirby, Woodworker,** PO Box 1065, Lawrence 66044 (913) 594-3849 *Furniture and architectural design and replication, all woods, metals and plastics.*

**Rex Kolste,** #3 Austin Ct., Colby 67701 (913) 462-2509

**Ted S. Komala, Komala Classics,** 5921 N. Hills Dr., Topeka 66617 (913) 288-1550 *Quality cabinetworks, furniture and other home furnishings.*

**Roger E. Mathews, M.W. & G. Inc.,** 132 N. Pinecrest, Wichita 67208 (316) 683-2071 *Doors, transomes and side lights.*

**(16) Will Orvedal, Woodworker,** Route 1 Box 95, Lecompton 66050 (913) 887-6578 *Design and construction of solid-wood furnishings.*

**Dan Quackenbush, Quackenbush Cabinets,** 1405 Lakestone Dr., Olathe 66061 (913) 782-0523 *Conservative contemporary furniture and cabinets.*

**Winchester Woodworks,** RR 1 Box 11C, Winchester 66097 (913) 774-7541 *Plantation shutters, custom laminate work and general woodworking.*

## Kentucky

**Mel Cole, Woodcarver,** RR 1 Box 206, Russell Springs 42642 (502) 343-3791 *Custom furniture and English chip carving.*

**(120) Robert Fry,** 1606 Greenup, Covington 41011 (606) 291-7053 *Custom furniture, woodturnings and wood sculpture.*

**Charles Harvey, Simple Gifts,** 201C North Broadway, Berea 40403 (606) 986-1653 *Shaker furniture and smallware—nesting oval boxes.*

**(146) Warren A. May, Woodworker,** 114 Main St., Berea 40403 (606) 986-9293 *Cabinets and Appalachian dulcimers, Kentucky styles and original designs.*

**Scott and Stacy Rowlette, Rowlette Brothers, Craftsmen of Fine Furniture,** Route 5 Box 589, Berea 40403 (606) 986-9557 *Wooden toys to classical furniture.*

**(24) Paul M. Sasso,** RR 1 Box 322B, Almo 42020 (502) 753-9330 *Art furniture.*

**Thomas R. Williams, Gwilym Ltd.,** Route 3 Box 440, Paris 40361 (606) 987-6225 *Carved and turned bowls, spoons, toys and electric folk instruments.*

**James E. Yule,** Route 3 Box 77A, Edmonton 42129 (502) 432-2945 *Hand-carved furniture, sculpture, coat of arms, clan badges and monograms.*

## Louisiana

**Michael Arbuckle, Arbuckle Originals,** 4323 Carondelet St., New Orleans 70115 (504) 899-5907 *Original, distinctive collectibles.*

**Rick Brunner,** 8108 Airline Hwy., Baton Rouge 70815 (504) 923-3011 *Contemporary wood furniture and accessories. Some commissions accepted.*

**Barry Champagne,** 14855 Stoneberg Ave., Baton Rouge 70816 (504) 275-7967 *Family-oriented furniture: clocks, desks, curios; storage and entertainment centers.*

**David I. Falkner, Bix Furniture Service,** 1120 Commerce St., Shreveport 71101 (318) 222-0060 *Refinishing, custom-made furniture, mirror resilvering, caning and antique restoration.*

**Alfred Neale Gordon,** 3732 South Lakeshore Dr., Baton Rouge 70808 (504) 343-7265

**Maryann McClain,** 27 Tradewinds Ct., Mandeville 70448 (504) 626-5931

**Ford Thomas, Benchworks,** 3057 Zeeland St., Baton Rouge 70808 (504) 344-1026 *Commissioned one-of-a-kind contemporary furniture.*

## Maine

**David P. Barresi, Hardwood Creations,** Box 75, New Vineyard 04956

**(73) Peter Barrett, Cabinetmaker,** 317 Cumberland Ave., Portland 04101 (207) 772-6137

**C.H. Becksvoort,** PO Box 12, New Gloucester 04260 (207) 926-4608 *Tables, desks, chairs, beds, cases and accessories.*

**Dan Bloomer, Designer/Craftsman in Wood,** 32 Western Ave., Waterville 04901 (207) 873-5865 *Fine custom furniture in hardwoods, architectural and residential cabinetry.*

**Tim Bogle,** Upper "A" St., Peaks Island 04108 (207) 766-5593 *Wood.*

**John Bryan,** 27 Bridge St., Yarmouth 04096 (207) 846-9379 *Investment-quality furniture, design and carving.*

**Louis J. Charlett,** Box 236, Kings La., Manset 04656 (207) 244-5643 *Custom design and building of conservation contemporary furniture.*

**Jonathan Clowes, Clowes Woodworking,** RFD 3, Waldoboro 04572 (207) 832-5191 *Custom-designed and crafted furniture, sculpture and particularly mobiles.*

**(21) Robert H. Effinger, Newport Reproductions,** 59 Main St., Fryburg 04037 (207) 935-3288 *High-style 18th-century reproductions.*

**Dari Forman, Dari's Custom Furniture,** Back Pond Rd., Alibon 04910 (207) 437-9368 *Custom furniture: bureaus, desks, cabinets, etc., original designs.*

**Robert Gassett, Custom Woodworking, Furniture and Cabinetry,** RFD 2, Oakland 04963 (207) 362-3873

**(19) Anthony Giachetti,** PO Box 504, East Boothbay 04544 (207) 633-3740 *One-of-a-kind cabinets, desks, tables, etc.*

**Jeff Hanna, Oat Canoe Co.,** RFD 1 Box 4100, Mt. Vernon 04352 (207) 293-2694 *Building and restoration of small wooden boats, especially wood/canvas canoes.*

**(65) Lee F. Harvey,** 252 Foreside Rd., Falmouth 04105 (207) 781-5479

**John R. Jandik, Heirlooms in Wood,** RR 1 Box 394, Gouldsboro 04607 (207) 963-7683 *Custom-designed hardwood furniture.*

**Jamie Johnston,** 74 Lincoln St., Portland 04103 (207) 773-5288

**(110) Darryl Keil, Maine Architectural Interiors,** 80 Second St., South Portland 04106 (207) 799-4603 *Furniture and custom interiors.*

**(77) Jeff Kellar,** PO Box 4770, Portland 04112 (207) 773-6269 *Furniture, sculpture.*

**(104) Gregg Lipton, In Wood,** 63 Spruce St., Portland 04102 (207) 772-1653 *Custom furniture on commission, design prototyping and limited production.*

**James McCarthy,** Box 208, Ocean Park 04063 (207) 283-1231

**Neal Meltzer, Woodworker,** RFD 1, Coffin Hill Rd., Limerick 04048 (207) 793-8617 *Individually designed and built contemporary furniture and custom cabinetry.*

**(13) Gordon R. Merrick, Woodsmith,** PO Box 1187, Kennebunkport 04046 (207) 283-0669 *One-of-a-kind veneered furniture, spiral staircases and custom interiors.*

**(149) R.J. Regier,** RR 1 Box 401, South St., Freeport 04032 (207) 865-6687 *Fortepiano and harpsichord construction, repair and restoration, instrument rental.*

**Cliff Rugg,** 45 State St., Gorham 04038 (207) 774-5111 *Precise reproduction of American, English and Oriental furniture, contemporary adaptations.*

**Gerald R. Sullivan, Cabinetmaker,** E-5 Maplewood Terrace, Freeport 04032 (207) 865-9394 *Cabinetmaking and fine furniture.*

**W. Turner, Woodworker,** Box 90, Old Harrington Rd., Walpole 04573 (207) 677-3749 *Custom commissions, one-of-a-kind and limited-edition pieces.*

**R.N. Winters, Cabinetmaker,** PO Box 10, La Grange 04453 (207) 943-7972 *Cabinetry, commissioned furniture, architectural woodwork.*

## Maryland

**(107) Kent Bailey, LTD,** 1856 Cherry Rd., Annapolis 21401 *Wood and metal sculpture.*

**John F. Christian,** 6502 Ridge Dr., Bethesda 20816

**Carl W. Clinton,** 8115 Raonoke Ave., Takoma Park 20912 (301) 587-0403 *One-of-a-kind traditional and contemporary furniture.*

**(15) Arnold d'Epagnier-Woodworking-,** 14201 Noltey Rd., Colesville 20904 (301) 384-1663 *Solid wood, inlays, boulle work, Greene & Greene style furniture.*

**David Haber, ABD Woodshop,** 523 Mill St., Lavale 21502 (301) 759-2929 *Custom furniture and architectural millwork.*

**Scott Blair Hubbard, Hubbard Designs,** Route 2 Box 579, Knoxville 21758

**Kenneth S. Kashkett,** 9453 Clocktower La., Columbia 21046 (301) 953-3543

**William W. Kinney,** 10520 Rolling Green Ct., Clarksburg 20871 (301) 831-6085

**Eric Lundberg, Craftsman,** 14221 Turkey Foot Rd., Gaithersburg 20878 (301) 840-1205 *Cabinetmaking, furniture, woodcarving, reproductions and restorations.*

**E. Scott MacLaren, Designer-Craftsman,** 6717 Old Stage Rd., Rockville 20852 (301) 881-3819 *Custom-designed, handcrafted furniture made to outlast its maker.*

**Richard McCarthy,** 5110 Hazelwood Ave., Baltimore 21206 (301) 866-1088

**Rupert Moure, Ciscon, Inc.,** 11629 Danville Dr., Rockville 20852 (301) 881-2627 *Desks, tables, cabinets of solids and/or veneers.*

**Victor J. Mullan, The Mullan Remodeling Company,** 4609 Schenley Rd., Baltimore 21210 (301) 243-1399

**Jerry Nelson, Woodworker,** 13211 Lutes Dr., Silver Spring 20906 (301) 946-3319 *Modern interpretations of Oriental, Egyptian and Colonial styles.*

**William Pierce, Woodworking,** 13915 Crest Hill La., Silver Spring 20904 (301) 384-3629

**George R. Pitman, Glen Mill Woodworks,** 10109 Bevern La., Potomac 20854 (301) 762-8851 *Design and build custom hardwood furniture.*

**Walter Raynes,** 2925 Guilford Ave., Baltimore 21218 (301) 625-1470 *Handcrafted period and contemporary furniture, antique restoration and conservation.*

**Stuart Sklas,** 2904 Taney Rd. 1A, Baltimore 21209 (301) 764-2193 *Sculptor and turner of fine woods.*

**Richard Snow,** 1294 Ritchie Rd., Capitol Heights 20743 (301) 350-8949 *From casework to carving contemporary furniture.*

**Lloyd Sussman, Sussman Woodworking,** Route 1 Box 95, Accident 21520 (301) 245-4466 *All facets of woodworking: millwork, cabinets, furniture, bending and carving.*

**Robert S. Teringo, Furnituremaker,** 2 Harrowgate Ct., Potomac 20850 (301) 424-7928 *Designer/craftsman of fine hardwood furniture.*

## Massachussetts

**(63) A.B. Acker, The Yankee Joyner,** PO Box 56, Cushman 01002 (413) 549-6640 *Period furniture and stringed instruments.*

**(107) James Adams, Woodworking,** 375 North Leverett Rd., Leverett 01054 (413) 367-2103 *Desks, beds, small runs and unique items by commission.*

**Philip Bird, Designer/Woodworker,** 23 Idaho St., Dorchester 02126 (617) 296-6673 *Contemporary furniture to satisfy your dreams.*

**Bill Brace, Woodworker,** 49 Liberty St., Concord 01742 (617) 253-3391 *Beds, tables, chairs, desks, chests and cradles.*

**(85) Jeffrey Briggs, Briggs Fantasies In Wood,** 17 Dalton St., Newburyport 01950 (617) 465-5593 *Imaginative woodcarving.*

**(70) Dale Broholm,** Box 653, Jamaica Plain 02130 (617) 524-0072 *Custom-designed furniture and cabinetry for the trade and individual.*

**(104) Tony Clarke,** 37 Old Stage Rd., W. Hatfield 01088 (413) 247-9803 *Fine furniture and architectural woodworking.*

**Gus Cournoyer,** 131 Brook St., Brookline 02146 (617) 566-4965

**Brian C. Donnelly,** Off Forest St., Manchester 01944 (617) 576-1066

**(24) Mark E. Del Guidice,** 12 Abbott St., Wellesley 02181 (617) 237-0161 *One-of-a-kind and limited-production furniture.*

**(20) Jeremiah de Rham, de Rham Custom Furniture ,** c/o Fort Point Cabinetmakers, 368 Congress St., Boston 02210 (617) 338-9487 *Custom furniture on commission, period pieces and modern design.*

**Brian R. Dyke,** 40 Lillian Terrace, Taunton 02780 (617) 822-9700

**Daryl Evans, Rick Hulme, Masterpiece,** 65 Budwell St., Avon 02322 (617) 580-0021 *Custom furniture and specialty finishes.*

**James J. Farrington,** 91 Prospect Hill Rd., Waltham 02154 (617) 894-6451 *Cabinetry, furniture and architectural woodwork.*

**Mary Ferraro, Cantebury Woodworking,** 70 Reed St., Cambridge 02140 (617) 491-7610 *Custom furniture, repair and restoration of antiques.*

**Kenneth H. Fischer,** 59 Minot St., Reading 01867 (617) 944-5112

**John Francis,** 13 Elm St., Brookline 02146 (617) 232-2061 *Custom-designed radiator enclosures.*

**Lorenzo Freccia, Designs in Wood,** 8 Dexter Ave., Seekonk 02771 (617) 336-7520 *Segmented and laminated turnings.*

**(74) Robert Freeman,** 6 Vernon St., Somerville 02143 (617) 625-8044

**Karen Frickenhaus,** One Cottage St., Easthampton 01027 (413) 527-9812 *Design and build one-of-a-kind and limited-edition furniture, commissions welcome.*

**(108) John Goodman, Joint Ventures Woodworking,** 9 Montague St., Cambridge 02139 (617) 876-2210 *Custom designs with a preference for quirky problems.*

**Glen G. Grant, Craft-Wood Products,** 70 Osgood St., Andover 01810 (617) 475-6686 *Custom-made furniture, one-of-a-kind.*

**Jock Harkness, Harkness Woodworks,** 72 Northampton St., Boston 02118 (617) 427-4414

**Tim Harkness, T.H. Cabinetmaker,** 72 Northampton St., Boston 02118

**(8, 59) Hartung/Mason,** 32 Clifton St., Somerville 02144 (617) 776-9110

**Robert Hoel, Hoel Studio,** 17 Robbons St., Waltham 02154 (617) 894-1255 *Custom wood sculpture in relief and in the round.*

**W. Howard, Fort Point Cabinetmakers,** 368 Congress St., Boston 02210 (617) 338-9487 *Contemporary and traditional one-of-a-kind furniture.*

**Emmy Howe, Woodworking,** 59 Linden St., Brookline 02146 (617) 731-2855

**Edwin Huff, Woodworking,** 87 Burt St., Boston 02124 (617) 288-6008

**Stephen Hynson, Sand Hill Woodworking Co.,** 440 Somerville Ave., Somerville 02143 (617) 625-2888

**Joseph S. Iannuzzi,** 31 Hawthorne St., New Bedford 02740 (617) 997-3129

**Tom Jenkins, Jr., Valley Woodworking, Inc.,** PO Box 1073, Easthampton 01027 (413) 527-5575 *Custom woodworking, one-of-a-kind, limited production, cabinetry.*

**Gregory Johnson,** 70 Linden St., Newton 02164 (617) 244-6220 *Custom finishing, woodworking and antique restoration.*

**Christopher Keane, Keane Furniture and Cabinet Shop,** 8 Dan. Carpenter Ct., Foxboro 02035 (617) 543-5074

**S. James Kentley,** 3 Oak St., Wayland 01778 (617) 653-9666

**Dimitrios Klitsas, Sculptures,** 705 Union St., West Springfield 01089 (413) 732-2661 *Hand-carved sculpture and furniture in wood.*

**Alex Krutsky, Fort Point Cabinetmakers,** 368 Congress St., Boston 02210 (617) 338-9487 *Custom furniture, turning and millwork.*

**(16) Scott Lefton, Design Innovation,** 59 Orient Ave., Melrose 02176 (617) 665-1528 *Specialized cabinets, gallery furniture, stained glass, sculptural jewelry, multimedia constructs.*

**(137) David Lilienthal,** PO Box 167, Barnstable 02630 (617) 362-9165 *Custom woodworking, cabinets and design.*

**(42) Thomas Loeser,** 16 Emily St., Cambridge 02139 (617) 661-9836

**Russ Loomis, Jr., Fine Furniture & Cabinetmaker,** RR 219B, Williamsburg 01096 (413) 628-3813 *Period and contemporary furniture of heirloom quality.*

**Pascal Luthi,** 31 Hawthorne St., New Bedford 02740 (617) 997-3121

**Robert March, March Woodworking,** 2 New St., Worchester 01605 (617) 752-3844

**Roy McAlister, McAlister Wood Design,** 8 Summer St., East Hampton 01027 (413) 527-7084

**Margot S. Menkel,** One Cottage St., Easthampton 01027 (413) 527-9812

**Matthew S. Newman, O.T.,** Box 46 Scott Rd., New Braintree 01531 (617) 867-3318 *The original, traditional wooden basket.*

**(27, 29) Lance Patterson, Fort Point Cabinetmakers,** 368 Congress St., Boston 02210 (617) 338-9487 *Traditional American furniture.*

**Woody Pistrich, Woody's Big Discount Furniture Factory Outlet,** 26 East St., Hadley 01035 (413) 586-8969 *Unique handmade hardwood furniture and woodenware.*

**James D. Price,** 31 Washington St., Charlestown 02129 (617) 242-0253

**Bruce H. Reitman,** RFD 1, Fosters Pond Rd., Andover 01810 (617) 475-1165 *Clock cases, small boxes and cabinets, wooden tools and instruments.*

**Scott Rikkers,** 137 Rockland St., New Bedford 02740 (617) 991-2230

**Jamie Robertson,** 16 Emily St., Cambridge 02139 (617) 864-7600

**Rita Roppolo,** c/o North Bennet St. School, 39 North Bennet St., Boston 02113 (617) 227-0155 *Custom-made furniture: contemporary and traditional.*

**Neil A. Rosenberg,** PO Box 2942, Nantucket 02584 (617) 228-3162

**Paul Ruhlmann,** 16 Avon Pl., Arlington 02174 (617) 646-8466 *One-of-a-kind and limited-edition furniture, sculpture and woodturning.*

**Jon Schmalenberger,** 70 School St., Acton 01720

**Pamela Slass,** 82 North St., New Bedford 02740 (617) 997-3282

**Ed Slattery,** 25 Fay St., Seekonk 02771 (617) 336-4617

**(60) David L. Smith,** 191 Elm St., New Bedford 02740 (617) 992-7167 *Avant-garde and three-dimensional designs.*

**Wendy Stayman,** One Cottage, PO Box 773, Easthampton 01027 (413) 527-8656

**Stan Stillwell,** 38 Lilly St., Florence 01060 (413) 584-6145 *Historical restoration and research a specialty.*

**(23, 100) Lee Trench,** 465 Medford St., Charleston 02129 (617) 242-2536

**Peter Van Benthuysen,** 34 Meadowbrook Dr., Easthampton 01027 (413) 527-8096

**Rob Warren, Warren Woodworks,** 72 Northampton St., Boston 02118 (617) 427-4414 *Custom furniture of original and traditional design.*

**Hugh Wesler,** 16 Churchill St., Springfield 01108 (413) 736-4828

**E. White Clocks,** 1575 Beacon St., Brookline 02146 (617) 738-1494 *Clocks and other wooden things.*

**(22) Mark R. White, Fine Line Woodworking,** 459 Liberty Square Rd., Boxborough 01719 (617) 263-4322 *Custom-made furniture, cabinetry and architectural woodworking.*

**Jeffery Wilkins, Wilkins Woodwork—Sculptured Furniture,** 333 Cabot St., Beverly 01915 (617) 922-9222 *Sculptured bedroom furniture, custom cabinets, truck racks.*

**Howard Wing, BH Craft,** 120 Cobleigh Rd., Boxboro 01719 (617) 263-4839

**(30) Jonathan R. Wright, Furnituremaker,** 16 Emily St., Cambridge 02139 (617) 868-7515 *Custom furniture and cabinets.*

**(62) William Tandy Young, Makers Kelly & Young,** PO Box 459, Stow 01775 (617) 562-4340 *Furnituremaking, restoration and finishes.*

## Michigan

**John M. Allen,** 910 Fifth St., Ann Arbor 48103 (313) 662-9856

**David G. Antoff, Against the Grain,** 545 Lovell, Troy 48098 (313) 879-2653

**John Baird,** 538 S. Fifth Ave., Ann Arbor 48104 (313) 996-3811

**Dennis A. Beatty, Marquetry by Beatty,** 70 E. Roosevelt, Zeeland 49464 (616) 772-4524 *Marquetry panels for banks, offices and homes, by commission.*

**Craig Brown, Woodwork,** 211 Garland, Traverse City 49684 (616) 941-7766 *Wholesale/retail. Jewelry boxes, bar, restaurants, furniture and displays.*

**Phil Dinehart, Harmonious Woods,** 411 Longshore Dr., Ann Arbor 48105 (313) 662-2413 *Solid-wood inlay using images from the natural world.*

**George Fisher,** 1410 Franklin Blvd., Ann Arbor 48103 (313) 668-2486 *Whittling, carving, small objects and sculptures.*

**Armin Gollannek, Northern Sun Woodworks,** Route 1 Box 765G, Munising 49862 (906) 387-4082 *Architectural specialties, circular and spiral stairs, railings—custom woodwork.*

**Tom Hagadone,** 1362 Ferndale Ave., Kalamazoo 49007 (616) 349-5496

**Russel Hare, Eclectic Designs,** 36461 Greene, New Baltimore 48047 (313) 725-2911 *Design and construction of fine furniture.*

**John C. Holtslander, Wood Plane Studio,** 2417 Fenton Rd., Flint 48507 (313) 239-4700

**(149) Steven M. Lash,** 4331 Geisler's Ct., Birmingham 48010 (313) 851-6255 *Eighteenth-century handmade furniture, none of which is for sale.*

**(129) Barry T. MacDonald, The Good Turn,** 1423 Berkshire, Grosse Pointe Park 48230 (313) 881-7097 *Custom turning.*

**Edith Maynard,** 910 Fifth St., Ann Arbor 48103 (313) 662-9856

**(109) Darryl Pfau, Graphic Images In Wood,** 444 Parkwood, Kalamazoo 49001 (616) 342-9060 *Wall reliefs, sculptural boxes and accessories.*

**Chris D. Podlaskowski,** 40770 Irval, Sterling Heights 48078

**Andre M. Poineau,** 5297 Behling Rd., East Jordon 49727 (616) 536-2725 *Custom doors and architectural artwork.*

**Ken Rambow, Guitars,** 3513 Fiesta, Kalamazoo 49008 (616) 375-3494 *Solid-body electric guitars utilizing premium-grade hardwoods.*

**Noah Roselander,** 5410 Collingwood Dr., Parchment 49004 (616) 345-4176 *Fine cabinetry, kitchens, interior design and remodeling.*

**Roger Szeszulski,** 1202 Adams Ct., Midland 49640 (517) 832-2574

**Alois von Matt, Al's Cabinet Shop,** 1118 W. Ceder, Gladwin 48624 (517) 426-2116 *Contemporary custom furniture, marquetry, handcrafted interior woodwork, Formica.*

**Dale E. Vorenkamp, Daze Guitars,** 5269 Fordham, Kalamazoo 49001 (616) 385-4623 *Custom guitars and basses, folding panels, short production runs.*

**Fred H. Wiman,** 2215 Packard #4, Ann Arbor 48104 (313) 995-9575

## Minnesota

**T. Anderson Woodworking,** 537 E. 4th Ave., Shokopee 55379 (612) 445-2750

**Amanda Berndt, Norbert Marklin, Simonetti Design,** 219 N. Second St., Suite 401, Minneapolis 55401 (612) 375-1185

**James Blackburn,** 4003 Hull Rd., Minnetonka 55343 (612) 935-3782

**Ronald Corradin,** 1625 Watson, Saint Paul 55116 (612) 699-7795

**Stephen P. DeSilva,** 1211 1st St. NW, Rochester 55901 (507) 288-0813

**Grey Doffin,** Box 114, Duluth 55801 (218) 726-0395 *Custom furniture, ornamental lathework.*

**(109) Jon Frost, Frost Cabinets, Furniture & Design,** 500 N. Robert St., Studio 432, St. Paul 55101 (612) 224-3745 *Fine cabinets and furniture.*

**Tom Gannon,** 4417 Oakley, Duluth 55804 (218) 525-3390

**R.A. Golden,** 1820 Oak Grove Rd., St. Cloud 56301 (612) 255-1723

**Glenn Gordon,** 3435 Cedar Ave. S., Minneapolis 55407 (612) 721-4332

**Robert Hedstrom,** 322 S. 4th St. #308, Minneapolis 55415 (612) 338-4628

**James B. Johnson,** 210 Sunset Blvd., Mankato 56001 (507) 345-8542

**Arthur Kliniske, Art Kraft Wood Products,** HCR 70 Box 387, Lake George 56458 (218) 266-3983 *Custom furniture, period reproductions, limited-run production and kitchen cabinets.*

**Erik Maakestad, Maakestad-Sculpture,** RR 5 Box 64, Northfield 55057 (507) 645-5918 *Sculpture plus occasional exotic furniture pieces.*

**Jay McDougall, McDougall Woodworks,** 1215 N. Union Ave., Fergus Falls 56537 (218) 736-7040 *Personalized designing and building of fine furniture.*

**(137) John Nesset, When Furniture Becomes Art,** 4744 5th Ave. S., Minneapolis 55409 (612) 827-4039 *Hand-tool built, one-of-a-kind originals.*

**(50) Michael P. O'Brien,** 513 South 6th St., Stillwater 55082 (612) 439-3301 *Custom furniture and cabinetry.*

**Tom Polacek,** RR 2 Box 68, Owatonna 55060 (507) 451-3391

**Charles W. Preble, Designs in Wood,** PO Box 844, St. Joseph 56374 (612) 363-4735 *Quality designs in wood for qualified customers.*

**Mary Redig, Red Elm,** 667 Harriet Ave., Shoreview 55126 (612) 483-3489 *Woodturning, one-of-a-kind commissions, miniatures.*

**Tim Schmitz,** 3415 East 40th St., Minneapolis 55406 (612) 724-8276 *Small boxes, shelves, custom desks, etc.*

**Stephen M. Schuweiler, Schuweiler Musical Boxes,** 3640 McKnight Rd., White Bear Lake 55110 (612) 426-3112 *Creation and restoration of fine-quality music boxes.*

**Adam Shinbrot, Ten Designs,** 2201 NE California, Minneapolis 55418 (612) 781-1299

**Richard E. Weiner, Weiner's Woodcraft,** RR 2 Box 219, Eyota 55934 (507) 288-3415

**Orville Williamschen, Orv's Carving Place,** Box 414, New London 56273 (612) 354-2864

**(55) Thomas Wood, Frost Cabinets,** 500 N. Robert St., Studio 432, St. Paul 55101 (612) 224-3745 *Fine cabinetry and furniture in all styles.*

## Mississippi

**Fletcher and Carol Cox,** PO Box 188, Tougaloo 39174 (601) 956-2610

**James H. Maclellan, Maclellan Cabinet and Millworks,** 1415 Main St. PO Box 1822, Columbus 39703 (601) 328-5075 *Architectural millwork, reproduction period pieces, one-off and custom pieces.*

**Ed Nichols,** Route 3 Box 363, Canton 39046 (601) 859-4652 *Custom-designed hardwood furniture.*

**Bill Rusk,** Route 3 Box 314-W, Jackson 39213 (601) 856-6227

## Missouri

**Michael Bauermeister, Meramec Woodworks,** Route 1 Box 310, St. Clair 63077 (314) 629-1775 *Design and build cabinets and furniture, carving and turning.*

**Kerry Boyd, Lincoln Co. R-4 Wood Shop,** 6th St., Winfield 63389 (314) 668-8130

**Linda Casady,** Box 282, Unionville 63565 (816) 947-3031

**Tom Cole, Heartwood Cabinet Shop,** Route 1 Box 219, Harrisburg 65256 (314) 875-1417 *Designers and makers of fine furniture and cabinetry.*

**(75) Ron Diefenbacher,** 12132 Big Bend, St. Louis 63122 (314) 966-4829 *Custom furniture.*

**Randy R. Elkins, Woodworker,** 1322 N. Benton, Springfield 65802 (417) 864-4264 *One-off tables and automotive woodworking.*

**Paul Gross, Albert Lewis, Wildwood,** 219 East Second St., Willow Springs 65793 (417) 469-4800 *Custom design and building of furniture and architectural woodwork.*

**Gary P. Korneman,** 1015 Isadore St., Joseph 64501 (816) 233-0866

**Paul E. Krautmann,** 7305 Maple, Maplewood 63143 (314) 645-8125 *Woodturning, furniture and casework.*

**(35) John Kriegshauser, Kansas City Woodworking,** 2030 Grand, Kansas City 64108 (816) 474-4618 *Furniture of original design and custom pieces made-to-order.*

**Ray Lawler, Ornamental Wood Works,** 6607 Ralston, Raytown 64133 (816) 358-1227 *Ornamental turning, interior doors, cabinets and furniture.*

**Charles Lippert,** 6907 Washington Ave., University City 63130 (314) 725-2325

**(90) Oscar Moreno,** Route 3 Box 560, Fredricktown 63645 (314) 783-6715 *Custom-designed handcrafted furniture, fine veneer work, restoration of veneers in antique furniture.*

**Lawrence Okrend, Jack Rees, Design Matrix,** 309 E. 66th St., Kansas City 64113 (816) 333-8948

**Lawrence R. Oliver, Tanglewood Studio,** Route 3 Box 196, Mansfield 65704 (417) 924-8683 *Sculpture.*

**Jay Stratton, The Dovetail,** 832 W. Burkhart, Moberly 65270 (816) 263-0867 *Unique, handmade furniture, sculpture and cabinetry, assembled with precision joinery.*

**Clarence Teed, Designer/Craftsman,** 6021 Central, Kansas City 64113 (816) 361-3428 *Furniture and accessories in wood.*

## Montana

**(102) Joel Bender,** 512 Little Sleeping Child Rd., Hamilton 59840 (406) 363-6818 *Steam-bent mirrors, carving, traditional timberframing.*

**Bill Clinton, Woodworker,** 216 Lindley Pl., Bozeman 59715 (406) 587-2529 *Custom furniture, cabinet design and fabrication.*

**Michael Dolny,** 2717 Woodland, Missoula 59802 (406) 728-7233

**Brian C. Duncan, Duncan Furniture,** Route 1, Highwood 59450 (406) 733-6741 *Custom furniture designs to fit specific needs and spaces.*

**(108) Steven J. Gray, Gray & Gray Wood Wrights,** PO Box 1884, Bozeman 59715 (406) 587-0383 *Objects of fantasy, kaleidoscopes, telescopes, furniture and accessories.*

**(10) Don Harrington, Specialty Woodwork,** 2111 Sunnyview La., Billings 59102 (406) 656-5687 *Distinctively detailed designs in commissioned furniture and limited architectural pieces.*

**Douglas N. LaMont, The Woodwright,** 1916 3rd Ave. N., Billings 59101 (406) 248-3393 *One-of-a-kind and custom fine furniture. Residential and commercial.*

**(66) West Lowe, Primrose Center,** 401 W. Railroad St., Missoula 59802 (406) 728-5911 *Primrose is a school for woodworking and furniture design.*

**Dan Mongold,** 327 S. Bozeman Ave., Bozeman 59715 (406) 586-3794

**Kent Perelman,** 401 W. Railroad, Missoula 59802 (406) 728-5911

**Janet L. Read, Fleur Nouveau,** Route 1, Meadow Creek Rd., Bigfork 59911 (406) 837-5324 *Turning and carving of functional wood sculpture.*

**E.K. Robertson,** 2345 S. 7th St. W., Missoula 59801 (406) 549-7685

**Ron Sinnema, Sinnema Wood Design,** 8155 Churchill Rd., Manhattan 59741 (406) 282-7449 *Custom cabinets and fine furniture.*

**Steven Speich, Furniture Design,** 321 Speedway, Missoula 59802 (406) 721-1057

**(80) Sandy Volkman, Designer/Craftsman in Wood,** SW 3395 Kramis Rd., Hamilton 59840 (406) 363-3750 *Fine furniture.*

## Nebraska

**R. Bruhn,** 1344 C St., Lincoln 68502 (402) 474-6434

**Michael Herres, Designer and Woodworker,** RR 1, Garland 68360 (402) 588-2412 *Original designs in solid woods for the home and office.*

**Michael McKibbin, Out Of The Woodwork,** Route 2 Box 88A, Peru 68421 (402) 872-4145

## Nevada

**Robert D. Davis,** 1580 Royal Dr., Reno 89503 (702) 747-0815

**Paul Haines,** 6621 Bristol Way, Las Vegas 89107 (702) 873-2466

**Edward Schairer, The Woodshire,** 5400 Mountain Vista, Las Vegas 89120 (702) 454-3485 *Custom furniture, cabinetry, repairs and architectural woodwork.*

**Harry Weinberg,** 320 W. Riverview Circle, Reno 89509 (702) 329-3141 *Sculpture, rocking horses, toys and furniture.*

## New Hampshire

**Russ Aubertin Furniture,** 53 Concord St., Nashua 03060 (603) 886-0663 *Design and build custom contemporary furniture.*

**Francis G. Blanchard, Tic Tac Shop,** RFD 2 Box 32, Maple St., Contoocook 03229 (603) 746-3055 *Handcrafted and painted mantel clocks and tall clocks.*

**Joy Bloomfield,** RD 1 Box 72, Contoocock 03229 (603) 746-4058 *Furniture and interior finishing.*

**Donna Bolduc, Creative Expressions,** 49 Main St., Pittsfield 03263 (603) 435-8165 *Original-design wood projects, carved, inlay and original quality quilts.*

**(96) Jeffrey Cooper,** 135 McDonough St., Portsmouth 03801 (603) 436-7945 *Designer of sculptural furnishings in wood.*

**Paul Demers, Woodgrains,** 79 Pillsbury St., Concord 03301 (603) 225-6838

**Chris Hardy, Cabinetmaker,** PO Box 390, Contoocook 03229 (603) 746-3586 *Custom cabinetry and furniture.*

**Kathleen C. King-Lueders,** 202 Main St., Sandown 03873 (603) 887-2430

**(105) Sherman E. LaBarge, LaBarge Studio,** Box 854, Conway 03818 (603) 447-5809 *Woodcarvings, hand-carved signage, doors, beds and bas-reliefs.*

**John McAlevey,** 100 Memorial St., Franklin 03235 (603) 934-3241 *Design and execution of furniture. Accept commissions on many levels.*

**Terry Miller, Craftsman,** 97 Prospect St., Jaffrey 03452 (603) 532-7504 *Custom-made furniture from colonial to contemporary.*

**(37) Terry Moore, Cabinetmaker,** 11 Summer St., Newport 03773 (603) 863-4795 *Uniquely designed furniture featuring beautiful woods and traditional joinery.*

**C.B. Oliver**, Box 204, Nottingham 03290 (603) 772-2010 *Versatility in hardwood furniture. Response given to interesting requests.*

**(70) Frederick Puksta, Designer-Craftsman,** 6 Elm St., Claremont 03743 (603) 542-6317 *Multimedia, custom-designed and produced furniture and architectural woodworking.*

**Mark Ragonese,** 22 Spring St., Newmarket 03857 (603) 659-3551 *Carved, shaped, found, wood furniture, fine joinery, minimalist design.*

**Reedy Design Associates,** RFD 4 Box 17, Pickpocket Rd., Exeter 03833 (603) 772-8774 *Design—custom redwood graphics, signature for corporations, business.*

**(62) Richard C. Ruppel, Cabinetmaker,** 219 B Durano Rd., Randolph 03570 (603) 466-2407 *Handmade chairs and accompanying furniture.*

**Michael Santomauro, Broken Tree Studio,** Main St., Route 302 Box 441, Bethlehem 03574 (603) 869-2077 *Jewelry boxes of all sizes in native and exotic hardwoods.*

**(91) Jeff Schall, Watersedge Design,** HCR 10 Box 66, Milan 03588 (603) 449-2912 *Custom-designed furniture and timberframes.*

**(128) John Serino, Tree Top Studio,** Carpenter Rd., Sugar Hill 03580 (603) 823-7028 *Turning, carving, some occasional cabinetry and wood bending.*

**David Shaw,** 5½ Saint Laurent St., Nashua 03060

**(127) Roland Shick, Ironwood Studio,** Box 733, Main St., Bethlehem 03574 (603) 869-5568 *Turning, carving and inlay. Showroom, public welcome, classes offered.*

**John G. Skewes, Fine Chairs & Woodwork,** RFD 2, Drinkwater Rd., Exeter 03833 (603) 778-7360 *Post and rung, Windsor chairs, carpentry and cabinets.*

**Paul Socha,** 1103 Smyth Rd., RFD 14, Manchester 03104 (603) 627-1223

**Paul Tuller, Ishiyama Company,** Box 64, Pierce Rd., Dublin 03444 (603) 563-8884 *Shoji maker, Japanese-style woodworking with traditional hand tools.*

**William Wingert, Woodworks Fine or Commercial,** RFD 2 Box 425, Tilton 03276 (603) 286-4985 *Fine or commercial woodworking as applied to furniture—interiors and exteriors.*

## New Jersey

**Matthew T. Barba,** 170 DeMott La., Somerset 08873 (201) 545-3940

**John Bonato, III, B & B Woodworkers,** 2180 Dante Ave., Vineland 08360 (609) 696-0070 *Custom wood and laminate design and fabrications.*

**Tom Bourdot,** 1200 Dorsett Dock Rd. Apt. A3, Pt. Pleasant 08742 (201) 295-9610 *Figurative sculpture, archetypal women.*

**George Brown, The Hoboken Wood Wright,** 201 Madison St., Hoboken 07030 (201) 659-7106

**Peter Brylinski, Custom Woodworking,** 23 DeVausney Pl., Nutley 07110 (201) 667-2514

**David Buchsbaum,** 4 Pine Ct., Westfield 07090 (201) 233-2273

**(42) Robert J. Chehayl,** 49 Harrison St., Hoboken 07030 (201) 798-3018

**(73) John Chiara,** 153 Mali Dr., North Plainfield 07062

**Richard W. Christie,** 87 Green Knolls Dr., Wayne 07470 (201) 831-0764

**Tom Gall, Wood 'N' Things,** Box 9, Arthur Rd., Belle Mead 08502 (201) 359-8717 *Bandsaw boxes and turnings from exotic woods.*

**Robert Gerish, R & J Gerish Wood Design,** 31 Harding Terrace, Irvington 07111 (201) 374-2932 *European cabinetry and furniture, lacquer finishings and carving.*

**J.T. Griffith, Creative Woodworking,** 34 East Mary La., Waterford Works 08089 (609) 768-0796

**John E. Hein, Fine Furnituremaker,** 46 Park Pl., Princeton 08542 (609) 921-3538 *One-of-a-kind solid hardwood furniture.*

**Bill Jackman, Wood Sculptor,** RD 4, 23 Foxsparrow Turn, Vincentown 08088 (609) 268-8152

**R.H. Karol,** 124 Sayre Dr., Princeton 08540 (609) 520-0010 *Laminated sculpture in wood, acrylics and metal.*

**(117) Joseph Kazimierczyk, Kazimierczyk Designs,** 163 N. Hamilton Ave., Mercerville 08619 *Furniture, small carved or turned objects.*

**Margaretta Lear-Svedman, Pingry School,** Teacher of contemporary woodworking, Martinsville 08836

**(120) Steven B. Levine,** PO Box 123, Dayton 08810 (201) 297-0131 *Segmented turnings creating unique designs of contrasting exotic woods.*

**Steve Levine,** 57 Wellington Rd., East Brunswick 08816 (201) 254-7188

**Lenno Mbaga, Lenno Woodworks,** PO Box 1662, Morristown 07960 (201) 538-0458 *General woodworking (furniture).*

**Robert Millenky Custom Furniture,** 225 Peyton Ave., Haddonfield 08033 (609) 429-5873 *Abstract or representational carvings integrated into furniture, executed as freestanding pieces.*

**Keith Naples, Woodworker,** 435 Spruce Ave., Garwood 07027 (201) 232-1385 *Furniture, interiors and sculpture.*

**Geoffrey Noden, The Titusville Woodworks Inc.,** 11 Park Lake Ave., Titusville 08560 (609) 737-1222

**William C. Nyberg,** 13 Essex Ct., Marlton 08053 (609) 596-0652

**(136) Paul Rochon,** 520 Cary St., Orange 07050 (201) 653-8096 *Designers and builders of furniture, interior woodwork and unique objects.*

**William Rothfuss, Design,** PO Box 135, Blairstown 07825 (201) 362-5105 *High-end custom design and cabinetry, art-deco veneer and inlay.*

**Allan Smith, Cabinetmaker,** 359 Stonybrook Rd., Hopewell 08525 (609) 466-1595 *Furniture and cabinets, designed and built to order.*

**(11) Todd Smith, Smith Woodworks & Design,** RR 1 Box 42, Farmersville Rd., Califon 07830 (201) 832-2723 *Custom-designed and made Shaker-inspired furniture and accessories.*

**Joseph Uhrhane,** 2 Millers Farm Rd., Morristown 07960 (201) 538-1445

**Mark Wescott, Luthier,** 301 W. New York Ave., Somers Point 08244 (609) 927-2486 *Steel-string concert and recording guitars.*

## New Mexico

**Harvey Buchalter, Sculpture,** 1615 Kit Carson SW, Albuquerque 87104 (505) 247-2602 *Sculpture for home, office and lobby in wood and stone.*

**(69) Larry and Nancy Buechley, Buechley Woodworking,** Box 21, El Valle 87521 (505) 689-2445 *Fine furniture, especially with open structures and bent-laminations.*

**Robert Chappell, El Cuchillo Woodworking,** PO Box 235, Arroyo Seco 87514 (505) 776-2419 *General custom work, one-of-a-kind orders, carving.*

**Lee E. Elgin, Leelgin,** PO Box 1750, Santa Fe 87504 (505) 471-1520 *Fine furniture and architectural crafts in wood, plastic and metals.*

**Frank Fernando, The Fernando Studio,** 2907 Commercial NE, Albuqueque 87107 *Specializing in custom fine woodworking and etched glass.*

**(76) David B. Fowler,** 12050 Candelaria NE, Albuquerque 87112 (505) 345-8735

**(14) Donald J. Gardner,** Box 683, Taos 87571 (505) 758-2345 *Designing one-of-a-kind pieces.*

**(13) Skip Sven Hanson,** 2028 Madeira NE, Albuquerque 87110 (505) 266-1333 *Custom home and office furniture, including showcases and reception desks.*

**Ron Hilgert, Mesasmith,** #53 RD 3133, Aztec 87410 (505) 334-6784 *Fine-carved southwestern furniture.*

**David L. Irion,** 921 East Lincoln Rd., Hobbs 88240 (505) 393-8172

**James Rannefeld Jawar, Media Seven Design Group,** PO Box 858, Taos 87571 (505) 758-8455

**Dan Lucero, D.L. Woodcrafts,** Star Route Box 27, Mesilla Park 88047 (505) 524-0354 *Antique restoration and custom woodworking.*

**(105) John Martinez, Phil Martinez and David Samora, Samora Woodworks,** 2873 All Trades Rd., Santa Fe 87501 (505) 471-5728 *Architectural millwork.*

**John Quinn Miles, Wood 'N' Art,** 6821 San Francisco NE, Albuquerque 87109 (505) 821-1840 *Custom-built to suit repairs, carved signs and art.*

**Jan Moore, Earth-Arts Studios,** Box 40, Torreon 87061 *Custom hand-carved doors, emphasis on Old World carving techniques.*

**Guy Wm. Nichols, The Renaissance Shop,** Star Route Box 27, Mesilla Park 88047 (505) 524-0354

**(33) Gerald D. Otis,** 4605 Compound Ct. NW, Albuquerque 87107 (505) 345-7202 *One-of-a-kind furniture pieces.*

**Bruce Peterson,** 6B Pilar Route, Taos 87571 (505) 758-4086

**Ada P. Rippberger, RB Woodworking,** 514 Apache Lp SW, Rio Rancho 87124 (505) 891-8713 *Custom woodworking of all types with emphasis on oil finishes.*

**Constance Starr,** 4605 Compound Ct. NW, Albuquerque 87107 (505) 345-7202

**Ron Wallace,** PO Box 35235, Albuquerque 87176 (505) 281-2801

**Greg Frye Weaver,** 1105 Florida NE, Albuquerque 87110 (505) 265-2719

**David Wendt, With The Grain,** 3420 Monterey Circle, Farmington 87401 (505) 325-9369 *Earring boxes, weed pots, small cabinets.*

## New York

**Domenick Abbate, Design-A-Mention,** 2 Hampton Way, Ridge 11961 (516) 924-0714 *Handcrafted hardwood furniture for the home or office.*

**(60) Fred Baier, Furnituremaker-Designer,** 80 Oakwood La., Scottsville 14546 (716) 889-1521 *One-of-a-kind furniture, speculative or commission.*

**Sy Balsen, New Chatham Joiner,** Route 66, Malden Bridge 12115 (518) 766-2829 *Windsor and Shaker chairs and custom cabinetmaking.*

**Ronald Banaszak, Woodgrains,** 1201 Prendergast Ave., Jamestown 14701 (716) 485-0028 *Custom furniture, residential interior renovation.*

**Neal Barrett, Woodworking,** 55 Railroad St., Rochester 14609 (716) 454-2276

**(40) William R. Bartoo,** 382 Chesnut St., Fredonia 14063 (716) 672-6466

**John Bickel,** 6 Grants La., Ossining 10562 (914) 941-5408

**Graham Blackburn, Furniture,** PO Box 487, Bearsville 12409 (914) 679-7632

**Joseph A. Bottigliere,** 109 Manila Ave., Staten Island 10306 (718) 351-5655

**John L. Bowen, Jr., Hudson River Boat & Cabinet,** 187 E. Market St., Rhinebeck 12572 (914) 876-3550 *Turnings, moldings, doors, architectural detail and fine handmade furniture.*

**Alexander S. and John Brewster, Brewster Coachworks,** Barmore Rd., PO Box 159, La Grangeville 12540 (914) 677-5088 *Handcrafted hardwood, classic automobiles, executive gifts.*

**Edgar A. Brown,** 72 Van Borgh Ave., Rochester 14610 (716) 482-9027 *Handmade furniture, custom-design and craftsmanship excellence.*

**Kenneth S. Burton, Jr., Designer-Craftsman,** 330D Audino La., Rochester 14624 (716) 889-5893

**(5) Ron Callari,** 173 Fillmore St., Rochester 14611 (716) 235-8879 *Contemporary wood furniture.*

**Gordon Campbell,** 131 LaRue Dr., Huntington 11743 (516) 421-5004

**Timothy C. Castine, Of The Earth,** Box 390 Ridge Rd., Chazy 12921 (518) 846-7585 *Functional and non-functional sculpture.*

**John Chandoha,** 2210 Mohansic Ave., Yorktown 10598 (914) 245-6951

**Roger Charles, Woodworks,** 344 Westervelt Ave., Staten Island 10301 (718) 447-0977 *Distinctive cabinetry and furniture made from exotic hardwoods.*

**Jim Christo,** 608 Charles St., Jamestown 14701

**Richard Cohen,** 18 Joyce Dr., Spring Valley 10977 (914) 425-6767 *Solid-wood furniture and cabinetry.*

**Janis Colella, Colella Custom Furniture,** Greenwich Rd., Bedford 10506 (914) 234-6969 *Design and build custom furniture of all types and styles.*

**(66) Tobias Dean, Furnituremaker,** RD 2 Box 326, Trumansburg 14886 (607) 387-9524

**Thomas DeVeau, Woodworker,** Manlius 13104 (315) 682-2805 *Chair caning, tables, chests, custom woodworking.*

**D.D. Doernberg, Lignum Design, Inc.,** 146 W. 25th St. N., New York 10001 (212) 242-3493 *Architectural woodworking, commercial/residential, furniture design, wall systems, craftsmanship.*

**James Dron,** 665 Webster Rd., Webster 14580 (716) 872-6048

**(5) Peter S. Dudley,** 18 Maple St., Scottsville 14546 (716) 889-1521 *One-of-a-kind specialty furniture.*

**(72) Thomas J. Duffy, Cabinetmaker,** 1 Commerce St., Ogdensburg 13669 (315) 393-1484 *Furnituremaking and architectural woodworking of first quality.*

**Glenn Enderby,** 228 Hardwood Circle, Rochester 14625 (716) 385-2691

**Anthony Farah, Big Twig Woodworks,** 550 Nassau Rd., Roosevelt 11575 (516) 223-4671 *Architectural woodwork, railings, furniture.*

**(24, 58) Kalle Fauset,** 115 W. 15th St., New York 10011 (212) 255-5486

**(67) Jim Fawcett, Experimental Craft,** PO Box 455, 4 River Rd., Highland 12528

**Leonard Feldberg,** 15 Wilshire Dr., Spring Valley 10977 (914) 356-0039

**Warren S. Fenzi, Fenzi Design Workshop,** 29 Everett St., Rye 10580 (914) 967-1527 *The design and execution of fine furniture.*

**Tracy A. Fiegl,** RD 1 Box 97D, Fillmore 14735 (716) 567-8734 *Early American and Shaker reproductions, artistic woodturning, custom furniture.*

**Sid Fleisher, Woodworker,** 384 2nd St., Troy 12180 (518) 272-1944 *Furniture and cabinet commissions, originals and reproductions.*

**Maurice Fraser Workshop,** 153 West 78th St., New York 10024 (212) 595-3557

**Antonio Freda,** 55 Bedford Ave., Westbury 11590 (516) 333-0546 *Custom-designed furniture and cabinets.*

**(57) Paul St. Germain, Furnituremaker,** PO Box 223, New Lebanon 12125 (518) 794-7105

**Kam Ghaffari,** 22 Pine Brook Dr., White Plains 10605 (914) 761-2606

**Rick Godlewski, Lief Larsen, Northern Designs Specialty Woodworking,** RD 4 Gower Rd., Scotia 12302 (518) 370-5105 *Custom furniture, commercial woodworking and refinishing.*

**Harvey Goldstein, Studio 1628,** 41 Union Square W., New York City 10003 (212) 989-0160 *One-of-a-kind furniture and sculpture.*

**B. Goode,** 460 Countess Dr., W. Henrietta 14548 (716) 359-4844 *Sculpture, fine art, paintings, carving and furniture.*

**(31) Michael A. Gregorio, Michael-Angelo Woodworking, Inc.,** 96 South Long Beach Rd., Rockville Centre 11570 (516) 766-4030 *Custom furniture, sculpture, one-of-a-kind pieces.*

**(138) Capt. Jon O. Grondahl, Grondahl's Treasures,** 83 Champlain Ave., Staten Island 10306 (718) 351-4032 *Custom-made furniture, rosemaling.*

**Robert F. Gudger, Gudger Industries,** 15 Oak St., Lk. Ronkonkoma 11779 (516) 588-0078 *Custom fabrications in wood, metals and synthetics.*

**Arthur C. Hastings,** 701 Pickering St., Ogdensburg 13669 (315) 393-2535

**Katherine E. Henry, Craft Artist in Wood,** 223 Main St., Hamburg 14075

**Jerry Hitchcock,** 208 Shademore Dr., Rochester 14626 (716) 227-0767

**Le Roy Hogue, Woodlands,** 27 Meadow Dr., Spencerport 14559 (716) 352-5610 *Sculptured jewelry boxes, laminated and hand-carved serving trays, hand mirrors.*

**Alan Holt,** 515 W. 110 St. #2A, New York 10025 (212) 222-8102

**Icarus Furniture,** 154 4th St., Troy 12180 (518) 274-2883 *Household and commercial furniture, liturgical woodwork, tongue drums and kalimbas.*

**Ann Jochems, A.J. Woodworking,** 179 Cottage Ave. #3, Mt. Vernon 10550 (516) 489-9412 *Woodworking and fine carpentry.*

**(6) James R. Johnson, Grey Haven Studios,** 1237 E. Main St., Rochester 14609 (716) 288-3050 *Residential and commercial furniture, design specialty woodworking.*

**Steven Johnstone-Mosher,** 3671 Hudson Manor Terrace, Bronx 10463 (212) 796-0988 *Antique restoration and conservation.*

**Lee F. Karkruff, Oasis Designs Unlimited,** 212 Walton St., Syracuse 13202 (315) 475-9565 *Custom-made furniture, woodworking, antique repair and restoration.*

**Kevin Kegler,** 286 Woodward Ave., Buffalo 14214 (716) 824-2463

**Andrew Cogan Kelly, Furniture and Cabinets,** 50 Douglass St., Brooklyn 11231 (718) 797-0898

**Peter M. Kenney, Chestnut Hill Woodworks,** 4993 Papermill Rd., Avon 14414 (716) 226-3959 *Custom furniture and fine cabinetwork.*

**(93, 95) William Keyser,** 6543 Rush-Lima Rd., Honeoye Falls 14472 (716) 533-1041 *Furniture and architectural embellishments for public, ecclesiastical, corporate and residential spaces.*

**Tom Kneeland, Kneeland Design,** 137 Benham St., Penn Yan 14527 (315) 536-8178 *Custom-designed hardwood furniture and distinctive wooden accessories.*

**Frank M. Knox,** No. 2 Tudor City Pl., New York 10017

**Iz Kopmar, Kopmar Wood Works,** 16 Baylor Circle, White Plains 10605 (914) 761-0163 *Unique expressions in wood from clocks to cabinets.*

**Bernd Krause, Autumnwood Instruments,** RD 2 Box 9, Fredricks Rd., Johnson City 13790 (607) 748-2941

**(55) Neil Lamens, NL Furniture Co.,** 180 South 6th St., Lindenhurst 11757

**(98) Robert Leach,** RD 2 Box 671, Fountain St., Clinton 13323 (315) 853-5714 *Bowls, boxes, clocks, segmented turnings, etc., from domestic hardwoods.*

**Gregg Lehman, Designs,** 23 Bellmawr Dr., Rochester 14624 (716) 889-9533

**Paul A. Lewis,** Twin Lakes Rd., South Salem 10590

**James Liccione, Sculpture Studio,** 232 West 42nd St., New York 10007

**(117) Steve Loar,** 6 East Court St., Warsaw 14569 (716) 786-5864 *Bowls and vessels, principally lathe or turned.*

**Mark A. Lockburner, Marks Woodworks,** RD 12 Box 314C, Unadilla 13849 *Custom-made furniture and molding toys.*

**M. Loret,** 13-29 Michael Pl., Bayside 11360 (718) 352-0742

**Eric P. Marczak, Marczak Woodheu's,** 338 Amsterdam Rd., Scotia 12302 (518) 374-3693 *Nets, musical instruments and custom furniture.*

**Brian A. Mayes, Below The Bark,** 155-E Hague Blvd., Glenmont 12077 (518) 767-9636 *Custom furniture, clocks, woodturnings and commissions.*

**John D. McCarthy, Custom Carving,** 805 Arden Ave., Staten Island 10312 (718) 984-0191

**Girvan P. Milligan,** RD 9 Daisy La., Carmel 10512 (914) 277-4905

**(8) Vicki Moss,** 115 W. 15th St., New York 10011 (212) 255-5486

**James Nagel,** Box W302 RD 1, Alexandria Bay 13607 (315) 482-3698

**John C. Packard, Cabinet Shop of Sea Cliff,** 266 Sea Cliff Ave., Sea Cliff 11579 (516) 671-1515 *Furniture made-to-order, restored or refinished.*

**R.J. Pellet,** 31 Wolf Rd., Croton on the Hudson 10520 (914) 271-6872

**Mike Pereira, Corner Of The Sky,** 21 Howe Pl., Bronxville 10708 (914) 337-0509

**(9) Susan Perry,** 269 W. 11th St., New York 10014 (212) 675-2361 *Fine furniture and cabinetry, architectural woodworking and handpainted surface treatments; instructor at the Craft Students League.*

**Ralph Peterman, Weathered Knot,** RD 4 Box 87A, Putnam Valley 10579 (914) 526-3125 *Realistic and scaled sculptural work, custom clocks and furniture.*

**(7) Gerald Plain, Productions,** 30 Doncaster Rd., Rochester 14623 (716) 475-1453 *Design and construction of contemporary furniture.*

**Michael Puryear,** 163 W. 22nd St., New York 10011 (212) 620-9607

**Doug Redmond,** 411 Bergen St. #4, Brooklyn 11217 (718) 230-0254

**Alan Reich, Designs In Wood,** 244 Riverside Dr., New York 10025 (212) 865-3614

**Kerry J. Rubin, Woodchips, Inc.,** 2611 Grand Ave., Baldwin 11510 (516) 546-1452 *Small, medium cabinets; music, jewelry boxes.*

**James Ryan,** 416 Seifert La., Putnam Valley 10579 (914) 526-3041

**Michael D. Sage, Artisan Wood Works,** 31 Pearl Ave., Blasdell 14219 (716) 828-0915 *Woodworks of past, present and future.*

**Terry Saye,** 119 Thayer St., Jamestown 14701

**Maurice Sewelson, Sewelson Woodcraft,** 391 Jervis Ave., Copiague 11726 (516) 789-1935 *Woodturning and decorative accessories.*

**Thomas Sterling,** PSC Box 6058, APO 09194 *Contemporary Netsuke—wood and ivory.*

**Peter J. Strasser,** 35 Hillside Ave., Monsey 10952 (914) 425-6400 *Woodworker carving directly in solid wood.*

**Charles Swanson,** 29 E. Cavelier Rd., Scottsville 14546 (716) 889-2849 *Custom-designed, handmade furnishings.*

**(41) Richard Tannen,** 1237 E. Main St., Rochester 14609 (716) 288-3050 *Custom furniture and interiors.*

**(40) A.J. VanDenburgh, Designer & Builder of Fine Furniture,** 31 Sumner Pk., Rochester 14607 (716) 271-8591

**(61) Naomi Vogelfanger,** 351 W. 24th St., New York 10011 (212) 989-5603 *Designer/maker.*

**Tom Volk,** Baptist Church Rd., Yorktown Heights 10598

**An-Khang Vu-Cong,** 4313 9th Ave. #4C, Brooklyn 11232

**Tom Watrobski,** 832 Merchants Rd., Rochester 14609 (716) 288-5537

**(103) Howard Werner,** Route 28, Mt. Tremper 12457 (914) 688-7024 *Direct-carved and constructed furniture and direct-carved sculpture.*

**(87) Tom Whitlow,** 52 Turkey Hill Rd., Ithaca 14850 (607) 272-6529

**(108) Harry Wilhelm, Designer & Craftsman in Wood,** 254 Luce Rd., Groton 13073 (607) 533-7221 *One-of-a-kind furniture.*

**Robert T. Wilson,** 4 Leuce Pl., Glen Cove 11542 (516) 671-5822

**Alan D. Winer, Woodworking,** 274 N. Goodman St., Rochester 14607 (716) 244-5678

**Mr. and Mrs. George H. Worthington, Worthington Woodworkers,** 1462 Wilson Rd., East Meadow 11554 (516) 489-3118 *Hand-carved wooden horses, rocking, relief and freestanding.*

**Christopher W. Wright, Woodwright,** 2 Riverview Heights, Rochester 14623 (716) 328-3456 *Custom furniture design and construction.*

**Barry R. Yavener,** 589 Breckenridge St., Buffalo 14222 (716) 882-5515

**Rhett M. Zoll,** RD 1 Box 226, Middletown 10940 (914) 386-9521

## North Carolina

**Robert Bailey, Cabinetmaker,** Route 1 Box 21B, Woodleaf 27054 (704) 278-4703 *Hardwood furniture, period and custom designs, architectural joinery and restoration.*

**Jim Barefoot,** 612½ N. Blount St., Raleigh 27604 (919) 829-1672

**Douglas N. Bechtol,** Box 25786, Raleigh 27611 (919) 833-5391

**Valerie Beckel,** 4630 Grinding Stone Dr., Raleigh 27604 *Design and build furniture, custom doors.*

**(46) John Clark,** Wood Resident, Penland School, Penland 28765 (704) 765-6647 *One-of-a-kind and some multiples. Commissions encouraged.*

**John R. Combs, Custom Furniture & Woodworking,** PO Box 1121, Lake Junaluska 28745 (704) 627-9959 *Original design and reproductions of furniture and architectural woodworking.*

**Dick Goehring,** RR 2 Box 6391, Timberlake 27583 (919) 364-2988

**Kate Gosnell Harrison, For The Love Of Wood,** Route 1 Box 1060, Hillsborough 27278 (919) 732-2275 *Building custom-designed, handmade furniture and accessories.*

**Paul Harrell,** 2406 Camellellia G-1, Durham 27705 (919) 471-6736

**Baird Hoffmire,** 9 Oak Park Rd., Asheville 28801

**Eddie Hovis,** 607 Battleground Rd., Lincolnton 28092 (704) 735-2503

**Doug Hurr, Melody Woodworks,** Route 4 Box 638, Boone 28607 (704) 262-5719

**K.W. Jamison, Woodworks,** Route 2 Box 170A, Sylva 28779 (704) 586-8507 *Open to all projects built of wood.*

**Steven Knopp Studios,** 506 Merrimon Ave., Asheville 28804 (704) 258-2586 *Period furniture, reproductions, carvings, turnings and custom architectural joinery.*

**Stoney Lamar,** 47 Thompson Rd., Saluda 28773 (704) 749-9561 *Lathe-turned wood vessels, sculptural woodturning and sculpture.*

**Drew Langsner,** 90 Mill Creek, Marshall 28753 (704) 656-2280

**P.A. Moore, Moore's Antique Shop,** 2800 Sunset Ave., Rocky Mount 27804 (919) 443-1298 *Antique furniture reproductions, handmade beds.*

**John Hamilton Morse, Hamilton Morse Originals,** Frost Rd., Saluda 28773 (704) 749-3321 *Native wood, bandboxing, one-of-a-kind.*

**George Nader, Nader's Pine Furniture Shop,** Oak Park, White Oak Dr., Arden 28704 (704) 684-9838 *Woodcarving models for furniture company.*

**Pete Nichol, Nantahala Studios in Wood,** PO Box 1191, Franklin 28734 (704) 528-4646 *Original works in Appalachian hardwoods.*

**(121) Wayne Raab Woodwork,** 307 South Richland St., Waynesville 28786 (704) 456-9376 *One-of-a-kind, commission, speculative furniture and accessory design.*

**Paul F. Ramshaw, Wood Designs,** 100 Industrial Park Dr., Waynesville 28786 (704) 452-0100 *Custom interiors and fine furniture to order.*

**Mark Strom, Loth Lorien Woodworking,** 244B Swannanoa River Rd., Asheville 28805 (704) 258-1445

**(19) Chad Voorhees,** PO Box 156, Saluda 28773 (704) 749-4901 *One-of-a-kind and limited-production furniture.*

**Mark H. Wessinger,** 525 Adans St., Hendersonville 28739 (704) 693-4520

**James E. Yarbrough, Jr.,** 921 Vernon Ave., Winston-Salem 27106 (919) 723-8391 *Small, functional wood objects, lathework, minor furniture repair and refinishing.*

## Ohio

**Tim J. Barnhart, Tri-Star Woodworking,** 1363 Albemarle Rd., Springfield 45504 (513) 325-7892

**E.L. Bauer, "Wooden Treasures",** 5501 San Paulo Dr., Toledo 43612 *Replicas of antique cars, boats and planes for play or display.*

**J. Douglas Bootes,** 3818 Mt. Vernon Ave., Cincinnati 45209 (513) 631-4119

**Kenneth S. Christy, The Wooden Rainbow Studio,** 1493 Rose Hedge Ct., Youngstown 44514 (216) 757-9133

**Doug Ellis,** 508 Orangewood Dr., Kettering 45429 (513) 223-6500

**R.E. Engel, Woodworking,** 2939 Bishop Rd., Willoughby Hills 28786 (216) 944-6746 *Custom furniture, accessories and architectural reproductions.*

**Randall K. Fields, Furnituremakers,** Box 206, Amesville 45711 (614) 448-2321 *Windsor chairs, stools and tables, contemporary styling with traditional techniques.*

**J. Hunter Fox, Designer/Craftsman In Wood,** 8345 Erie Ave., Canal Fulton 44614 (216) 854-4774 *One-of-a-kind furniture and accessories.*

**Joseph M. Herrmann,** 87 East Walnut St., Jefferson 44047 (216) 576-7697

**David J. Hostetler, Sculptor,** PO Box 989, Athens 45701 (614) 593-8180 *Carved wood and polished bronze figures of "The American Woman."*

**Stephen P. Latta, Valley Woodwork,** 225 S. Willow, Kent 44240 (216) 628-5866 *Contemporary and traditional hardwood and lacquer reproduction.*

**Robert Ludwig,** 1314 West 39th St., Lorain 44053 (216) 282-5120

**Voicu Marian, Custom Wood Design,** 2711 S. Union Ave. Apt. 17, Alliance 44601 (216) 821-4482 *One-of-a-kind pieces of my own design.*

**Greg Maxwell, Legacy Benchworks,** 155 Letts Ave., Sunbury 43074 (614) 965-2501 *Grandfather clocks and rolltop desks featuring highly figured accents/inlays.*

**R.D. Morrow Woodworking-Woodturning,** 661 Eastside Dr., Carrollton 44615 (216) 627-7472 *Fine furniture by commission, reproductions, restorations, accessories and custom picture frames.*

**Vasil Nastev, Old World Master Cabinet Maker,** 2805 E. Fifth Ave., Columbus 43219 (614) 237-4545 *Custom woodworking, repairing and refinishing.*

**Ralph Z. Neff,** 1616 Greenway Rd. SE, North Canton 44709 (216) 499-4946 *Custom woodworking. "That odd piece you can't find."*

**(5) Rob O'Reilly,** 4549 Hilldom Rd., Kingsville 44048 (216) 224-0053 *Handcrafted furniture and cabinets done on commission.*

**Gary L. Perkins, Artistic Woodturning,** 422 Sixth St., Fremont 43420 (419) 334-4771

**L.W. Pillot,** 32950 Ledge Hill Dr., Solon 44139 (216) 248-6695

**Robert S. Pinter,** 10 Ash Ct., Tipp City 45371

**(11) Joseph Pirogowicz, Stephen Latta, Liberty Custom Furnishings,** 2166 Swartz Rd., Suffield 44260 (216) 628-5866 *Individual design and reproduction.*

**Gary Ransick,** 209 5th St., Loveland 45140

**Chip Rosenblum,** 111 N. Roosevelt Ave., Columbus 43209 (614) 235-7732 *Sculpture, indoor or outdoor, wood and metal, commissions accepted.*

**(148) Charles M. Ruggles, Pipe Organs,** 24493 Bagley Rd., Olmsted Falls 44138 (216) 826-0097 *Custom, handcrafted pipe organs of all sizes and styles.*

**Bernard Salzman, Design & Construction,** Route 1 Box 125AA, Millfield 45761 (614) 797-4172 *Passive solar homes, custom woodworking, interior design, signmaking, stained glass.*

**Stan Schaar Custom Furniture,** Route 1 Box 103B, Amesville 45711 (614) 448-6665 *Custom hardwood furniture, specializing in hand-carved panels.*

**Tom Stadler, Stadler's Custom Furniture/Woodworking,** 14 East Crawford, Toledo 43612 (419) 476-9557

**John Wilkinson,** 51 Warner Rd., Hubbard 44425 (216) 759-8311

## Oklahoma

**Jerry Brownrigg, Industrial Education Department,** Northwestern Oklahoma State U., Alva 73717 (405) 327-1700 ext. 309

**Chris Christensen,** 1013 NW 41st St., Oklahoma City 73118 (405) 528-3708 *Tables, small cabinets and display systems.*

**Matthew Heitzke,** 13008 Red Eagle Pass, Edmond 73013 (405) 478-3875

**(7) James L. Henkle, Designer,** 2719 Hollywood, Norman 73072 (405) 321-7353 *Design and construction of contemporary furniture.*

**Ben Imel, Imel Woodworks,** Route 3 Box 155, Wellston 74881 (405) 356-2505 *Contemporary office furniture, conference tables, antique reproductions and hand-carved details.*

**Robert Jackson,** 509 E. Pecan, Altus 73521 (405) 477-2261

**Alan Lacer, Worker of Wood,** 715 W. Symmes, Norman 73069 (405) 364-9180 *Woodturning, specifically turned decorative bowls.*

**John C. Lowery, L & W Wood Products,** 516 N. J.M. Davis, Claremore 74017 (918) 342-0422 *Design and production of fine furniture and cabinetry.*

**Tom Temple, The Turning Point,** 1230 NE 70th, Oklahoma City 73111 (405) 478-4936 *Custom and production woodturning.*

**Mark Tindle, Tindle Furnishings & Lutherie,** PO Box 690021, Tulsa 74169 (918) 437-8501 *Custom furniture, accessories and fine mountain dulcimers.*

**Stephen Tindle,** 2247 S. Darlington, Tulsa 74114 (918) 744-5894

**Bob Watson, Watson Cabinets and Millwork,** 801 S. Stockton, Ada 74820 (405) 436-0352

## Oregon

**(134) Ken Altman,** 109 Rock St., Silverton 97381 (503) 873-6015 *Boxes: production, limited-edition, one-of-a-kind.*

**David W. Anderson,** 2215 Jeldon St. NE, Salem 97303 (503) 363-8426

**Christian Burchard, Cold Mountain Studio,** 14670 Hwy. 66, Ashland 97520 (503) 482-1077 *Furniture, turned bowls, sculpture, carving and refinishing.*

**Vincent P. Carl, New Trends,** 900 Templin Ave., Grants Pass 97526 (503) 476-2031 *Design and fabricate cabinets and furniture.*

**Rob Chambers, Music Chambers,** 5340 NW Skyline Blvd., Portland 97229 (503) 297-5064 *Stringed instruments, specialty items and French polishing.*

**Cory Colburn,** 655 Rose Ave., Vernonia 97064 (503) 429-0900

**Rick Cook, Wood Studio, Gallery,** 705 Oregon St., Port Orford 97465 (503) 332-0045 *Original furniture designs in local northwest woods.*

**David Crawford,** 305 E. Park, Enterprise 97828 (503) 426-3335

**Diedrich Dasenbrock, Sculpture In Glass & Wood,** 1161 NW Taylor St., Corvallis 97330 (503) 753-4178 *Wood sculpture, lighting units of glass and wood, architectural glass.*

**Michael deForest Woodworking, Oregon Fine Joinery,** 1104 NE 28th, Portland 97232 (503) 288-9903 *Commercial and residential furniture and cabinets; specialty architectural work.*

**(63) Michael Elkan, Michael Elkan Studio,** 22364 N. Fork Rd., Silverton 97381 (503) 873-3241 *Maple burl boxes and accessories, rockers and dining chairs, custom furniture using highly figured Oregon wood.*

**H. Curtis Finch,** 2711 Lakeview Blvd., Lake Oswego 97034 (503) 222-1661

**(98) Tom Freedman, Beth Yoe, Cutting Edge Woodworking,** 4406 SW Corbett, Portland 97201 (503) 236-6056 and (503) 294-0927 *Commercial, residential and art furniture, lighting fixtures and specialized color finishes.*

**Stephen R. Grove, Furniture Maker,** 2844 SE 70th Ave., Portland 97206 (503) 774-2139 *Custom-designed residential and commercial furniture.*

**(133) Lee J. Herold,** PO Box 230252, Tigard 97223 (801) 972-5249

**Clyde Hofflund,** 1633 NE Diablo Way, Bend 97701 (503) 389-0555

**(17) Nancy Horne (Flagstol), Custom Woodworking,** 3135 SW Grace La., Portland 97225 (503) 292-1928 *Office furniture, computer desks, entertainment centers and quality furniture.*

**(110) Walter Huber and Sam Bush, The Swiss Cabinetmaker,** 10355 SE Hwy. 212, Clackamas 97015 (503) 655-9911 *Custom millwork.*

**Thomas Hughes, Woodworking,** PO Box 104, Tolovana Park 27145 (503) 436-1701 *Custom-designed furniture, doors, finishwork, specialty cabinets.*

**Michael and Rebecca Jesse, Jesse Woodworks,** PO Box 15075, Salem 97309 (503) 370-9183 *Interior architectural woodwork for the home and office.*

**Lane D. Johnson, Broadleaf Designs,** 3308 SE Belmont, Portland 97214 (503) 235-2054 *Fine handcrafted furniture, American and Oriental antique reproductions.*

**Robert J. Klein,** 2140 SW 184th Terrace, Aloha 97006 (503) 294-6604

**Randy and Shelly Knapp,** 75 NW 6th St., Ontario 97914 (503) 889-2361 *Rocking chairs and one-of-a-kind in exotic hardwoods.*

**(130) Dan Kvitka,** 2655 NW Fillmore, Corvallis 97330 (503) 754-8744 *Turned forms in exotic woods.*

**(105) Tony La Morticella,** 301 N. Willamette St., Coburg 97401 (503) 484-5580 *Custom furniture, doors, cabinets and window frames.*

**Judy Lewis, Made In Jefferson,** 3259 Jeff Scio Dr., Jefferson 97352 (503) 327-2543 *Custom furniture: bedroom, dining room, living room, office.*

**Kim W. Lewis, Crown Carving,** 16561 SE Marna Rd., Clackamas 97015 (503) 658-8519 *Hand-carved doors, fireplace mantels, murals, sculpture, barrels, signs and refinishing.*

**Dave Maize, Wood Originals,** PO Box 1015, Ashland 97520 (503) 482-1436 *Hand-carved doors, custom woodcarving and custom furniture.*

**Dargan H. Marr, Naphtali Creations,** 1935 Wriston Springs Rd., Coos Bay 97420 (503) 267-6293 *Woodturning, furniture restoration and refinishing.*

**(134) Jeffrey T. McCaffrey, McCaffrey Designs,** 1404 SE 26th Ave., Portland 97214 (503) 239-5367 *Custom and limited-edition woodworking specializing in bentwood.*

**Larry McEntee,** 1435 24th St. NE, Salem 97301 (503) 363-4106

**Lynn Midkiff, Artist in Wood,** 15266 S. Maple Hill Dr., Molalla 97038 (503) 829-4278 *Custom-carving, cigar-store Indian reproductions, animals, signs and totem poles.*

**Ken Moran, Oregon Fine Joinery,** 1104 NE 28th, Portland 97232 (503) 288-9903 *Residential and commercial furniture.*

**Wayne Morrow, Very Handmade Furniture,** 26969 Cantrell Rd., Eugene 97402

**Russell Osterloh, Osterloh's Originals,** 1312 Jefferson, La Grande 97850 (503) 963-8879 *Custom hardwood furniture, dining room, bedroom, rolltop desks and hope chests.*

**Edward C. Overbay, Cabinetmakers,** 2095 SE Airport Rd., Warrenton 97146 (503) 861-1379 *Custom and limited-edition furniture, entry doors and interior design.*

**Chris Peterson, Great Western Woodworks,** 1852 Charnelton, Eugene 97401 (503) 342-8405 *Furniture, architectural woodworking and finish carpentry.*

**(75) Ralph Phillips, Woodworking,** 407 Jefferson, Sisters 97759 (503) 549-1521 *Custom-designed and built furniture and cabinets.*

**Janet Geib Pretti,** PO Box 295, Port Orford 97465 (503) 348-2482

**Mark Rehmar, Fine Furniture and Cabinetry,** PO Box 39, 1249 Waldo Rd., O'Brien 97534 (503) 596-2393 *Custom-designed and crafted fine furniture, architectural woodwork.*

**William Roach, Designer/Builder,** 182 W. 5th, Eugene 97402 (503) 687-9021 *Custom furniture, curved folding screens and traditional Shoji.*

**Gary Rogowski, Furniture Design,** 1104 NE 28th, Portland 97232 (503) 284-1644

**Rosemary Rupp, Woodchuck Studios,** 514 NW Furnish, Pendleton 97801 (503) 276-2807 *Kitchen and serving-ware using North American hardwoods, usually fruitwoods.*

**Jennifer Schwarz,** 2806 SE Taylor, Portland 98502 (503) 235-0537

**Jeff and Rena Segebartt, Oregon Wagon Co.,** PO Box 8545, Coburg 97401 (503) 686-0301

**Fred F. Siedow, Furniture Craftsman,** 5744 E. Burnside St., Portland 97215 (503) 236-0336 *Antique furniture restorations, refinishing, custom-made furniture, antique furniture reproductions.*

**(46) John Simon, Finish Carpentry and Custom Woodworking,** 11615 SW Center #9, Beaverton 97005 (503) 626-6728

**Randy Skyberg,** PO Box 557 (680 Oak St.), Willamina 97396 (503) 876-4902

**Barry Slaughter, Slaughter 'N Wood,** 61425 Brosterhous Rd., Bend 97702 (503) 389-4118 *Affordable handmade custom furniture.*

**Sheldon K. Smith,** 1321 Ranch Rd., Reedsport 97467 (503) 271-3701 *Doors, entertainment cabinets, presentation cases, jewelry boxes and outdoor furniture.*

**Tim Spear, Designs In Wood,** PO Box 6724, Bend 97708 (503) 389-6383 *Functional, one-of-a-kind, contemporary and original designs.*

**James Stettler,** 6540 Yampo, Amity 97101

**William Storch, Custom Woodworking,** 5710 SW West Hills Rd., Corvallis 97333 (503) 757-8717 *Custom furniture and specialty woodworking.*

**Kirk Szymanski,** 17925 SW Arbor Crest Ct., Aloha 97006 (503) 642-4771

**Brian H. Tarrant, Tumalo Woodworks,** 61502 Camelot Pl., Bend 97702 (503) 389-8867

**Emmett Turner,** 5224 Gaffin Rd. SE, Salem 97309 (503) 370-0183

**Dan Zaiss, DC Zaiss,** 1325 West 5th, Eugene 97402 (503) 342-3028 *Custom furniture, cabinetry and trinkets.*

## Pennsylvania

**Tim Abbott, Strictly Top Shelf,** 59 Reeder Rd., New Hope 18938 (215) 862-5476 *Architectural details, woodworking and furniture.*

**Kurt D. Althouse, Althouse Woodworking,** 512 W. 3rd St., E. Greenville 18041 (215) 679-7615

**Allen D. Androkites, Woodworking,** 328 Weymouth Rd., Norristown 19401 (215) 279-9344

**(20) Kevin R. Arnold, D. Douglas Mooberry, Kinloch Woodworking Ltd.,** Route 82, Unionville 19375 (215) 347-2070

**Ken Baumert,** 793 Spruce St., Emmaus 18049 (215) 965-6974 *Custom furniture design and construction.*

**(9) Thomas J. Beck, Designer-Craftsman,** 3029 Fanshawe St., Philadelphia 19149 (215) 332-3385 *One-of-a-kind furniture.*

**(76) Yale Bruce Berman, I Design,** 2107 Mary St., Pittsburgh 15203 (412) 481-3600 *Difficult design problems requiring fine craftsmanship with innovative solutions.*

**Jeff Biddle's Woodworking,** 521 W. Main St., Boalsburg 16827 (814) 466-7720 *18th- and early 19th-century restorations and reproductions, architectural millwork.*

**Dick Boak, Church of Art,** 14 South Broad St., Nazareth 18064 (215) 759-7100 *Custom musical instruments, woodworking, graphics, ceramics, recording and live music.*

**James Britland,** 50 Woodside Ave., Levittown 19057 (215) 943-9942 *Furniture and custom woodworking.*

**Don Bucci,** RD 2 Box 324, Mertztown 19539 (215) 682-4184

**Steven Buggy,** 1901 W. Walnut St., Shamokin 17872 (717) 640-4921

**Don Burkey, Cabinetmaker,** 795 Route 271 N., Ligonier 15658 (412) 238-7697 *Period and contemporary furniture, traditional joinery, woodcarving, guilded carved signs.*

**John Eric Byers, Furniture Maker,** 416 S. 15th St., Philadelphia 19120 (215) 875-1084 *Custom, one-of-a-kind furniture and accessories.*

**Marion H. Campbell, Cabinetmaker,** 39 Wall St., Bethlehem 18018 (215) 865-2522 *American period casework furniture and architectural woodwork.*

**Raphael Canizares,** Louis E. Dieruff High School, Allentown 19512 (215) 820-2200

**(4) Peter Chamberlain,** 2994 Eastburn Rd., Broomall 19008 (215) 353-8051 *Custom-designed, traditional and contemporary furniture.*

**David Cloud, Designer/Woodworker,** 1412 Rainer Rd., Brookhaven 19015 (215) 874-5554 *One-of-a-kind design to suit the environment of the client.*

**Andrea Deardorff, Designs in Wood,** Box 96, Worchester 19490 (215) 584-4858

**Carl Desko,** 211 Woodlawn Ave., Willow Grove 19090

**Richard G. Diehl,** 1340 Hamilton St., York 17402 (717) 755-3804 *Turnery: wooden eggs, chess sets, goblets, vases.*

**Christopher Ditlow, Oak Park Cabinetry,** 4410 Lexington St., Harrisburg 17109 (717) 545-9616 *Custom cases and doors for homes and office, light millwork.*

**Emily Eckel, Creative Enviroments, Inc.,** 2107 Mary St., Pittsburgh 15203 (412) 488-3336 *Custom furniture, architectural and furniture design.*

**(48) Glenn Gauvry, Heartwood Craftsman, Inc.,** 312 W. Columbia Ave., Philadelphia 19122 (215) 236-3050 *Furniture, cabinetry and millwork.*

**J.H. Geisel,** RD 4 Box 343A, Muncy 17756 (717) 546-6340 *Early American reproductions, gun cabinets, blanket chests, mirrors.*

**Barry C. George Woodworking,** 16767 Holly Rd., Wescosville 18106 (215) 395-3847

**Geo A. Getty,** 543 Schoolhouse Rd., Johnstown 15904 (814) 269-3533

**W. Gerry Grant, Custom Furniture,** 455 Rupp Rd., Gettysburg 17325 (717) 528-4496

**Jeffrey Greene, Design Studio,** 94 New St., New Hope 18938 (215) 862-5530 *Fine solid-wood furniture with pegs and interlocking wood joinery.*

**Guido,** RD 3 #198, Chicora 16025 (412) 894-2194 *Use of organic forms and domestic hardwoods.*

**Robert H. Haffner,** 811 W. Beaver Ave., State College 16801 (814) 234-0837

**Jim Haynes,** Box 479, Trexlertown 18087 (215) 398-1609

**A.T. Heicher, Restorations,** 219 Second St., High Spire 17034 (717) 564-0205 *Restoration of 18th- and 19th-century houses.*

**(52) Steven J. Hirsh, Hirsh, Brothers and Lavine, Inc.,** A-91 RD 2, Eagle Rd., New Hope 18938 (215) 598-3556 *Dining rooms, living rooms, desks and occasional furniture.*

**Max Hunsicker,** 68 Pine St., PO Box 316, Mt. Gretna 17064 (717) 964-3108

**(78) Michael Hurwitz,** 627 N. 3rd St., Philadelphia 19123 (215) 875-1048 (days) / 238-9660 (evenings)

**(76) Bob Ingram, Ingram Design Studio,** 1102 E. Columbia Ave., Philadelphia 19125 (215) 739-7253 *Furniture designed and developed for industrial production, gallery sales and/or commission.*

**Keck Jackson, Jackson's Cabinet Shop,** 2879 Wildwood Rd. Ext., Allison Park 15101 (412) 487-1291 *Reproduction of period American and English furniture.*

**Douglas Jones,** 240 N. Broad St., Doylestown 18901 (215) 340-1179

**(46) John Kennedy, Heartwood Craftsmen, Inc.,** 312 W. Columbia Ave., Philadelphia 19122 (215) 236-3050 *Designing and building limited-editions of residential and commercial furniture and cabinetry.*

**Jerry Lilly,** 119 N. Homewood Ave., Pittsburgh 15208 (412) 241-1649

**Bud Mall, Fancy Pickles,** 1017 Perry Hwy., Pittsburgh 15237 (412) 366-6054

**W.G. Matthews, Matty Cabinet,** 811 Rossmore Ave., Pittsburgh 15226 (412) 561-6441

**Thomas P. Maurer, Custom Woodworking,** 2750 Mountain Rd., Danielsville 18038 (215) 837-6266

**Jon S. Mehl, Period Furniture Maker,** 544 Schoolhouse Rd., Aspers 17304 (717) 528-8647 *Queen Anne and Chippendale chairs and case furniture.*

**(32) Thomas L. Merriman, Cabinetmaker,** 2093 Constitution Blvd., McKeesport 15135 (412) 751-8295 *Residential and corporate custom furniture.*

**Michael Milner,** 1617 Porter St. 1st Fl., Philadelphia 19145 (215) 875-1048

**(129) Micheal D. Mode,** RD 2 Box 133A, Zionsville 18092 (215) 679-2386 *Spindle and faceplate turning, production work, architectural turning, special commissions.*

**Ron Morgan, Cabinet and Furniture Designs,** 31 St. Pauls Rd., Ardmore 19003 (215) 642-1262 *Custom-designed wood furniture and fine cabinets.*

**Robert F. Mullan, Moon's Dust Shop,** 417 W. 18th St., Tyrone 16686 (814) 684-1328

**Thomas J. Noone,** RD 1 Box 96, Uniondale 10470 (717) 222-4334

**Ed Nordberg, Custom Woodwork,** RD 5 Box 522B, Bellefonte 16823 (814) 355-9112 *Custom furniture, architectural woodwork.*

**Debra L. Oltman,** 209 N. 6th St., Perkasie 18944 *Small functional ware in exotic woods, sculpture and sculptural cabinetry.*

**James L. Otstot, Jim's Woodworking,** 711 Noble Blvd., Carlisle 17013 (717) 243-4287 *Small cabinetwork, inlay, woodcarving and signs.*

**Robert Rosand, Dutch Hill Woodturning,** RD 1 Box 30, Bloomsburg 17815 (717) 784-6158 *Woodturning, primarily one-of-a-kind, some spindle-turning.*

**(25) Richard Rose,** 29 Sunnyside La., Yardley 19067 (215) 493-6915 *High-tech custom design and fabrication.*

**Mark Sfirri,** RD 2 Box A143, New Hope 18938 (215) 794-8125 *Experimental turning; bowls, furniture, one-of-a-kind pieces.*

**Robert W. Shields,** Box 239, Fairfield 17320 (717) 642-5907

**(73) Joanne Shima,** 13 S. State St. Apt. E, Newtown 18940 (215) 860-7156

**Jonathan S. Simons, Jonathan's Spoons,** PO Box 4, 81 Penn St., Lenhartsville 19534 (215) 562-5480 *Hardwood kitchen utensils, custom designs and production lines, wholesale and retail.*

**Carter Jason Sio, Designer/Builder,** George School, Newtown 18940 (215) 968-3811 *Contemporary designs using all available mediums.*

**(53) Scott C. Smith, Smith Works,** 125 Elysian St., Pittsburgh 15206 (412) 362-0149 *Originally designed furniture and sculpture.*

**Carl E. Spaeder,** 623 Sommerheim Dr., Erie 16505 (814) 838-3612

**William E. Stowe,** 2592 Springfield Rd., Broomall 19008 (215) EL6-7445 *Woodworking of all kinds, laminations and veneer work.*

**Jay Taylor,** 5 Riviera Rd., Pittsburgh 15239 (412) 793-9346 *Furniture and sculpture in wood.*

**Mark Taylor,** 404 S. Union St., Kennett Sq. 19348 (215) 444-3158

**Steve Temple,** 2802 Homer Ave., Erie 16506 (814) 838-2265 *Carving, furniture and objects. Architectural installation (custom).*

**Richard Webster,** 143 Inland Rd., Ivyland 18974 (215) 357-3339

**(96) Christopher Weiland, Designer-Craftsman,** RD 1 Box 127A, Penn Run 15765 (412) 349-8917 *Individual design and construction of residential, corporate and institutional works.*

**Tui and Zvi Weinman, TZ Design,** RD 4 Box 176, Bethlehem 18015 (215) 866-8194 *Custom furniture for the home and office.*

## Rhode Island

**(89) Richard Chalmers,** 92 East Manning St., Providence 02906 (401) 751-5165 *Furniture design and construction services, contemporary motifs.*

**Keith Crowder,** Box E2, RISD, Providence 02903 (401) 331-3511

**(131) Thomas Davin, Davin & Kesler,** PO Box 87, Slocum 02877 (401) 295-7515 *Fine wooden gifts and accessories.*

**(99) Bruce Decker, Hardwood in Design,** Dorset Mill Rd., Slocum 02877 (401) 294-2235 *Architectural woodworking.*

**Bruce Decker, Woodworker, Mark McDonnell, Designer,** 95 North Rd., Peace Dale 02883

**Jeff Hannon, Woodworker,** 206½ Columbus Ave., Pawtucket 02861 *Custom cabinets and tables, items from roots, stumps and burls.*

**John Holscher,** 12 Manton St., Warwick 02818 (401) 885-5453

**Robert B. Materne Co.,** PO Box 925, Bristol 02809 (401) 253-9974 *Custom woodworking and furniture design.*

**Timothy S. Philbrick,** PO Box 555, Narragansett 02882 (401) 789-4030

**A. Tavares, Acts In Wood,** PO Box 7232, Cumberland 02864 (401) 333-4835 *Custom woodworking, country and Shaker styles, hand-carved signs, folk sculpture.*

**(84) Stephen Turino, Designer/Craftsman,** PO Box 343, Fort Ninigret Rd., Charlestown 02813 (401) 364-3511 *One-of-a-kind furniture, fine cabinetry and special architectural details.*

**John Weeks, Weeks Woodworking,** 149 Lancaster St., Providence 02906 (401) 351-0363

## South Carolina

**Lucius M. Cline, Jr.,** 2407 Augusta St., Greenville 29605 (803) 233-3205

**(66) Tim Gorka, Artistry In Wood,** PO Box 7741, Hilton Head 29938 (803) 681-3008 *Children's furniture and interiors—sculptural, architectural, marine woodcarving and joinery.*

**Tom Haffner, Haffner Woodworking,** 208 Loblolly La., Greenville 29607 (803) 297-3865 *Hardwood furniture, leaded bevel glass, stained glass and general woodworking.*

**(84) John Jeffers, JMO Woodworks, Inc.,** 1859 Summerville Ave., Charleston 29405 (803) 747-5102 *Furniture and millwork.*

**Stephen Loper, Woodworks,** PO Box 791, Bluffton 29910 (803) 757-4243 *Custom woodworking, fine furniture and cabinetry.*

**Jackson A. Parris, Lourcraft Woodworks and Fine Cabinets,** Route 4 Box 219, Hwy. 183 E., Pickens 29671 (803) 878-4489 *Custom furniture and cabinets, custom and reproduction millwork.*

**C. Edward Singletary, Jr., Singletary Woodworking,** 413 Fleming Rd., James Island, Charleston 29412 (803) 795-4285 *Designer/craftsman of fine contemporary furniture.*

## South Dakota

**Edmund J. Bucknell, Prospect Mountain Crafts,** 3027 Roxbury Circle, Rapid City 57702 (605) 343-9522 *Carved birds, gunstocks and framing.*

**Joe VanDeRostyne, Prairie Woodworking,** 12 SE 8th Ave., Aberdeen 57401 (605) 226-2444

**Roger Wermers, Woodcarvings,** 522 NE 3rd, Madison 57042 (605) 256-9827 *Carousel animals and western art carvings.*

## Tennessee

**David and Harvey Baker, Dunmire Hollow Woodshop,** Route 3 Box 449, Waynesboro 38485 (615) 722-9201 *Custom woodworking—furniture and architectural millwork.*

**(88) Jan Bell,** 8875 McCrory La., Nashville 37221 (615) 646-5611 *Innovative custom furniture and functional art.*

**Richard H. Busey, Custom Furniture,** 106 S. Tampa La., Oak Ridge 37830 (615) 483-5024 *Antique reproductions and contemporary designs.*

**(64) Stephen B. Crump, Handcrafted Original Furniture,** 2127 Young Ave., Memphis 38104 (901) 276-6918 *Contemporary furniture, designed and built on commission.*

**Jack Davis, Jeananlee Schilling,** PO Box 8, Crosby 37722 (615) 487-5543 *Hammer dulcimers, mountain dulcimers, bowed and plucked psalteries, doorharps and woodcrafts.*

**Grover W. Floyd, III,** 6800 Ball Camp Pike, Knoxville 37931 (615) 690-2973 *18th-century furniture recreations and restorations with traditional joinery used exclusively.*

**Randall Grace,** Route 6, Summers Rd., Franklin 37064 (615) 791-1832 *Shaker and southern reproductions, custom design for home and office.*

**John Jordan, Gray Acres Woodworking,** 446 Battle Rd., Antioch 37013 (615) 776-1247 *Original and commissioned wood furniture—custom woodwork.*

**E. Jeff Justis, Justis Reproductions,** 4209 Walnut Grove, Memphis 38117 (901) 767-1697 *Commissions for period reproductions.*

**Lida J. Mayer,** Route 45, Babelay Rd., Knoxville 37924 (615) 688-8458 *Primarily small pieces: jewelry, hairpins, boxes, tone drums and laminated items.*

**Brian F. Russell, Three Dimensional Designs,** 2537 Broad St., Memphis 38112 (901) 327-1210 *Limited production and custom one-offs in wood and metals.*

**Phillip A. Stafford,** 4231 Canada Rd., Arlington 38002 (901) 372-9518 *Fine furniture and architectural specialties.*

**Ross Trotter, Trotter's,** 2309 Wagon La., Knoxville 37920 (615) 577-1122 *Contemporary wood objects and furniture.*

**David N. and Jack Vaughn, Acorn Acres Woodshop,** 179 S. Col-Arl Rd., Collierville 38017 (901) 853-4112 *Custom-made hardwood furniture.*

**Gerry Victory,** 516 Golden Harvest Rd., Knoxville 37922 (615) 966-8604

## Texas

**Frank Andrews,** 171 Maeiposa, Mercedes 78570 (512) 565-5502

**Dean Arnold, The Wood Factory,** 2328 Sul Ross, Houston 77098 (713) 522-9117 *Remodeling, custom cabinets, custom doors, etched glass.*

**William Kelly Bailey, Handcrafted Furniture & Custom Woodworks,** 5239 Ripplebrook, Houston 77045 (713) 433-9550 *Custom furniture and cabinets (original or custom-designed) and reproductions.*

**(23) Morgan Rey Benson,** 811 Wyoming, El Paso 79902 (915) 532-1077 *Custom designing and manufacturing, prototype research and development.*

**John Blair,** 106 E. Schubert, Fredericksburg 78624 (512) 997-3161

**Michael Colca, Summertree Woodshop,** Route 1 Box 112, Manchaca 78652 (512) 282-0493 *Design and build custom furniture, cabinetry and architectural woodwork.*

**Larry DeVinny, Live Oak,** PO Box 223, Brownsboro 75756 (214) 852-6954 *Original designs in hardwood boxes, tables and chests, enhanced by a balance of function and form.*

**(142) Tom H. Ellis, Ellis Mandolins,** 7208 Cooper La., Austin 78745 (512) 442-4941 *The finest custom mandolins and banjos, custom inlay and restorations.*

**Richard Epstein, Designer/Craftsman,** 2413 Riverside Farms Rd., Austin 78741 (512) 385-0629 *Designer of hardwood interiors and furniture.*

**(147) Charles R. Ervin, Charles Ervin Violins,** 903 E. 38th St., Austin 78705 (512) 467-2277 *Violins, violas, cellos, basses and bows made and repaired.*

**Richard Fisher Woodworking,** 4601 Ave. D, Austin 78751 (512) 453-2029 *Custom furniture, cabinetry and accessories.*

**(115) Clay Foster,** Route 1 Box 2640, Krum 76249 (817) 458-3839 *Faceplate turning.*

**Louis Fry, Woodsong,** 1345 W. Mary St., Suite H, Austin 78704 (512) 447-4000 *Fine custom furniture and entry doors.*

**Ted Gowin, Craftsman,** 2810 Bowman Ave., Austin 78703 (512) 477-6602 *Functional sculpture, mantels, doors, restorations, commercial interests.*

**George A. Greider, Woodwork by George,** 8425 Cheswick, Houston 77037 (713) 931-8871

**Martin Grunow, The Woodwork Shop,** 4009 Belford Ave., Fort Worth 76103 (817) 536-3352 *Design and construct one-of-a-kind furniture.*

**Don Hart, Hartwoods,** 1230 Kappa, Pasadena 77504 (713) 487-5484 *Woodturnings, bowls, nonfunctional.*

**Kim Herry, Doug Smith,** 2014 Goodrich, Austin 78704 (512) 443-9303 *Custom lathe turning, design and build custom furniture.*

**Larry Hulsey,** 418 N. Fillmore, Amarillo 79107 (806) 372-7261 *Raised panel doors, moldings, custom furniture, fireplace mantels, kitchen cabinets.*

**Peter Hutchinson, Hutchinson Woodworking,** 13818 St. Marys, Houston 77079 (713) 493-6697 *18th-century reproductions and woodturned objects and bowls.*

**Lewis A. Jewell, Family Tradition Ponys,** 105 N. Forest, Lewisville 75067 (817) 430-8107

**Mike Kelly, Woodworker,** 11907 Marrs Dr., Houston 77065 (713) 890-1825 *Clocks, hardwood toys, bowls, small furniture and knicknacks.*

**David H. Kievit, That's Woodwork!,** 18 Mossy Cup Ct., Conroe 77304 (409) 756-0791 *Custom hardwood furniture and decorating accessories.*

**Philippe Klinefelter, Robert Mather, Klinefelter Company,** 800 Gullet St., Austin 78742 (512) 476-1360 *Innovative design/constructions using wood, marble and metal.*

**S.C. Larson, Custom Furnishings,** 1306 Ludlow Terrace, Austin 78723 (512) 451-9213 *Custom furniture for office and home interiors.*

**Richard L. Lazear,** 19407 Gagelake La., Houston 77084 (713) 492-0680

**Dean Luse, Woodworker/Architect,** 3716 Julian, Houston 77009 (713) 869-0303 *Custom furniture and store fixtures—design and manufacture.*

**Tony McKinney, Heartwood,** 707 Turtle Hill, Driftwood 78619 (512) 847-5362

**Shep Miers, C.S.M. Designs,** 1606 Maple, Irving 75060 (214) 438-6188

**Eddie Norman, Hand Feats,** Route 2 Box 87, Wimberley 78676 (512) 847-5351 *Antique pine, no nails, tacks, staples, interlocking joints, natural contours.*

**(12) Daniel Peck, Timberworks, Inc.,** 5606 W. Prue Rd., San Antonio 78240 (512) 697-9903 *Custom furniture design and manufacturing.*

**Jonathan K. Percy, Hotspur Hardwoods,** 2205 Tanglevine Dr., Austin 78748 (512) 282-7669 *Furniture, accessories and picture frames.*

**Ken Picou, Design in Wood,** 5508 Montview, Austin 78756 (512) 454-3425 *Custom and production woodwork, turning and functional design.*

**Thomas J. Proch, Cabinetmakers,** 9603 Meadowhill Dr., Dallas 75238 (214) 348-7750 *Design concepts to completion, problem solution and reproductions.*

**Robert Robertson, R & R Millworks,** 1604B S. Congress, Austin 78704 (512) 441-4111 *Custom-arch millwork, residential and commercial, executive and conference-room furniture.*

**Tony Sauer,** 912 Cherry Hollow Rd., Fredericksburg 78624 (512) 997-4315

**Keith Schindler, Wooden Wonders,** 1325 Princeton Ct., Denton 76201 (817) 566-4727 *Wooden toys and custom oddities.*

**F.W. Schmidt,** 12901 Oak Creek Circle, Austin 78727 (512) 244-0602 *Bowls and weed pots from native woods.*

**Robert F. Stamm,** 216 Crestwood Dr., Fredericksburg 78624 (512) 997-3639 *Functional as well as decorative items.*

**Shane Stock, Top CounterTops,** 1115 Speer La., Austin 78745 (512) 462-1697 *Custom countertops—new and restorations.*

**Larry Templeton, Temple Contracting,** 518 N. Oak Cliff, Dallas 75208 (214) 942-9461 *General contracting, custom cabinet/built-in and interior finish.*

**Larry Verner, Woodwork,** Route 12 Box 871, New Braunfels 78130 (512) 438-4086 *Furniture, accessories and specialties.*

**(48) Jim Wallace, J.C. Design,** 1105 South Riviera Cr., Cedar Park 78613 (512) 258-2075 *Veneered tables.*

**Barry Ward,** 3814 Glencove Circle, Missouri City 77459

**H. Weathers, Shade Tree Craftsman,** 420 Norvel, Beaumont 77707 (409) 866-7155 *Custom furniture, porch swings and boxes.*

**Paul H. Whelchel, Heartwood Transition,** 10815 Piping Rock, Houston 77042 (713) 785-7701 *Custom furniture, tables, chairs, cabinets and accessories.*

**John Yount, Wood Artist,** 3855 Wosley Dr., Fort Worth 76133 (817) 292-7690

## Utah

**Clead Christiansen, The Turning Post,** 3086 N. 150 E., No. Ogden 84404 (801) 782-5105 *Custom and decorative woodturning.*

**Kent Korgenski, Korgenski Woodworks,** 2311 East 3740 S., Salt Lake City 84109 (801) 278-3993 *Custom woodturning and woodworking.*

**Richard Marshall, Marshall Woodworks,** 170 Olympus St., Midvale 84047 (801) 255-3829

**Richard Packer, Forest St. Wood Designs,** 538 Holiday Dr., Brigham City 84302 (801) 723-7786 *Miniature houses, miniature furniture and woodworking plans.*

## Vermont

**(135) David Bayne,** 134 S. Main St., Northfield 05663 (802) 485-7466

**R.W. Chatelain, Woodworker,** RD 1 Box 105, Huntington 05464 (802) 434-2542 *Maker of turned wood, bowls, custom-made croquet mallets and "Shoji-ish" screens.*

**George De George,** RR 1, Fairfield 05455 (802) 524-3059 *One-of-a-kind turned, covered bowls.*

**Robert M. Gasperetti, Fine Wooden Furniture,** PO Box 603 Route 7A, Manchester Village 05254 (802) 362-1985

**(146) H.F. Grabenstein, Bowmaker at the Tourin Music,** Box 575, Duxbury 05676 (802) 244-5557 *Viola da gamba and other historical string instruments and bows.*

**(43) Steven Holman,** Box 572, Dogpatch Rd., Dorset 05251 (802) 867-5562

**David Holzapfel, Applewoods,** Route 9 PO Box 66, Marlboro 05344 (802) 254-2908 *Subtractive furniture and sculpture in native burl and spalted woods.*

**(118) Michelle Holzapfel, Applewoods,** Route 9 PO Box 66, Marlboro 05344 (802) 254-2908 *Turned/carved objects in Vermont burl and spalted hardwoods.*

**James Ludwig,** RFD, Randolph Center 05061 (802) 728-4232 *Sculpted and very large turned bowl forms.*

**(53) Dan Mosheim,** Box 2660, Red Mountain Rd., Arlington 05250 (802) 375-2568 *Custom furniture, traditional, painted, Windsor chairs.*

**Stewart Ruth,** 14½ Decantur St., Burlington 05401 (802) 863-6531

**(81) John Ryan and Ray Mullineaux, Techne Design,** BCIC Building, Water St., North Bennington 05257 (802) 447-2407 *Original-design furniture, lacquer and veneer work, restoration and unique casegoods.*

**(119) Peter Szymkowicz, Heartwood Treenworks,** RR 1 Box 185, Shoreham 05770 (802) 897-2657 *Sculptural burl vessels, hand-carved utensils and interior accessories.*

**Richard Taub, Furnituremaker,** RFD Box 123, Waitsfield 05673 (802) 496-7643

**Edward Tetreault, Wildacre Enterprises,** HCR Box 18, Grafton 05146 (802) 843-2324 *Custom-designed furniture built to suit all needs.*

**Tom Tugend, Tugendworks,** RR 1 Box 594M, Huntington 05462 (802) 434-4236 *Producer of high-quality custom woodwork, fine furniture and cabinets.*

**Wall/Goldfinger, Inc.,** 7 Belknap St., Northfield 05663 (802) 485-6261 *Contract furniture in wood and granite with custom capabilities.*

**D. Lowell Zercher,** PO Box 117, Waterbury Center 05677 (802) 244-7255 *Individually designed furniture and accessories.*

## Virginia

**John F. Balko, Jr., Cabinetmaker,** 1713 Jackfrost Rd., Virginia Beach 23455 (804) 460-2563 *Cabinetry, furniturebuilding, boat joinery, wood sculpture and woodturning.*

**Mac H. Barnes, III,** 14670 Endsley Turn, Woodbridge 22193 (703) 680-4183 *Violins and other stringed instruments.*

**(50) Hugh Belton,** 1154 Bellview Rd., Mc Lean 22102 (703) 759-2216 *Freestanding furniture of contemporary design.*

**Craig A. Biddle,** 2504 Floyd Ave. #3, Richmond 23220 (804) 358-0686

**(126) Nigel B. Briggs,** PO Box 4642, Falls Church 22044 (703) 237-2494 *Turned wooden bowls.*

**Marty Britt,** 660 West Union St., Wytheville 24382

**Andy Buck,** 121 N. Lombardy St., Richmond 23220 (804) 355-0417

**(61) Graham Campbell,** V.C.U. Crafts Dep., 221 Shaffer St., Richmond 23220 (804) 353-3574

**Peter Chapman, Woodworker,** PO Box 45, Bent Mt. 24059 (703) 929-4848 *Custom furniture, Windsor chairs and bowlturning.*

**Stephen A. Clerico, Woodworker,** PO Box 192, Free Union 22940 (804) 978-4109 *Mirrors for wall and floor, wall hangings, small furnishings.*

**Jeffrey Dahlquist, Dahlquist Studios,** 1946 Creek Crossing Rd., Vienna 22180 (703) 255-1451 *Custom furniture and interiors.*

**DeSantis Designs, Inc.,** 314 Victory Dr., Herndon 22070 (703) 759-2222 *Designing and building hardwood furniture, wooden signs, murals and etched glass.*

**Wright Deter,** 1805B Inglewood Dr. #28, Charlottesville 22901 (804) 296-1376

**Ronnie Ferguson, Ferguson's Custom-Designed Furniture,** 512 Nottingham Rd., Portsmouth 23701 (804) 465-0280 *Custom furniture using exotic hardwoods.*

**Rob Grant, Contemporary Woodcrafts,** 220 S. Henry St. (rear), Alexandria 22314 (703) 548-1741 *Quality, custom-built furniture and wall units.*

**William Hammersley, Hammersley Fine Arts, Wood,** 2206 E. Main St., Richmond 23219 (804) 343-1750

**(30) Jaeger & Ernst , Inc.,** Route 1 Box 145, Barboursville 22923 (804) 973-7018 *Custom furniture—client-oriented design.*

**Gove M. Johnson, Mountain Woodworks Fine Furniture,** PO Box 56, State Route 151, Nellysford 22958 (804) 361-2357 *Custom furniture and architectural joinery.*

**Landon Kines,** Route 1 Box 177, Midland 22728 (703) 788-4161

**Joanne L. Knaebel,** 411 Alamosa Dr., Highland Springs 23075 (804) 737-3862

**Stephen R. LaDrew, Custom Furniture and Interiors,** Old Reliance School, Route 1 Box 1920, Reliance 22649 (703) 869-6710 *Custom contemporary hardwood furniture.*

**Marty MacVittie, MickBeth Design,** 6200 Impala Dr., Richmond 23228 (804) 261-4158 *Cabinetmakers, staircases, doors, windows and reproductions.*

**Sarah McCollum,** Box 18, Free Union 22940 (804) 823-1128 *Furniture and accessories: one-of-a-kind and limited edition.*

**Pepe Mendez,** 11720 Blue Smoke Trail, Reston 22091 (703) 860-0559

**David W. Narum,** 2611 Rothland Dr., Richmond 23229 (804) 270-1838 *Design and construction of custom furniture and wood sculpture.*

**Jessie and James Payne, Payne Construction,** Route 29, Rustburg 24588 (804) 821-2159

**Paul Pyzyna, Woodworks,** Box 43, Free Union 22940 (804) 978-1639 *Prototype/custom pieces and small-production runs.*

**David Ramazani, Custom Woodworking,** 33 Westwood Dr., Ruckersville 22968 (804) 985-2154 *Handmade furniture from exotic hardwoods.*

**J.W. Rose,** PO Box 1865, Middleburg 22117 (703) 955-1364 *Furniture to fit traditional settings, carving and toolmaking.*

**Larry Smith, Woodsmith Furniture,** Route 1 Box 210, Pilot 24138 (703) 651-6185 *Original design, handmade furniture.*

**Robert Sonday,** Box 18, Free Union 22940 (804) 823-1128 *Bowls, furniture, accessories: one-of-a-kind and limited edition.*

**(53) Craig E. Steidle,** PO Box 202, Waterford 22190 (703) 455-9581 *Custom woodworking, fine furniture and clocks.*

**Sidney N. Stone,** 7741 Merrimac Dr., Mc Lean 22101 (703) 522-8875

**(119) George Van Dyke, Arborcraft,** 3628 Danny's La., Alexandria 22311 (703) 379-8277 *Bowlturning.*

**Brad Warstler, Northwind Woodworks,** Route 3 Box 154A, Floyd 24091 (703) 745-3595 *Accessories, furniture and turnings.*

**(63) John A. Weissenberger, Windsor Chairs,** 23 East Monmouth St., Winchester 22601 (703) 667-1627 *All kinds of Windsor chairs and settees.*

**Roger Neil White, White's Woodworking,** Route 3 Box 1157, Blacksburg 24060 (703) 951-2223

**(62) B. Randolph Wilkinson, Windsor Chairs,** 5208A Brook Rd., Richmond 23227 (804) 264-5585 *Windsor chairs and settees in a variety of styles.*

**Henry Wise, Custom Woodworking,** Route 2 Box 315, Edinburg 22824 (703) 984-8180 *Chests, cabinets, shelves, clocks.*

## Washington

**Lou Almasi, Tanglewood,** 12618 36th St. NE, Lake Stevens 98258 (206) 334-7061 *Custom woodworking—furniture, cabinets and woodcrafts.*

**(86) Judith Ames, Furniture,** 625 Western Ave., Seattle 98104 (206) 343-2332 *Custom and limited-production furniture, steam-bent and laminated forms (a favorite), carving and veneering.*

**Gert Becker,** 462 East Lake Sammamish Rd., Redmond 98053 (206) 868-4553 *Sculptures and hand-carved furniture in historic styles.*

**Marianne Bond, Wood You Like,** 3014 60th Ave. SE, Mercer Island 98040 (206) 236-2469

**Geoffrey Braden, Braden Design,** 4207 Burke Ave. N., Seattle 98103 (206) 632-6955 *Furniture design and production, general woodworking.*

**Larry L. Brooks,** 20408 NE Bridlewood Rd., Battle Ground 98604 (206) 687-4663 *Custom-designed fine furniture.*

**Pete Bruce,** 16950 Olympic View Rd. NW, Silverdale 98383 (206) 692-6816

**(69) Jonathan Cohen,** 3410 Woodland Pk. N., Seattle 98103 (206) 632-2141 *Custom furniture focusing on bent-lamination/exotic hardwoods.*

**Martha Collins, Lost Mountain Editions, Ltd.,** PO Box 304, 754 Lost Mountain Rd., Sequim 98382 (206) 683-2778 *Cabinetry and furniture, gaming tables, etc.*

**(25) Emmett E. Day, Creations in Precious Materials,** 5126 Woodlawn N., Seattle 98103 (206) 547-9676 *Combinations of precious metals and woods on commission, furniture, jewelry and sculpture.*

**(17) Ross Day,** 3134 Elliott Ave. #220, Seattle 98121 (206) 283-2586 *Custom-wood furniture.*

**Scott Dinges, Design,** 1023 NW 196th St., Seattle 98177 (206) 546-8154 *Custom furniture, cabinets and turnings.*

**(37, 144) Rion and Kathleen Dudley,** 405 Cedar St., Seattle 98121 (206) 448-1642 *Commercial and residential interior design and custom-furniture design.*

**Gary Gilbert,** 1918 N. 44th St., Seattle 98103 (206) 547-9881 *Sculpture, furniture and design.*

**(144) Robert Girdis, Luthier,** 368 Edens Rd., Guemes Island 98221 (206) 293-2227 *Custom acoustic guitars.*

**(34) David Gray, Fine Furniture,** 208 3rd Ave. S., Seattle 98104 (206) 625-9081 *Desks.*

**Matthew Healey,** 726 Taft St., Port Townsend 98368 (206) 385-4850

**Don Hennick, Whispering Wood,** 9547 Wallingford N., Seattle 98103 (206) 522-5380

**Erik Rist Holt, Nordic Dragon Woodworks,** 20716 78th Pl. W., Edmonds 98020 (206) 776-4190 *Turning, carving and custom cabinetry with use of figured woods.*

**(33) Robert (Hank) Holzer, Holzer Furniture,** 625 Western Ave. 4th Fl., Seattle 98104 *Group shop of ten members making fine furniture and cabinetry.*

**Mike Jackson,** PO Box 974, Bellingham 98227 (206) 676-4039 *One-of-a-kind work using traditional joinery.*

**(87) Ralf Keeler,** 7341 13th NW, Seattle 98117 *Custom handmade furniture and cabinets.*

**Ed Kirchner,** 9738 14th NW, Seattle 98117 (206) 784-2434 *Oriental lamps, custom orders taken.*

**Jack Kizer,** 4336 Baker St., Seattle 98107 (206) 789-6238

**David Knobel, Knobel Woodworks,** 4826 17th NW, Olympia 98502 (206) 866-0544 *Maker of custom furniture and fine cabinets since 1975.*

**Armand E. Larive,** NE 1500 Stadium Way, Pullman 99163 (509) 332-2332

**Towner D. McLane, Woodworker,** PO Box 34, Lummi Island 98262 (206) 758-7295 *High-quality traditional wooden boats and furniture.*

**Earle McNeil, Serendipity Art Works,** 1909 Bowman, Olympia 98502 (206) 943-5735 *Lathework, custom furniture and kaleidoscopes.*

**(137) Curt Minier,** 210 3rd St., Seattle 98104 (206) 625-9081 *Custom hardwood furniture, one-of-a-kind/my own designs.*

**Michael Neiman,** E. 2414 63rd, Spokane 99223 (509) 448-4165 *Short-run production and one-of-a-kind furniture.*

**Fred Paxson, Furniture As Form,** PO Box 222, Trout Lake 98650 (509) 395-2426

**Michael Peterson, Sculptured Woods,** 15120 73rd Ave. W., Edmonds 98020 (206) 745-0547 *Sculptural bowl and vessel forms—lathe-turned and hand-carved.*

**Tim Place,** 1578 Mt. View Rd., Big Lake 98273 (206) 424-8815

**Floyd E. Rank, Rank's,** Box 127, Seaview 98644 (206) 642-2407 *Custom-built hardwood furniture—traditional to contemporary.*

**(123) R.E. Renner, Geppetto's Woodworks,** 6304 Kansas St., Vancouver 98661 (206) 693-6566 *Turning, inlay, reproductions, carving and cabinetry.*

**Dwayne Roeder, Woodworking,** 060L Woodard Creek Rd., Stevenson 98648 (509) 665-3596 *Aesthetic wooden mechanical furnishings and contraptions.*

**Alan Rosen,** 3740 Legoe Bay Rd., Lummi Island 98262 (206) 758-7452 *Fine furniture, antique reproductions to contemporary originals.*

**(145) Richard Schneider, Lost Mountain Editions, Ltd.,** PO Box 304, 754 Lost Mountain Rd., Sequim 98382 (206) 683-2778 *Classical and steel string guitars of the Kasha design, wood jewelry, cabinetry and furniture.*

**Dave L. Shilton, Shilton Designs,** 625 Western Ave. 4th Fl., Seattle 98104 (206) 624-4869 *Commercial and residential furniture from selected imported and domestic hardwoods.*

**(37) Stephen Stokesberry, Crag Studio,** 7723 17th Ave. NW, Seattle 98117 (206) 782-8394 *Innovative and expressive furniture for individuals.*

**Bob Street, Woodworks,** 100 W. First, Aberdeen 98520 (206) 532-8215 *One-of-a-kind specialty pieces in rosewood.*

**(77) Michael Strong,** 718 Highland Dr., Bellingham 98225 (206) 671-9952 *Chairs, custom chairs, other seating and dining tables.*

**(97) Malcolm Suttles,** 5136 Ballard Ave. NW, Seattle 98107 (206) 789-5253 *Fine furniture and woodturning.*

**Paul Swanson,** PO Box 541, Clear Lake 98235 (206) 855-1938

**Timberwolf Custom Woodworking,** 3740 Legoe Bay Rd., Lummi Island 98262 (206) 758-7452 *Fine cabinetry—commercial and residential, custom millwork and wooden boatwork.*

**Ron Vanbianchi, Adria Design,** 7035 Crawford Dr., Kingston 99346 (206) 297-3068

**(52) Andy Webster, Cloudy Mountain Woodworks,** 4497 Minaker Rd., Sumas 98295 (206) 988-6695 *Furniture, cabinetry and design.*

**Charles J. Woodruff,** 5507 55th Ave. S., Seattle 98118 (206) 723-8487

## West Virginia

**A.E. Bennet, Genes Woodcraft,** Route 1 Box 35, Cottageville 25239 (304) 372-9988 *Clocks and various craftshop items.*

**Richard Cobos,** Broad Run, Centerpoint 26339 (304) 782-1016 *Custom wood-work—furniture, cabinets, murals, etc.*

**Ameen Dahdah Bakula Das, New Vrindaban Woodcarving,** RD 3 Box 177A, New Vrindaban 26003 (304) 242-9552 *Custom-only woodcarving, inlay gold leaf, etc.*

**Lost River Woodworks,** Box 1A, Lost River 26811 (304) 897-6379 *Custom-designed and built hardwood furniture and cabinetry.*

**(98) Bert Lustig,** Route 3 Box 194, Berkeley Springs 25411 (304) 258-1195 *Custom furniture, accessories and architectural work.*

**Kermit R. McCartney, Woodwork,** Route 3 Box 288A, Buckhannon 26201 (304) 472-8484 *Custom-design furniture and other woodwork.*

**Jim Probst, Probst Woodshop,** Route 1 Box 46D, Hamlin 25523 (304) 824-5916 *Custom-designed and built furniture.*

**Richard Sink,** PO Box 25, French Creek 26218 (304) 924-6819 *Designer, custom cabinetry, blacksmith, fine furniture.*

**Thomas Swift, Pin Oak Design,** Route 1 Box 122B, Paw Paw 25434 (304) 947-7109 *Fine modern furniture for both residential and commercial interiors.*

**Fred Williamson, Woodcraft,** Route 4 Box 20, Webster Springs 26288 (304) 847-5814 *Green woodturned bowls and custom furniture specializing in rocking chairs.*

## Wisconsin

**Dennis A. Allen,** Route 1, Green Bay 54301 (414) 866-9227 *Toys, wood vases, music boxes, hand mirrors.*

**Joseph Antolak,** 1043 W. Elm St., Chippewa Falls 54729 (715) 723-2206

**Mark G. Arnold,** 5433 Colonial Crest, Waunakee 53597 (608) 849-7274

**Alan C. Atwood, Atwood Design,** 805 Hewitt St., Neenah 54956 (414) 772-4364

**Phyllis Bankier,** 2738 North Stowell Ave., Milwaukee 53211 (414) 964-5280 *Custom furniture, jewelry boxes.*

**Judi Bartholomew, Wood-Ivory-Antler Sculptor,** 3858 South 57th St., Milwaukee 53220 (414) 541-1132 *Sculpture: wood-ivory-antler relief, in the round.*

**Else Bigton, Phillip Odden, Norsk Woodworks,** Highway 63, Barronett 54813 (715) 822-3104 *Traditional Norwegian woodcarving and furniture.*

**Richard Bronk, Chrysalis,** Route 3, Plymouth 53073 (414) 893-5581 *Rockers, art, furniture and accessories.*

**Rich Butusov,** Route 3 Box 640, Spring Green 53588 (608) 588-2617 *Finish carpentry and custom furniture in the style of Greene & Greene.*

**Sam Caldwell,** 5542 Riverview Rd., Waunakee 53597 (608) 849-7341

**Sheila Canning, Marcelien Fens, Planeworks,** 157 E. Wilson St., Madison 53703 (608) 256-3338

**Trish Collins,** 2152 Linden Ave., Madison 53704 (608) 241-7097

**(114) Rod Cronkite, Cronkite's Woodworks,** 2812 Wright Ave., Racine 53405 (414) 633-6303 *Turned bowls and vessels, built-in and freestanding cabinets.*

**Timothy Dalton,** 2217 Fish Hatchery Rd. Apt. A, Madison 53713 (608) 255-5235 *Veneer work and hardwood construction.*

**Norm Doll,** 1409 N. 67th St., Wauwatosa 53213 (414) 257-2878

**Mark Duginske,** 1010 N. 1st Ave., Wausau 54401 (715) 675-2229 *Custom design and architectural restoration.*

**(35) Hugh Foster, Furniturebuilder,** 848 N. 6th St., Manitowoc 54220 (414) 684-6065 *Computer furniture, bedroom suites, your interesting projects.*

**James Gentry Furniture,** 303 East Wilson, Madison 53703 (608) 251-2549 *Tables, chairs, casework and concept pieces.*

**David H. Haessig,** PO Box 22, Verona 53593 (608) 222-4380

**Michael J. Hanley, Autumn Woods Studio,** W63 N655 Washington Ave., Cedarburg 53012 (414) 375-1912 *Custom furniture, architectural work and wood bowls. Classes available.*

**Dan Hein, Flambeau Woodworks,** Route 1 Box 799, Phillips 54555 (715) 339-3871 *Executive furniture, wood/canvas canoe, construction and repair.*

**Ansel Heram, Heram Custom Woodworking,** 228 S. 11th St., La Crosse 54601 (608) 784-2626 *Custom cabinets, furniture, church fixtures and craft items.*

**Ken Hosale, Contemporary Works,** 11022 N. Cedarburg Rd., Mequon 53092 (414) 242-4157 *Resawn veneers used in original furniture, custom paneling and doors.*

**Rus Hurt, Woodworking,** Box 116, Flagg River Rd., Port Wing 54865 (715) 774-3528 *Functional, nonfunctional and architectural woodturning.*

**Tim B. Inman, Inman Furniture Restorations,** 1019 South Main St., Lake Mills 53551 (414) 648-2533 *Quality restorations of fine furniture, specializing in veneers and finishes.*

**C.R. (Skip) Johnson, Cjon Wood,** 3496 Hwy. 138, Stoughton 53589 (608) 873-5237

**Richard Judd, Furniture,** 192 State St., Oregon 53575 (608) 835-7699 *Original designs using the finest hardwoods.*

**Dale Karow,** 518 Norton St., Lake Mills 53551 (414) 648-8463

**Bill Keenan,** 729 W. Main, Madison 53715 (608) 251-6089

**Mark T. Kerr, Northern Furniture Designs,** Spread Eagle 54121 *One-of-a-kind custom furniture.*

**R.C. Kidd, Woodworking,** 1430 N. Torun Rd. #323, Stevens Point 54481 (715) 341-3515 *Creative designs and commissioned pieces, large and small.*

**Joseph Kleinhans,** 1714 Helena St., Madison 53704 (608) 241-7107

**Robert Krantz, Krantz Design,** N47 W28270 Lynndale Dr., Pewaukee 53072 (414) 367-0806 *Specialty cabinetry, furniture, trick designs.*

**John Michael Linck,** 2550 Van Hise Ave., Madison 53705 (608) 231-2808 *Fine hardwood toys for your children's children.*

**Steven Lockhart,** 2408 S. Harmon, Appleton 54915 (414) 733-2347

**Dave L. Martin,** 3220 N. 13th, Sheboygan 53083 (414) 458-5381

**James L. Masko, Jr.,** 629 Grove, Racine 53405 (414) 632-3913

**Mark J. Matthews,** 316 W. LaCrosse St., Tomah 54660 (608) 372-9051

**Bob McCurdy, Eden North Gallery,** Door County 54202 (414) 839-2754 *Woodcarving, custom handcrafted furnishings.*

**Michele Moushey-Dale,** 2616 Gregory St., Madison 53711 (608) 233-2304

**(46) David A. Munkittrick, Design Woodworks Inc.,** Route 2 Box 274, River Falls 54022 (715) 425-1799 *Custom woodworking.*

**Michael Olp, Olp Miniatures,** Route 2 Box 66A, Brooklyn 53521 (608) 455-1381

**Neal O'Reilly, O'Reilly Woodworking,** 504 S. 76th St., Milwaukee 53214 (414) 476-1909 *Furniture, lighting and accessories.*

**Bruce Petros, Luthier Custom Woodworking,** Route 4, County Trunk CE, Kaukauna 54130 (414) 766-1295 *Custom guitars, musical instruments, repair and restoration, custom woodworking.*

**William and Peggy Riemer,** Elm Valley Rd., Ogdensburg 54962 (715) 467-2748

**Paddy Rose,** 626 N. 9th St., La Crosse 54601 (608) 784-9683

**Enrique Rueda-S., Inca Music,** 432A State St., Madison 53703 (608) 256-5273

**Herb Schmidt,** 640 E. Kinder St., Richland Center 53581 (608) 647-2393

**Stephen Spiro,** 2829 Perry St., Madison 53713 (608) 271-0840 *Functional and ceremonial furniture in wood.*

**(147) James Woods, Woodworker,** Main Rd., Washington Island 54246 (414) 847-2250 *Musical instruments, furniture, cabinetry, carpentry, commissioned works of all sorts.*

## Wyoming

**Michael Clapper, High Design,** Box 878, Wilson 83014

**Robert W. Lichvar, Lichvar Studios,** 1216 West 31st St., Cheyenne 82001 (307) 632-0158 *Distinctive furniture designed and handcrafted for your home or office.*

## Australia

**(36) Henry Black,** 28 Lord St., Botany, NSW 2019 Australia (02) 666-8959 *Fine work in solid, veneered or painted wood, prototyping and patternmaking.*

**W. Cyril Brown,** 22 Kirk Rd., Point Lonsdale, Victoria 3225 Australia (052) 52-1797

**Richard Crosland,** 20A City Rd., Chippendale, Sydney, NSW 2008 Australia (02) 211-5114 *Teacher of woodwork at my own school; custom-built commissions, possible and impossible.*

**M.J. Darlow, Woodturning,** 20A City Rd., Chippendale, Sydney, NSW 2008 Australia (02) 212-5782

**Kevin Gilders,** 13 Champion Crs., Glen Waverley, Vic 3150 Australia (03) 233-9686 *Maker of useless wooden articles.*

**Ray Lilford,** 13 Champion St., E. Doncaster, Vic 3109 Australia (03) 848-4544

**Helmut Lueckenhausen,** 10 Suffolk Rd., Surrey Hills, Vic 3127 Australia (03) 836-3447

**Rodney Madam,** 22 Dalrymple St., Mackay, QL 4740 Australia 011-61-7-957-6767

**Geoff Mason,** 143 Ashburn Grove, Ashburton, Vic 3147 Australia *Children's toys, custom furniture.*

**(50) Michael Penck, Penck Design,** 33 Sunvalley Dr., Glenalta, SA 5052 Australia, (08) 278-7455 *One-offs to limited editions of modern furniture in solid native timbers.*

**(135) Gary Pye,** 39 City View Dr., Lismore, NSW 2480 Australia (066) 21-5040 *One-off woodturning, workshops and sculptured containers.*

**Gary M. Rizzolo,** 113 York St., Sand Bay, Hobert, TA 7005 Australia

**Brendan Stemp,** 2/27 Larnook St., Prahran East, Victoria 3181 Australia (03) 51-2311

**John Patrick Tobin, Windermere Woodcrafts,** RSD 1190, Windermere, TA 7252 Australia (003) 28-1476 *Woodcarving, functional pieces incorporating sculptural forms.*

**(104, 122) Grant Vaughan, Designs in Wood,** Quilty Rd., Rock Valley via, Lismore, NSW 2480 Australia (066) 29-3277 *Original designs, furniture, carving and sculpture. Commissions undertaken.*

**Edward Watt,** PO Box 46, Waratah, NSW 2298 Australia (049) 68-2327

**Ken Wilcox, Design & Reproduction Furniture,** 20 MacFarlane St., Davidson, NSW 2085 Australia (02) 451-1441 *Reproduction of 17th- and 18th-century English furniture.*

## Canada

### Alberta

**Victor Clapp,** 13620 117 Ave., Edmonton, AB T5M 3J2 Canada

**Nick Dobish,** 21150 Twp. Rd. 530A, Androssan, AB T0B 0E0 Canada (403) 922-2600 *Quality handcrafted solid hardwood tables, chairs and small cabinets.*

**Douglas A. Haslam, Kodama Woodworking,** 1709A 2nd Ave. NE, Calgary, AB T2N OG3 Canada (403) 270-3195 *Furniture, small objects, designed and fabricated using domestic and exotic woods.*

**Michael Mulvey, The Furniture Maker,** 1322 Hastings Crescent SE, Calgary, AB T2G 4C9 Canada (403) 243-7672 *One-of-a-kind furniture, specializing in inlay and carving.*

**Gary Potter,** 3220 1st St. SW, Calgary, AB T25 1R1 Canada (403) 287-2680

**Martin Rehn, Martin's Handcraft,** 74 Raven Dr., Sherwood Park, AB T8A OC8 Canada (403) 467-8058

**H.J. Schlosser,** 7207 Farrell Rd., Calgary, AB T2H OT7 Canada (403) 255-7372 *Contemporary modern furniture, one-of-a-kind only.*

**Jeffrey Wharton, The Oak Tree,** 9914-109 Ave., Grande Prairie, AB T8V 3A5 Canada (403) 539-7080 *Custom cabinetry and millwork, curved staircases, custom furniture.*

## British Columbia

**Peter Barkham, Telperion Furniture Designs,** 296B E. Esplanade, N. Vancouver, BC V7L 1A3 Canada (604) 980-3389 *Contemporary hardwood furniture, commercial and residential cabinetry, structural problem solving.*

**(105) Daniel Boudreau, Free Form Woodcraft,** PO Box 314, Clearwater, BC V0E IN0 Canada (604) 674-3718 *Custom solid-wood furniture, doors and cabinets.*

**Ron David,** 2044 McBride Cres., Prince George, BC V2M 124 Canada (604) 564-3993

**Jack Ferguson, Harmony Woodworkings,** 3284 140th St., Surrey, BC V4A 4J7 Canada (604) 536-2267 *Staircases, railings and custom furniture.*

**Graham Hall, Graham's Custom Woodworking,** Box 776, Bella Coola, BC V0T IC0 Canada 982-2455

**Harry Kublik,** 152 E. Carisbrooke Rd., N. Vancouver, BC V7N 1M9 Canada (604) 986-0929

**(94) Sean Ledoux, Designer/Creator,** 2090 Balsam St., Ste. 102, Vancouver, BC V6K 3M7 (604) 738-3301 *Innovative woodworking solutions, corporate and residential commissions and venturous art-furniture.*

**Paul Malakoff, Creative Wood,** RR 1, Naramata, BC V0H 1N0 Canada (604) 496-5627 *Lathe turning of local exotics.*

**(130) Jason Marlow, Woodturner,** 33508 Huntingdon Rd., Abbotsford, BC V2S 4N5 Canada (604) 854-3646 *Free-form bowlturning, and one-day turning course from studio.*

**David Peacock, Peacock Billiards Etc.,** 834 Johnson St., Victoria, BC V8W IN3 Canada (604) 384-3332 *Billiard and other large-game tables.*

**Brent Pfefferle, B & B Woodworking,** 363 N. Maquinna Dr., Tahsis, BC V0P 1X0 Canada (604) 934-6279 *Custom kitchens, furniture and turnings.*

**Roderick Robertson,** 2825 Edgemont Blvd., N. Vancouver, BC V57 2H3 Canada (604) 987-7687 *One-of-a-kind commissions and design consulting.*

**John J. Smith,** Box 894, Sparwood, BC V0B 2G0 Canada

**Ken Voth,** 9260 Walden St., Chilliwack, BC V2P 6H4 Canada (604) 792-1220

**Katherine Woods,** 1786 Chandler Ave., Victoria, BC V85 1N6 Canada (604) 595-8508 *Sculpture and woodturning (bowls).*

## Manitoba

**John W. Hiebert,** 43 Dunbar Crescent, Winnipeg, MB R3P OW6 Canada (204) 204-8895 *Crafted one-of-a-kind furniture, woodturning and ornamental work.*

**Walt Lysack,** 2 Ghent Cove, Winnipeg, MB R3R 3K2 Canada (207) 837-1235

**Kenneth J. Rerie, Rerie's Specialties In Wood,** 814 Government Ave., Winnipeg, MB R2K 1X7 Canada (204) 667-0308 *Custom design and construction, duplicating and repair.*

## New Brunswick

**M.D. (Mac) Campbell, Custom Woodworking,** RR 3, Harvey Station, NB E0H 1H0 Canada (506) 366-5794 *All types of commission work, including reproductions and original designs.*

**(122, 124) Wayne Hayes,** 205A Brunswick St., Fredericton, NB E3B 1G8 Canada (506) 459-5871 *Functional and sculptural woodturning.*

**Ross Phinney, Seaside Woodworks,** Group Box #35, Fishermans Rd., Saint John, NB E2M 4Z2 Canada (506) 672-8465 *Designing and making furniture, signs or whatever.*

## Nova Scotia

**David Burton, The Curio Cabinet,** Box 538, Wolfville, NS B0P 1X0 Canada (902) 542-5830 *Custom furniture and accessories in all woods.*

**John Comer, Cabinet Maker,** Site 14, RR 2 Box 54, Windsor Jct., Halifax, NS B0N 2V0 Canada (902) 861-1972 *Custom furniture design and fabrication.*

**Bill Hutten,** RR 1, Kentville, NS B4N 3V7 Canada (902) 678-7088

**Leo MacNeil,** RR 3, Sydney, NS BIP 6G5 Canada (902) 562-1510 *18th-century reproductions and original-design pieces handmade.*

**David J. Saunders, D.J.S. Woodworking,** Ketch Harbour PO, Halifax, NS B0J 1X0 Canada

## Ontario

**(78) Manivalde Aesma, Manivalde Woodworking,** Box 520, Burks Falls, ON P0A 1C0 Canada (705) 382-2026 *Household furniture, furniture accessories and toys.*

**Robert Anderson, Wood Works,** RR 2, Clarksburg, ON N0H 1J0 Canada (519) 599-5655 *Furniture and cabinets, design and building, traditional and contemporary.*

**Douglas S. Angle,** RR 1, Sydenham, ON K0H 2T0 Canada (613) 376-3908

**Dan Barrett,** 1477 Mississauga Valley Blvd. Apt.19, Mississauga, ON L5A 3Y4 Canada (416) 896-9180

**Bruce Beck,** RR 1, Queensville, ON L0G 1R0 Canada (416) 478-4740

**(19) Allan Bell, Allan Bell Designs,** 866 Davenport Rd., Toronto, ON M6G 2B6 Canada (416) 653-2987 *Occasional pieces and decorative boxes.*

**S. Scott Bland, Lensco,** 15 Sherwood Dr., Guelph, ON N1E 1R7 Canada (519) 823-2964

**Peter W. Boeckh, Winfield Construction Limited,** RR 1, Alton, ON L0N 1A0 Canada (519) 941-3775

**Edward V. Dick,** 68 Cameron Ave., Ottawa, ON KIS OW9 Canada (613) 738-0068 *Building and repair of stringed instruments.*

**(77) Robert Diemert, Robert Diemert Designs,** 135 Tecumseth St., Toronto, ON M6J 2H2 Canada (416) 947-1684 *Custom design and fabrication.*

**Joe Edwards,** 52 Manchester Ave., Toronto, ON M6G IV3 Canada (416) 537-5591 *Designer and maker of fine furniture, custom cabinetry and specialized gifts.*

**(97) Kim Fleming,** Box 254, Grauenhurst, ON P0C 1G0 Canada (705) 687-2157

**(39) Peter Fleming,** 12 South Dr., Toronto, ON M4W IRI Canada (416) 947-1684 *Commissioned furniture and related objects.*

**(81) Michael Fortune, Designer/Maker,** 278A Gladstone Ave., Toronto, ON M6J 3L6 Canada (416) 532-4607 *One-of-a-kind and limited-edition furniture.*

**Ian Fraser, Nth Degree Woodworking,** 719 Clermont Ave., London, ON N5X 1N5 Canada (519) 438-5994 *Furnishings and custom woodwork, original design, reproduction, restoration, batch production.*

**Brahm Friedlander, Evergreen Design Workshop,** RR 1, Kaministiquia, ON P0T 1X0 Canada (807) 767-2479

**R.M. Gibbons, Contrad Ltd.,** 7673 Kennedy Rd., PO Box 581, Milliken, ON L0H IK0 Canada (416) 294-1578

**(11) Mark and Norman Gillespie, M.G. Enterprises,** 185 Richmond St. W., Toronto, ON M5V IV3 Canada (416) 979-5523 *Custom cabinets, furniture and architectural woodworking.*

**Michael Grace, Designer/Maker,** 932 College St. (Rear), Toronto, ON M6H 1A4 Canada (416) 531-8146 *Designer and maker of fine furniture, commissioned work.*

**David Hadley,** RR 4, Omemee, ON K0L 2W0 Canada (705) 799-6648

**(113) Ted Hodgetts,** RR 2, Millbrook, ON L0A 1G0 Canada (705) 932-5545 *Lathe-turned objects in burled and exotic woods.*

**(102) Ted Hunter, Wood Studio Co-Operative,** 2388 Dundas St. W., Toronto, ON M6P 1W9 Canada (416) 535-5096 *Sculptor specializing in large turnings with textures taken from nature.*

**(39) John Ireland, Artifice Woodwork,** 135 Tecumseth St., Toronto, ON M6J 2H2 Canada (416) 947-1684 *Design and making of furniture and architectural fitments.*

**(109) Terry Johnston,** 142 Duke St. Apt. #4, Hamilton, ON L8P 1X7 Canada (416) 522-4453 *Furniture design and custom building.*

**Peter Koenig,** RR 1, Duntroon, ON L0M IH0 Canada (705) 445-0203

**Paul Konrad, Konrad Furniture,** RR 3, Wheatly, ON N0P 2P0 Canada (519) 825-7709 *Custom-built furniture and refinishing.*

**Randy J. Krishka, Eva Lake Woodworks,** Box 402, Eva Lake, ON P0T 1C0 Canada (807) 929-2163

**James Krueger, Cabinetmaker,** 60 Gilley Rd., Downsview, ON M3K IL5 Canada (416) 630-3957

**William (Grit) Laskin,** 192 Dupont St. (rear), Toronto, ON M5R 2E6 Canada (416) 923-5801 *Guitarmaker.*

**Paul L. Legere, Heirloom Woodworking,** 139 Mill St. W., Acton, ON L7J 1G7 Canada (519) 853-2041 *Solid-wood furnishings from original designs.*

**Gordon MacKenzie,** RR 3, 111 Topol La., Carp, ON L0A 1L0 Canada (613) 839-3022 *Personal projects mostly. Custom contemporary furniture.*

**Donald Lloyd McKinley, Designer-Craftsman,** 1460 S. Sheridan Way, Mississauga, ON L5H 127 Canada (416) 274-0114 *Prototype, custom and limited-production furniture and accessories.*

**(4) Mike McNerney, McNerney Woodworking,** RR 1, Ompah, ON K0H 2J0 Canada (613) 479-2211 *Custom furniture and kitchens.*

**D.W. McTaggart,** 12 Innis Crescent, Richmond Hill, ON L4C 5K2 Canada (416) 884-1865 *Bagpipe manufacture and repair.*

**Walter Olenych,** 37 Hewitt Ave., Toronto, ON M6R 1Y4 Canada (416) 537-5406

**(71) Sven Pavey, Designer/Maker,** 1496 Indian Rd., Mississauga, ON L5H 157 Canada 274-9342 *Residential and commercial furniture.*

**Maureen Peets,** 36 Linelle St., Toronto, ON M2N 2J3 Canada (416) 785-8322

**Gord Peteran, Fine Innovative Furniture,** 104 Crawford St., Toronto, ON M6J 2V2 Canada (416) 361-5037 *Finely crafted solid wood, one-off or limited-edition pieces.*

**Sherry Pribik,** 2154 Dundas St. W. #301, Toronto, ON M6R IX3 Canada (416) 531-7840

**Marcel Rivard,** PO Box 155, Pain Ct., ON N0P 1Z0 Canada (519) 354-9163

**Dave Roberts,** 463 Harwood Dr., Oshawa, ON LIG 2V2 Canada (416) 723-1096

**Joel Robson, Design Access,** 135 Tecumseth St., Toronto, ON M6J 2H2 Canada (416) 947-1684 *Limited-production items, speculative endeavors for galleries and small pretensious objects.*

**Michael N. Ruff, Designs In Wood,** 2354 Long Lk. Rd., Sudbury, ON P3E 5H5 Canada (705) 522-9673

**Paul Shulist, Woodworks,** Wilnd, ON K0J 2N0 Canada (613) 756-3873

**Paul F. Starita,** 65 Harbour Square, Toronto, ON M5W 1P9 Canada

**Paul R. Tellier,** 221 Barclay Rd., Ottawa, ON KIK 3CI Canada (613) 744-6588

**Michael Uhthoff, Wood Studio,** 2388 Dundas St. W., Toronto, ON M6R 1H2 Canada (416) 535-5096 *Furniture-building and design. High-quality commercial cabinetry.*

**Ian Uphohn, Designer/Woodworker,** 932 College St. (Rear), Toronto, ON M6H 1A4 Canada (416) 531-8146

**Alasdair G.B. Wallace, Wallace Workshops,** Box 547, Lakefield, ON K0L 2H0 Canada (705) 652-8697 *Elizabethan and Jacobean brown-oak reproductions, one-of-a-kind creations.*

**Allan Westlake Designs,** 56 Meldazy Dr., Scarborough, ON MIP 4GI Canada (416) 438-6601 *Shoji screens and custom furniture.*

**(80) Philip Whitcombe, Woodworking,** 2388 Dundas St. W., 4th Fl., Toronto, ON M6P 1W9 Canada (416) 535-5096 *Custom furniture.*

**(143) David Wren, Wren Guitars,** 121 Oakcrest Ave., Toronto, ON M4C 1B4 Canada (416) 698-1491

**Robert S. Young, Chase of Toronto,** 90 Nolan Ct. Unit #33, Markham, ON L3R 4L9 Canada *Custom solid-wood furniture, unusual projects are our specialty.*

## Prince Edward Island

**(47) Steven G. Stairs, Designer-Maker,** RR #3 Hunter River, PE C0A 1N0 Canada (902) 964-2531 *Residential furniture, limited-production objects.*

## Saskatchewan

**Wayne Cameron,** RR 3, Saskatoon, SK 37K 3J6 Canada

**John & Rick Fedun, Cabinetmakers,** 131 Ontario, Yorkton, SK S3N 2A2 Canada (306) 783-3174 *Sixty years of experience in fine furniture and antique restorals.*

**Michael Hosaluk, Woodturner/Furniture Maker,** RR 2, Saskatoon, SK S7K 3J5 Canada (306) 382-2380

**Gerald W. Johnston, Creative Woodworks,** Box 222, Pennant, SK S0N 1X0 Canada (306) 626-3545 *Innovative woodturning techniques and furniture designing.*

**Don Kondra, Kondra's Kabinets,** RR 2 Site 1 Box 73, Saskatoon, SK S7K 3J5 Canada (306) 382-7385 *Design and manufacture of custom woodwork.*

**Ralph Reid, Wood for Life,** 2316 Lorne Ave., Saskatoon SK S7J 0S3 Canada (306) 664-4605 *Custom woodturning and custom furniture.*

**Jamie Russell,** Box 43, Ruddell, SK S0M 250 Canada (306) 389-4813 *Custom contemporary furniture and short-run production accessories.*

**Ray Schmuck, Custom Wood Carving,** 263 Stl. Ave. N., Yorkton, SK S3N 0Z7 Canada (306) 782-2001 *Wildlife carving excluding wild fowl.*

**Lynne Shuya,** Box 837, Kamsack, SK S0A 1S0 Canada (306) 542-4437

## Quebec

**Peter-John Ball,** 387 Bord du Lac, Dorval, PQ H9S 2A5 Canada (514) 631-8927 *Custom furniture and restoration.*

**(54) Jeannot Belanger,** 2952 de Vincennes St., Ste.-Foy, PQ G1W 2E4 Canada *Design and period furniture reproduction, woodcarving.*

**Jean-Pierre Cayer,** 6613 2nd Ave. Rosemont, Montreal, PQ H1Y 2Z5 Canada

**Alain Desaulniers,** 100 Pope St., Box 520, Cookshire, PQ J0B 1M0 Canada (819) 875-5235

**Jean-Luc Fauvel, Ebeniste Concepteur Enrg.,** 4440 Jeanne-D'Arc, Montreal, PQ HIX 2El Canada (514) 259-3623 *Fine design of custom-made cabinets.*

**(90) Barrie Graham,** RR 1, Arundel, PQ J0T 1A0 Canada (819) 687-2795 *Custom-designed furniture.*

**Paul-Emile Guilbert, Cabinetmaker,** 11 Massicotte, Cap de la Madeleine, PQ G8T 5K5 Canada (819) 378-3334 *Furniture design, exclusive woodworking, reproduction of ancient and inlaid work veneering.*

**Jacques Morin,** 3692 Ethel, Verdun, PQ H4G 1S3 Canada (514) 768-5770 *Functional sculpture and exclusive custom-made furniture.*

**Gerald Paquet,** 5070 A Capri, St. Leonard, PQ H1R 1Z2 Canada (514) 322-4242

**Marc Richardson, Finewoods Designs,** 386 Le Moyne, Montreal, PQ H2Y 1Y3 Canada (514) 849-1964

**Jean Soumis, Ebeniste-Concepteur Designer in Wood,** C.P. 136, St. Mathias, PQ J0L 2G0 Canada (514) 658-8089

## East Germany

**J.W. Volmer,** Salzstrasse 94, Karl-Marx-Stadt, German Democratic Republic 9003 *Oval-turned facework and centerwork.*

## England

**Suzanne Marquess Cartwright, Marquetry By Marquess,** 63 Church La., Sproughton, Ipswich IP8 3AY England *Original marquetry compositions, pictorial and applied.*

**(72) Tony Devonald,** The Cottage, Gayton Le Wold, Louth, Lincolnshire LN11 ORA England (050-781) 641 *Furniture design and development especially made to measure chairs.*

**Alan Dixon,** 1 Underidge Close, Paignton DE TQ3XU England

**(135) Ernie Ives, Marquetarian,** 63 Church La., Sproughton, Ipswich 1P8 3AY England *Marquetry and parquetry pictures, boxes and small woodenware.*

**Charles Stirling, Bristol Design,** 14 Perry Rd., Bristol BS1 5BG England (0272) 291740 *Secondhand tools, custom furniture.*

## France

**Pierre Stockemer,** 100 Chemin de Belle Vue, St. Vincent de Barbeyrargues 34980 France 33 67 59 60 19

## Holland

**(36) Bert Aalbers, Memo Meubelmakery Kopshout,** Groenestraat 294 Holland, 09-3180-227149 *Modern design in solid wood.*

**Chris Van Aar, Memo Meubelmakery Kopshout,** Groenestraat 294, 6531 Jc Nymegen, Holland 000-567055 *Modern design in solid European wood.*

## Ireland

**Liam O'Neill, Woodturning Studio,** Bay 19A, Smithstown, Shannon, Ireland 353-61-363055 *Functional and artistic one-of-a-kind woodturnings.*

## New Zealand

**Garry Arthur,** 63 Rose St., Christchurch 2, New Zealand 325-668

**Marc Zuckerman,** RD 1, Hokitika, New Zealand KOG 277

## Norway

**Rune Torp,** Tennisvn. 10, 0386 OSLO-3 Norway 02-143933

## Scotland

**John Wright, Woodworker,** Lyneriach, Ballindalloch, Banffshire AB3 9EB Scotland 08072 303 *All types of quality woodwork, including bentwork.*

## Sweden

**Hans Ahnlund,** Tangovagen 4, Genesta S-15400 Sweden

**Bengt Eliasson,** Villagatan 24 F, Dorotea S-91070 Sweden

**Poul Middleboe,** Hjalmaryd, FA 330 12 Sweden 0370-432 40

## Switzerland

**Boucard Yves,** ch. Montaux, Lonay 1027 Switzerland (021) 71-3942

## Virgin Islands

**J.C. Simon,** Box 37 Cruz Bay, St. John, Virgin Islands 00830 (809) 776-6922 *Custom hardwood furniture, antique restoration and yacht interiors.*

## West Germany

**David Delthony,** Zossenerstr. 10, 1000 Berlin 61 West Germany (030) 693-4164 *Laminated sculpture to be used as furniture.*

**Mack Stewart,** Comeuisstrasse 1, 8 Munich 80 West Germany (089) 280-0165

# Index

# Acknowledgments

## About the essayists

**Chairs** Tom Hurley is a writer and designer-craftsman. He lives and works in Toronto.

**Desks, Tables** Glenn Gordon is a free-lance writer and furnituremaker and an occasional contributor to Fine Woodworking magazine. He lives in Minneapolis.

**Boxes, Cabinets** Fletcher Cox lives in Tougaloo, Miss. where, in addition to building furniture and turning wood, he also writes.

**Beds** A.U. Chastain-Chapman is a woodworker, teacher and writer in Northfield, Mass. He is currently researching a book about the history of the contemporary craft movement. He is an occasional contributor to Fine Woodworking.

**Accessories** Richard Ewald is a free-lance writer and woodworker who lives in Westminster West, Vt.

**Bowls** Richard Raffan is a professional woodturner and the author of Turning Wood with Richard Raffan, published by the Taunton Press. He lives and works in Canberra, Australia.

**Instruments** William "Grit" Laskin makes classical, steel-string guitars and flamencos in his shop in Toronto. He has just completed a book about musical instrumentmakers, available from Mosaic Press, PO Box 1032, Oakville, ON, Canada L6J5EG.

## Magazine staff

Editor: *Paul Bertorelli*
Associate Editors: *Dick Burrows, Jim Cummins, Roger Holmes*
Assistant editors: *Roy Berendsohn, Sandor Nagyszalanczy*
Editorial assisants: *Mary Ann Colbert, Susan Gardner, Kelly Strasburger*

## Books staff

Publisher: *Leslie Carola*
Managing editor: *Mark Feirer*
Copy/production editor: *Mary-Caryl Goff*

## Art staff

Design director: *Roger Barnes*
Layout artist: *Marianne Markey*
Art/Production Technician: *Margot Knorr*

## Production staff

Manager of pre-press: *Austin E. Starbird*
Manager of production services: *Gary Mancini*
PC coordinator: *Rolland Ford*
Production services coordinator: *Dave DeFeo*
System operators: *Dinah George, Nancy Knapp*
Darkroom: *Cathy Cassidy, Mark Coleman, Deborah Cooper, Celeste Fallon, Krista Sterling*

Typeface: *ITC Garamond*
Printer: *Mondadori*